THE COMPLETE
ENCYCLOPEDIA OF
MUSICAL
INSTRUMENTS

THE COMPLETE ENCYCLOPEDIA OF
MUSICAL INSTRUMENTS

A comprehensive guide to music instruments
from around the world

BERT OLING, HEINZ WALLISCH

CHARTWELL
BOOKS, INC.

© 2003 Rebo International b.v., The Netherlands

Text: Bert Oling, Heinz Wallisch
Production and layout: Studio Imago, Amersfoort, The Netherlands
Cover design: Minkowsky Graphics, Enkhuizen, The Netherlands

ISBN 0-7858-1870-7

This edition published in 2003 by
CHARTWELL BOOKS, INC.
A division of BOOK SALES, INC.
114 Northfield Avenue
Edison, New Jersey 08837

Contents

...MAN PROPOSES AND DISPOSES ...

One of the ways in which mankind is distinct from all other living species on Earth is in the propensity to collect and arrange. Throughout history, there have been people who strived, as a result of their collecting mania, to create order in an often overabundant supply— whether of butterflies, lichens, or aerosol sprays. They wracked their brains to find just the right classification system, and were often forced to justify themselves to the skeptics.

The world of musical instruments is no exception. Starting in the sixteenth century, scholars such as Agricola, Praetorius ,and Mersenne made intriguing and desperate attempts to create order amid the profuse overabundance. The *Syntagma Musicum* by Michael Praetorius, and in particular, its second section, *Organographia*, captures in a highly encyclopedic manner, the state of affairs that prevailed in the sixteenth century .

It was not until the second half of the nineteenth century that the study of musical instruments, also known as organology, arrived at a precise definition and classification of families of musical instruments, based on their similarities and their distinguishing features. It is therefore not surprising that there is still no hard-and-fast classification of musical instruments. Put simply, we still know too little about the phenomenon.

Scholars who have studied this field exhaustively include Victor Mahillon, a Belgian academic (1841-1924), Curt Sachs (1881-1951), and Hans Heinz Draeger (1909-1968). Musical instruments are now consistently classified on the basis of the following principles:

1. The nature of the instrument's resonating material
2. The way in which it is made to vibrate
3. The shape of that part of the instrument that is important for generating the tone.

In this *Illustrated Encyclopedia of Musical Instruments*, the instruments are dealt with in the context of the family to which they belong.

What process is involved in the (chiefly) human perception of sound in general, and music in particular? What are the marginal phenomena in this development? How important are sound and music when viewed objectively, and what possible consequences do they have in a strictly subjective sense? We also discuss the development of music and how it is experienced, together with what people have thought about music, from the earliest times to the present day, resulting directly in the creation and the development of musical instruments that began in a primitive form.

Alongside the oldest and most perfect instrument—the human voice—primitive instruments sometimes evolved into extremely complex "constructions." Nor should the impact of electronics be understimated, especially in the twentieth century. Without this factor, a variety of appliances that we have accepted as musical instruments—sometimes with a certain amount of difficulty, it is true—would not even exist.

Before the instruments are discussed, in family groups and individually, there is an introductory chapter to explain the classification of the instrumentarium. In the main, the musical instruments that are covered in this encyclopedia belong within the setting of the classical symphony orchestra. However, it is obvious that this book will also include exceptions to the rule.

The Schnitger/Ahrend organ in the Martinikerk in Groningen, Netherlands (restoration completed in 1948) survives as an outstanding example of the neo-baroque style in Northern Europe.

Foreword

... MAN PROPOSES AND DISPOSES—THE URGE TO CLASSIFY

One of the ways in which mankind is distinct from all other living species on planet earth is in the propensity to collect and arrange. Throughout history, there have been impassioned collectors who have striven to create order in an often overabundant supply—whether of butterflies, lichens, or even aerosols. They wracked their brains with the systematization thought necessary, and often attempted to justify themselves to a skeptical outside world.

The world of musical instruments is no exception. Since the sixteenth century, scholars such as Agricola, Praetorius, and Mersenne have devoted time and energy to creating order among the chaos and profuse overabundance. The *Syntagma Musicum* by Michael Praetorius, and its second section, *Organographia*, in particular, is a valliant attempt to capture the state of affairs in the sixteenth century in a very orderly manner.

It was not until the second half of the nineteenth century that the study of musical instruments, also known as organology, arrived at a precise definition and classification of families of musical instruments, based on their similarities and distinguishing features. So it's not surprising that there is still no hard-and-fast classification for them.

Latter-day organologists include Victor Mahillon (a Belgian academic, 1841–1924), Curt Sachs (1881-1951), and Hans Heinz Draeger (1909–1968). Musical instruments are now classified on the basis of the following principles:

1. The nature of the instrument's resonating material
2. The way in which it is made to vibrate
3. The shape of the part of the instrument that is important for generating the tone.

(after Theo Willemze—*Prisma Compendia*)

The instruments covered in this *Illustrated Encyclopedia of Musical Instruments* are discussed in the context of the family to which they belong. The entries are listed alphabetically, and are followed by an essay about the electronic music—a development of which the end is still nowhere in sight. In conclusion, there is a detailed entry about electronic audio equipment This encyclopedia covers the processes involved in the (chiefly) human perception of sound in general, and music in particular, marginal phenomena in the evolution of musical instruments. The importance of music when viewed objectively, and the possible consequences that musical instruments have in a strictly subjective sense. The encyclopedia also deals with the development of music and how it is experienced. Music-makers have thought about how best to reproduce sounds from the earliest times to the present day, with as a direct consequence the creation and the development of musical instruments, from the most primitive to the most complicated and sophisticated.

Following and imitating the oldest and most perfect instrument—the human voice—music instruments gradually involved. The next musical revolution was the advent of electronics, especially in the late twentieth century. Thanks to electronics, a variety of devices that we have accepted as musical instruments—sometimes with some difficulty, —would not even exist.

Before the instruments are discussed in the encyclopedia in families and individually, there is an introductory chapter that explains the classification of the instrumentarium. In the main, the musical instruments covered in this book belong within the setting of the classical symphony orchestra, but jazz and popular music are not left out forgotten. Nor are certain instruments used for ritual purposes. It should come as no surprise that the ram's horn (*shofar*, q.v.) and the *lur* (q.v.), a Norwegian instrument similar to the *alpenhorn* (q.v.), are also included, considering that all these "modern" instruments—up to and including those that are now electrically amplified—even the Fender Stratocruiser electric guitar and moog synthesizer—have their origins in Antiquity. The editors have also included the references to the music written for certain instruments, especially the unusual ones. In principle, references to the familiar repertoire have been kept brief, while unusual compositions—for example, those requiring 14 trumpets or with 15 extra trumpets alongside the usual complement—are given a mention. Anyone with even a passing knowledge of classical music knows that almost all the great composers wrote at least one violin concerto, but not everyone is aware of the equally interesting works for that particular instrument with orchestra that have been penned by less well-known composers. That is why you will occasionally find examples of this type throughout this volume.

Collection of stringed instruments

1. Perception and reception

Culture and the cult of listening

Music is the most magical and mysterious of all the arts and thus also the most difficult to describe. Our word "music" has its roots in the Ancient Greek *mousikè technè*, which means "the art of the muse." We understand music to mean a collection of physical sounds, which must somehow be organized so that the ultimate objective—creating a specific effect—is achieved by means of gestures and motion.

The nine muses

The origins

As far back as the classical era, many thinkers applied themselves to the phenomenon of music and tried to "classify" it. The Greek philosopher Plutarch (46-120 A.D.), for example, made a distinction between harmony, rhythm, and meter. A few centuries earlier, Aristoxenos—a student of Aristotle who lived in Athens around 350 B.C. and to whom we owe a great deal of our theoretical knowledge of Greek music—stated that the notion of music is dependent upon two fundamental factors, perception and memory. This statement is undoubtedly true, because under all circumstances someone must be able to perceive what is in the process of being created (the conception) and must later be able to remember how this has come about or was organized.

A Roman philosopher, Ancius Boethius (c. 480-524), subdivided music, in the sense of a principle of order and unity, into *musica mundana* (a harmony of the spheres, of the physical world), *musica humana* (harmony of the human soul and body), and *musica instrumentalis* (instrumental music). Other relationships were proposed in Oriental philosophies. Music from Japan and China originally had a great many features in common. Music was linked with philosophy and cosmology. People tried to gain an understanding of the world order through music, which was then considered to be symbolic of heaven and earth, and held to exemplify the principle of balance and harmony.

According to the beliefs of the Brahmans, mankind originally existed in an indivisible union, or harmony, with the world and with sound. According to this view it was as im-

Engraving with musical instruments

> ## TO TAME THE HEART AND THE EMOTIONS
>
> *The genesis of music lies in the far distant past, and it is a very old tradition.*
> *The purity and the clarity of music are as those of heaven, music's wisdom and munificence as those of earth. Music's beginning and end is as the four seasons, its rhythmic movement as that of the two heavenly bodies (sun and moon). There are five notes in the scale associated with the five elements as well as with the five colors. There is nothing with which music cannot find an analogy. In addition, there are two further notes, making seven in all. Though there are many kinds of melody, none of them, neither the crystal-clear nor the darker sounds, goes beyond the "five notes."*
> *In the gardens, in which people praise Buddha and honor the Shinto deities, and on the sitting-mats, in other words the convivial meetings at which people hold ceremonies and celebrate with drinking, these are always accompanied by the sound of music. There is nothing better than music for taming the heart and the emotions, and may its reputation and glory continue for posterity.*
>
> *From Kokonchomonshu by Tachchibana Narisue (1254), a Japanese chronicle*

rhythm, loudness, and timbre, as well as the possibility of arranging tones in different ways. These are all aspects that characterize the phenomenon of music.

All the sounds that combine and harmonize to make music are physical vibrations, but that is also the case for sounds that do not

The Sad Orpharion, an unusual member of the lute family with a distinctively shaped body.

possible for a man to perceive an independent sound as it was to imagine an independent world. In the Brahmanic story of creation, mankind increasingly "turned towards" the earth, so all that remained of that original and indivisible harmony was mankind's own voice.

Organized sound

The composer Edgard Varèse (1883-1965) described his own music as "organized sound," a notion that may well inspire aversion among many traditionally minded music-lovers, but it still comes reasonably close to reality in every respect and under all circumstances. After all, music is a combination of simultaneous sounds, tones with a set sequence of pitches (melody), the combination with other sounds (harmony),

Devil's Pegs. Seven servants of the Devil, a gamba made by the luthier Gesina Liedmeier.

constitute music. We also define vibrations that are audible to the human ear as sound. This definition is not absolute, because a cat, for example, can hear vibrations that are inaudible to human beings, though this can also be defined as sound according to the human value system, at least viewed objectively.

The term "sound" can in itself lead to confusion. That is why it is necessary to make a distinction between "productive sound" and "receptive sound."

Even though music is a specific form of sound, this does not mean that we can simply state that all sound is music. After all, sound that is produced without human intervention is not music. Only humans can elevate sound to music, and they can do so in two ways—directly through the voice or

The Musician from *100 Illustrations of the Occupations*, by Johannes and Capaares Luiken, Amsterdam 1694.

De Musikant
Is 't Dropie soet, Staat naa de vloed.

Het Maatgesang en Spel der mensen,
Soolieflijk als men ooit kon wensen,
Is maar een Staaltie van 't Geluid,
Dat opgaat uit der Eng'len Kooren,
Voor d'Eeuw'ge oorspronck van het hooren,
Daar vreugde nooit een Einde sluit.

Saraswhita, wife of Brahman, goddess of study and music.

indirectly by means of a musical instrument. This means that the human voice is the oldest, most versatile, and most complete source of music. In using the voice, after all, it is the human being that becomes the sound source. Humans can produce a sung note at any time and in any place without any tools. In conclusion, it can be said that

15

the human being is the starting point for all music, and that his or her relationship to the notes (sound) is the point of departure for all musical appreciation.

A Magical Dimension

Even in this age of increasingly generalized development and a practically unstoppable stream of information, there are obviously still a great many music lovers who are not in the least interested in all these theories, so long as they are in a position to "consume" what they want to hear and gain satisfaction from it. That applies as much to a live performance of music in a hall, church, or in the open air, as to a performance reproduced via an audio system, for example in one's own living room. Viewed objectively, under almost any circumstances, an audio reproduction system is in no way inferior to a "live" music performance, but an enjoyable performance by live musicians always does more justice to the great mystery of music: the metaphysical element. This magical dimension is precisely what it will never be possible to capture technologically. Such a palpable aspect of music is done no justice by even the most advanced audio technology.

A youth string orchestra in action.

Sound and Tone

In terms of physics, the difference between a (musical) note and a (non-musical) sound lies in the distinction between regular and irregular stimuli. With a tone the vibrations are regular: the compression and decompression of the air occurs at a constant rate, x times per second. A sound, on the other hand, causes the air to vibrate irregularly. The difference can be illustrated using the following comparison. Sound vibrations are like the surface of a pond with a gust of wind blowing across it, but pitched vibrations are like the circles on the surface of still water when a stone is thrown into it. A precise demarcation of tones and sounds is not so easy, especially when human emotion, which is interpretative, plays a role. A phenomenon experienced as an "unpleasant sound" can, indeed, be an example of the most highly sophisticated music, while the sound of lapping waves can have such a pleasing effect that it is like music to the ears of the listener. Various contemporary composers have integrated "real-life" sounds of this kind in their work, a technique known as "musique concrète," and they present these sounds as part of the music. By no means every listener, however, actually perceives such "technical" components of a composition as music.

Hearing

Hearing is part of the "sensorium" (the five senses) of humans and animals, and it is a sense that also functions at a distance, unlike taste and touch. Just like the sense of sight, the sense of hearing is a "higher sense," because it enables humans to sharpen their general perceptions and, relatively speaking at least, to gain much more rational information than from the "base senses" of smell, taste, and touch, that provide a great deal of information that is emotionally tainted. In contrast to the sense of touch and visual perception—that primarily provide spatially structured information—hearing also offers decisive answers to the temporal aspects of stimuli, as well as offering spatial information.

The human ear picks up vibrations and converts them into nerve impulses. That does not mean that the reception of the vibrations and their conversion into nerve impulses necessarily leads to a classification or even basic recognition of those stimuli. Traveling via the outer ear (the earlobe and the auditory canal), the vibrations are detected by the eardrum, then the air-filled middle ear transfers them to the inner ear. The chief function of the middle ear in this process is the adjustment of the pressure (impedance), thus protecting the highly sensitive, fluid-filled inner ear.

Range

The frequency range audible to humans lies between 16 hertz and 20,000 hertz (Hz). The decibel (dB) is the unit of measurement, a ratio, that is used to compare the intensity levels (amplitude or loudness). If the lowest sound intensity is given the value 0 dB, the upper limit is about 120 dB. Music usually exists within these two extremes, i.e. between 50 and 12,000 Hz and between 20 and 100 dB.

Anatomy of the human ear, one of three unpublished drawings by Max Brödel
(W.B. Saunders Company, Philadelphia & London).

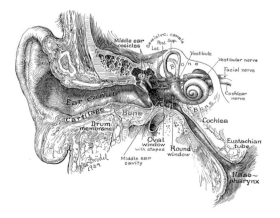

Musical Appreciation

Musical appreciation is the extremely complex ability to distil a meaningful cohesion from the configurations of musical sounds that are heard. In the first place, it is based on pitch, timbre, dynamics and duration, while on a higher level it entails the ability to perceive cohesion in the melodic, harmonic and rhythmical aspects of the music.

Localization of Sound

An essential aspect of the auditory perception of humans is the ability to localize sound. The function and importance of this depends on the way and the degree to which listeners orientate themselves in their surroundings. The process of an orientational reaction is characterized by two phases. The first phase is the localization: this is the result of the fact that the human ear is able to register sound waves from all directions. This is almost automatically followed by the second phase: a human being moves his or her head in the direction of the place where the registered sound originated.

Selective Listening

In localizing sounds we are further aided—should it be necessary—by listening selectively, which makes it possible to concentrate on one specific sound (for example, the voice of a single speaker) when various sounds are audible simultaneously (when more than one person is speaking, for example). This is called the "cocktail-party effect."

Sound waves

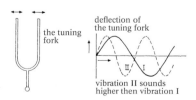

Something similar can present itself when listening to instrumental music: during *tutti* passages, a listener who loves a particular instrument can potentially focus more attention on that instrument than on the others. This is obviously more difficult when the fundamental requirements for the localization are not (sufficiently) available, for example when one is hard of hearing in one ear. It has also been established that selective listening is made easier by turning one's gaze in the appropriate direction.

Determining direction

In the horizontal plane the direction that sounds are coming from can be determined fairly accurately. That is the result of the so-called "interaural differences" (the differences between the two ears). When a sound source is not situated exactly in the middle to the front, behind, or above the listener, the sound not only reaches the closer ear earlier than the other but also with greater intensity—a consequence of the fact that the higher frequencies reach the ear that is further from the source in a slightly weakened form. This is because the head of the listener acts as an obstacle, creating a "sound shadow" that shields the ear furthest from the source.

Determining distance

Determining one's distance from a sound source is much more difficult than determining the direction from which a sound has originated. Research has shown that determining distance with any degree of accuracy is only possible in familiar spaces and with familiar sounds. That is because distance has only a limited effect on distortions to the sound before it reaches the ears of the listener. It is true that the intensity of the sound decreases and the sound also changes—it is primarily the high frequencies that are distorted—where the distance between the sound source and the listener is more than ten meters (33 feet)—but all in all those changes have a minimal impact on our perception.

Concert halls

We consider a concert hall to be a "normal" space in which to listen to sounds, because there we realize that the direct sounds—the ones produced on the podium and heard in the auditorium—are accompanied by other indirect "sounds," such as the reflections from walls, ceiling, and floor, and in some cases supplemented with sound reflectors and baffles that are placed above and at the sides of the stage.

These reflections reach the audience a few fractions of a second later than the direct sound. It is not uncommon for the reflected sound to be louder than the direct sound, but this generally seems to have no effect on the localization of the sound source. Normally the reflections are not noticed at all, unless they are much stronger—more than 100 dB greater—than the direct sound. If this is the case, then certain groups of instruments suddenly seem to sound "shrill." In the worst case of delay between direct sound and its reflections, an "echo effect" can occur.

Headphones

Users of headphones will notice that every point of orientation for the localization of sound disappears. The filter function of the earlobes is then eliminated. There are still differences in intensity and delay between the two ears. The distance aspect has usually "disappeared" completely, which makes it seem as if the sound is being produced right inside the listener's head.

Pomp and splendour in the concert hall

Manipulation

Nowadays it is possible to manipulate the situation electronically. It is possible—and that is also the case in practice—to simulate spatial reflections using electronic means. Laboratory tests have proven that it is also possible to influence how the direction is determined by playing off the differences in loudness and delay against each other when a subject is listening via headphones. It has thus been demonstrated that when one ear hears the sound earlier and the other ear hears the sound with a higher volume, then the listener is convinced that the sound must be localized in the middle.

Over the course of the centuries, sound has come to play an ever-greater societal role, but that role has never been so great as in our times. The fact that it is possible to manipulate sound, has over the years frequently been proven, and in a variety of ways. Dictators in particular have always been aware of the power of sound, and then primarily of the power of the crystallized sound in the form of music. The more forcefully the music is used in a manipulative fashion, the closer the specter of the totalitarian state comes to the fore.

Slowly but surely a mood this has created an atmosphere in which people have become dependent on the influencing effects of music for all kinds of actions. It is a form of dependency that is comparable to addiction to narcotics. In both instances it is possible to demonstrate the physical and mental effects, which may be harmful and in certain respects are even more dangerous than those of drugs. Often the victim does not even notice the effect, because this specific manipulation with sound—if it is applied in the manner intended—leads to demotivation and utter indifference. As a consequence, the inability to adopt a critical stance is to a large extent reinforced.

The manipulation of sound was, for example, applied by the Nazi regime during the twentieth century, originally for the voices of its orators, but also as regards the types of music deemed suitable for influencing the masses. Joseph Goebbels was a past master at this technique, and the driving force behind the one-man propaganda machinery of the Third Reich. The musician Peter Kreuder once told a story about how he had to play the piano during his meetings with Goebbels, but that Goebbels was not really happy with the result and took a seat at the keyboard himself in order to play. Goebbels then explained to Kreuder that shifting the accentuation and deviant intervals would undoubtedly have an effect on the mob.

Musical terrorism

Music can be heard practically everywhere where there are people. The onward march of sound is unstoppable. The phenomenon of music being played during work has been familiar for decades. Such background music is no longer limited, however, to factories in which the work is tediously repetitive. Hairdressing salons, department stores, restaurants, swimming pools, subway stations, airplanes, elevators, and even public transportation have not been spared the onslaught. The leading German weekly news magazine, *Die Zeit,* referred to a "veritable plague" and the more conservative German daily, the *Frankfurter Allgemeine Zeitung,*

Headphones

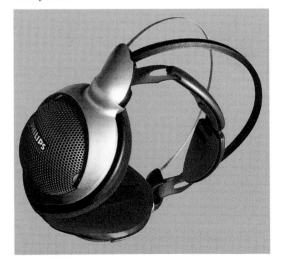

Street music: enjoyable or musical terrorism?

half of the 1980s, the management of the Hamburg subway system briefly used music at five of its stations in order to achieve two objectives simultaneously, to kill two birds with one stone. It was used for advertising (jingles and ads interspersed with the music) and to deter the groups of skinheads who hung out at the subway stations. The choice of music was of the "easy listening" type.

Cars and traffic

A study by the Technical University of Berlin indicated that 85.7% of all automobile drivers listen to music while driving. The research also revealed that there is a correlation between the choice of car model and musical preferences. For example, Opel drivers like folk music, people who drive a Citroen 2CV prefer to sing along with the music, and people with a Porsche prefer to listen to the growl of their engine. Traffic alone has already caused such an increase in noise levels in big cities and rural communities that it is no surprise that people want to do something to counteract all that noise, even if only in the form of alternative noise.

A while ago it was revealed that a police car in a big city in the United States in 1912 already needed a siren producing 88 dB in order to be heard above the traffic. Nowadays that has increased to about 120 dB.

Music therapy

Positive manipulation with music has also been put into practice, as in the case of music therapy—an area that is (still) undiscovered or underdeveloped in many countries, though interest in this discipline is growing. Music can have positive results in many cases where treatment with allopathic medication and other therapeutic means has been ineffective or failed to work completely. In a German hospital where sports injuries are treated, comprehensive research has shown that goal-specific music therapy can reduce

described this newest environmental pollution problem as "pure arbitrariness."

The restaurant owner who receives complaints from patrons trying to enjoy their food about his canned music will defend his "congenial musical wallpaper" by pointing out to customers that they also immediately switch on music of some kind whenever they first enter their home. Nevertheless, those who churn out Musak and its imitators are all too well aware that it also functions as a stimulus to greater consumption and that is the reason why canned music is so ubiquitous in department stores and supermarkets. When the first metro line in the Netherlands was opened, there were reports in the media about non-stop music at the metro stations. Research had apparently indicated that music would considerably reduce the chance of people feeling claustrophobic. In the second

the use of allopathic painkillers by half.
In more practical terms, sensitive people have already known for a long time that music can have a calming effect. Some fine examples of this were evidenced on the silver screen more than four decades ago. In Claude Chabrol's "À Double Tour" ("Double Twist") the crazed murderer is repeatedly calmed down by the music of Mozart. A traumatized policeman also listens to Mozart while he is convalescing in Alfred Hitchcock's "Vertigo."

Dentists were quick to recognize the calming effect of (certain kinds of) music. For a long time already, piped music has no longer been restricted to the waiting room in order to put the patients "at ease," but has also invaded the actual surgery.

As early as the 1980s, the *New York Times* reported that music was increasingly being used as a "medical aid" in operating theaters in the United States. In Europe this trend continues to spread, even though there are still physicians who protest against it, such as the anesthetist who commented that he found it very difficult to concentrate on the electrocardiogram with music playing in the background. "Anesthetizing sounds" are now played for patients undergoing general anesthetic, fairly restrained music during the first phase of the operation, and energetic music during the closing up of the wound.

Music and work

Listening to music while at work functions as a stimulus for work performance. Studies have shown that work productivity increases by as much as twenty percent as a result of the relaxation induced by music. It is not only humans who "work" better with music, but cows tend to produce more milk when they listen to Beethoven. As a result, a stereo installation in the cowshed is no longer an exception. After all, the investment is worth it.

Long ago, the Volga boatmen sang their famous songs, because the song had a positive effect on the functions and strength of the

Music therapy with bowl gongs

body. It charged them up, which is almost certainly what was intended. The same was true of sailors who had to heave anchors up and down by hand, or wind mooring-ropes around a capstan.

Plants

It is not only humans and animals that react to aural stimuli, and especially to musical stimuli, but plants as well, and in some cases with extremely positive results. Experiments in Canada have demonstrated that wheat in the field is terribly taken with the music of Johann Sebastian Bach, in particular by his violin sonatas.

Another experiment demonstrated that pumpkins liked the music of Haydn and Brahms, but they did not like rock music whatsoever. The plants grew enthusiastically towards the loudspeakers so long as the music was by Haydn and Brahms, but they promptly grew in the opposite direction when rock songs were played.

Slaughter

It is common knowledge that soldiers sang songs in order to overcome their own fear. And they also made music during battle. The drummers and trumpeters did their work in order to drum or blast more courage into the brave fighters, and because the blood ran more freely with music. Music is not only used in this manner on the "Elysian fields." Nowadays the music emanating from loudspeakers in the modern-day abattoir fullfils the same function.

Emotions

Music is still the most intense form of emotional expression that humans have created within their culture, and this form of emotion seems to satisfy an extremely existential need.

Unfortunately, the art of music is no longer exclusively an expression of the traditionally elevated emotions, and music now also plays a role of decisive significance in the somewhat more base passions. Everyone can sample music on a daily basis, whether they want to or not, for example if the neighbors open their windows and have the radios on full blast, perhaps blaring out some heavy metal, garage, or acid house music, to the anguish of classical music lovers.

Even the rhythm of the telephone ringing can have an effect on the body. The

The hunting horn is an instrument of great antiquity.

Wolfgang Amadeus Mozart, portrait by J.N. della Croce.

rhythm selected by the British for the distinctive ringing of their (fixed) telephones was originally intended to be as irritating as possible, to encourage people to answer the phone!

Rhythm

The rhythm in music has a relaxing effect on the human body, providing it coincides with the rhythm of the heartbeat. Experience shows that many rock songs and even some classical music, has a predominant rhythm of two short and one long beats, and is thus the diametrical opposite of the natural rhythm of the human heart, which has two long and one short beat. Music thus induces fatigue as opposed to pleasant.

People are hardly able to insulate themselves from these sorts of sounds, because—even if people consciously put up a mental

Ludwig van Beethoven (portrait by Joseph Stieler, 1819–1820.)

Johann Sebastian Bach (portrait dating from c. 1715, attributed to Johannes Ernst Rentsch senior, who was connected with the court of Weimar at the time. Now in the Städtische Museum, Erfurt, Germany).

barrier—there are still influences that filter through. It has been shown in tests on fetuses that they react to external aural stimuli while still in the womb. Music causes a change in the rhythm of their breathing and heartbeat. It is not yet entirely clear whether this should be seen as a positive or negative phenomenon, opinions are still divided.

Melody

The power of the melodic element in music is considerable. In the positive sense, there are a few features that are immediately noticeable. The melody improves the human activity level, has a favorable effect on the mental balance, and it increases a person's energy levels and sense of wellbeing. In a negative sense, "melodic influences" alter human perceptions, and thus also human behavior. A variety of studies have shown that people listening to music that is very melodious send out signals of surrender and rapture—of sensual pleasure—in their body language.

Youth

It was a characteristic of youth to seek "alternative" music, even in previous centuries. The contemporary composers provided it to some extent and who can be seen as the "rock musicians" of their time. According to some of their contemporaries, Beethoven and Schubert wrote deafening or unplayable music. Mozart himself composed music just for his own amusement (his *Divertimenti* for example). During

The flute, tambourine, trumpet, harp, and psalter are a literal illustration of the text of Psalm 81.

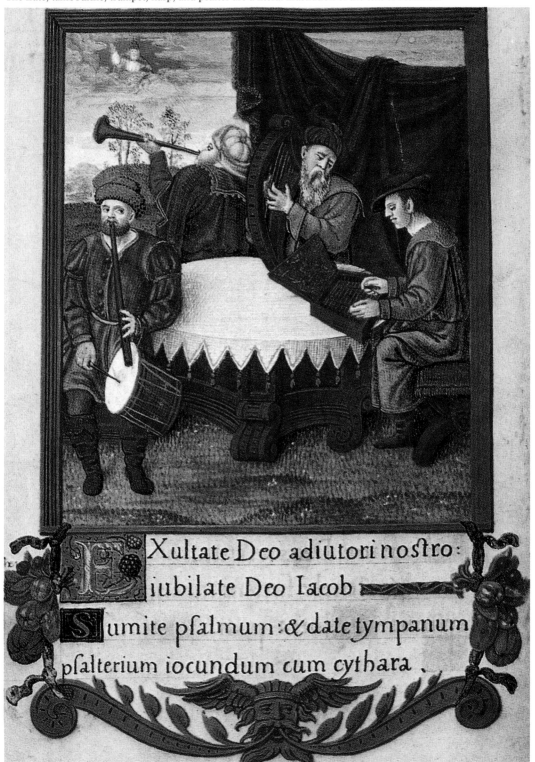

The sound of the Surdo will travel through any wall

Making music can be a passion

performances of *Eine Kleine Nachtmusik* people ate and drank, or even played card games. In the more recent past, the gypsy violinist, serenading the patrons of a Balkan restaurant functioned in the same way.

Modern young people face an increasing lack of communication—especially verbal communication—and as a result they have an increasing need to take refuge among people of their own age and where the disco beat or mellow background music form the element that binds them together. The increasing communication possibilities of the mobile phone, however, are doing little to improving verbal communication skills between young people and their peers or between young people and the older generation.

Sound

In pop music, in particular, technology has made a big contribution to the "degeneration" of music's original aim. Audio equipment is achieving greater and greater perfection and can provide a deafening sound level. Certain governments insist that portable devices such as the Walkman carry a warning that keeping the sound turned to maximum for any length of time may damage the hearing of the listener. Many pop music fans have a preference for a lot of bass when listening in the den or bedroom and want their stereo system to reproduce far more of the bass tones than

they would hear in a concert hall or other live performance.

Video Clips: Listen, Watch, Shut Up

Halfway through the 1980s, experts thought that the video clip represented the greatest menace to the music industry, because in video clips the sound is subordinated to the image. They were not totally wrong, because sound-on-video is boosted and distorted sound, contributing further to musical illiteracy, since the music makes fewer demands on the listener's critical faculties. as regards the music because the attention is divided between the visual and audio signals.

Young people also enjoy music ...

... in various ways.

Herbert von Karajan, whose musical career has included conducting the Berlin Philharmonic Orchestra, an orchestra renowned for its technical perfection.

Elite

The question remains as to whether the current music scene represents and deterioration and degeneration, as some critics claim. Good music has always been something enjoyed by the educated elite, in the sense that only a minority of people consciously listen to music. This elite has always had a marked preference for music that sometimes, even when performed by famous orchestras, became reduced to ordinary background melody.

Yet more people than ever before are enjoying classical music, at least on the radio, as shown by the classical music stations that are enjoying unprecedented popularity, that translates itself in terms of advertising revenue. The high quality of reproduction systems—quadriphonics, Surround Sound and other high fidelity forms of reproduction— enable the listener to enjoy a performance in his or her own living-room that is as good as or even better than a performance heard in the concert hall or other live performance, even assuming that the listener is in one of the best seats in the house. Nevertheless, live performances remain a favorite with music-lovers, for the same reason that the music video has been such a success—the combination of sight and sound is irresistible.

The public applause after a concert.

2. Classification

Organology: the Scientific Study of Musical Instruments

Long ago, musical instruments and their players did not enjoy the status they have today. Flutes, harps, and drums were never originally intended for musically pleasing purposes. Their original use had nothing to do with listening for pleasure. When first invented, they were tools, to be used in hunting, food preparation, and communication, to ward off enemies or evil spirits, to please the gods, and to allay fear. They were there to assist in the physical and mental survival of the human race.

Music emerged as a bonus from these tools for everyday survival. The more easily people adapt to their environment, the more likely they are to survive. Humans have proven to be ingenious adapters, aided by the surprisingly rapid growth of their cerebral cortex. In situations in which they were physically inadequate to the task, they invented extensions of their bodies, such as the spear, the bow and arrow (for hunting), and the drum (for communication). These tools were useful, in and of themselves, but they were to become more than that.

As a result of the rapidly growing, restless human mind, people were inspired to fur-

The theater at Epidaurus. In the foreground there is the circular orchestra, located in front of the proscenium (to the right). To the right of that is the stage (*skene*). The audience would be seated around the orchestra, amphitheater-style.

A "Consort Lesson".

The literature that has been handed down from Antiquity theorized extensively about music, but the only instrument involved was the so-called "monochord" (Greek for "one string"), a didactic aid for teaching intervals. Instruments of the period prior to the fifteenth century should preferably be categorized by their use or function, rather than by their sound, structure, or materials, of which we sometimes know little.

Musical instruments largely retained their practical and ritualistic functions until late into the Middle Ages. They were used in order to produce specific signals prescribed by the authorities for countless rituals, the unifying force in medieval society. The sounding of trumpets and drum rolls accompanied court ceremonies as well as battles. In both cases, they were intended to sound as intimidating as possible. Drums, trumpets, and rebecs were used in religious processions to accompany marching and the human voice.

The voice was the main "instrument" whenever the art of making music was practiced which was mainly in churches and at the courts of kings and nobles. Instruments were of secondary importance. At best, the harp or hurdy-gurdy was used by troubadours and minnesingers to accompany their poetry and church choirs availed themselves of wind instruments. The organ was played in church. The other use to which musical instruments were put was to accompany dancing. Hardly any instrumental scores existed, since they were not needed; musicians improvised on a limited repertoire of melodies. Even the way stringed instruments were played was in slavish imitation of the human voice, which was held in higher esteem than any instrument, until the baroque period. During the Renaissance, the instruments, their players, and the craftsmen who fashioned them became increasingly important. Slowly but surely, the musicians' subservient position in relation to the singers changed into the Renaissance artist's self-assured position as associated with painters, sculptors, and poets of that

ther explore the tools on which their lives often depended. For instance, the harp began as a lethal weapon—the bow. Music is the accidental by-product of a powerful mechanism for survival. With all their purposeful inventiveness, humans continued to live constantly in fear, and surrounded themselves with the organizing and stabilizing effect of magic and ritual. The human voice served well for this purpose, as did, to an increasing extent, the sounds discovered when from blowing through hollowed-out tree trunks or hollow reeds, the sounds made by using the bow and arrows, the pestle and mortar, and so on.

Certain tools thus acquired functions for sending *signals* and for *ritual purposes*. Over the course of thousands of years, these tools evolved into musical instruments.

In Europe, in Antiquity and during the Middle Ages, music developed into an esthetic art, borne on the wings of ritual and religion. For a long time, it was dominated by the sound of the unaccompanied human voice. Although musical instruments existed, they were not described in any detail.

era. Instrument building was spurred on by the flourishing economy of the times. This was also the Golden Age of contemporary instrument collections, such as those of Constantijn Huygens in the Netherlands, Ridolfo Sirigatti in Florence, and Duke Albrecht of Bavaria. These instruments were not preserved in glass cases, however. On the contrary, they were very much in use. The first printed anthologies of instrumental music were published in Italy in the early sixteenth century, and were direct transcriptions of vocal music.

The period coincided with the introduction of experimental science arose, when, for the first time knowledge was acquired through accurate observation and calculation. The new science engaged actively in organology, the scientific study of musical instruments. After the Renaissance, organology did not keep pace with the overwhelming growth and technical development of musical instruments. Attention shifted from science to advanced professional training, and many instruction books were published on how to play the various instruments. (It was not until the late nineteenth century that the classification of musical instruments was again seen as being important .) During the baroque period, instrumental music came into its own, bringing with it the accelerated technical development of various instruments. This development continued undiminished into the nineteenth century. Progress was made, especially in the mechanics of playing the piano and wind instruments until, by the late nineteenth century, the range of instruments were used that are still being played today in modern symphony orchestras.

In the latter half of the twentieth century, a growing number of musicians felt the need to become proficient in instruments from an earlier period, in order to better approach pre-eighteenth century music. This impulse was expressed in an authenticity movement whose was motto "back to the roots." This trend strove to create historically correct performances of the music of the Renais-

sance, baroque, and classical periods. It would not have been a viable proposition, however, had it not been for interest in scientific collection, description, and classification, which reached its peak in the mid-nineteenth century, though its roots were in the Renaissance.

In the course of the nineteenth century, when interest in the history of musical instruments developed into a science, people first began collecting historical instruments on a large scale and putting them into museum collections. Sometimes older private collections were acquired. Study also focused on works of art from previous centuries that depicted musical instruments, as well as the discovery and study of treatises on musical instruments of the Renaissance and later periods. The first catalogues of musical instruments were published in the late nineteenth century, produced by musicologists who attempted to describe all the well-known and lesser-known instruments as accurately as possible. Their history was recorded and they were classified systematically.

Such systematic classification had already been performed during the Renaissance, although not from an historical perspective. Attempts at classification can also be found in the works of ancient Chinese theoreticians, who based the categories of the instruments of their time on the materials of which they were made. The ancient Indian text, *Natyashashtra,* used the

acoustic properties of resonant materials as the criteria for a classification system.

In medieval Europe musical instruments were of minor importance. The scientific study of instruments, or *organology*, remained a neglected field until the Renaissance. As a result, little information survives about musical instruments of former times, although they are depicted in woodcuts, miniatures, and frescos, and there are reports of them by medieval poets, philosophers, and thinkers.

In the tenth century, Odo, abbot of the renowned and wealthy French abbey of Cluny, devoted a small study to the construction of the hurdy-gurdy, and in the thirteenth century the monk Hieronymus of Moravia, wrote in Paris, France, about

Page from Sebastian Virdung's *Musica Getutscht und Ausgezoge*.

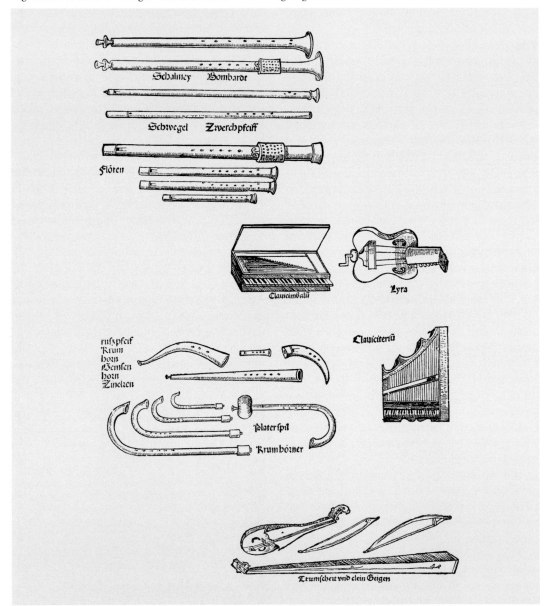

the tuning of medieval fiddles, in his *Tractatus de Musica*. One hundred years later, around 1325, Jean de Muris not only described several instruments but also created a classification system, the first in European history. This professor at the Paris Sorbonne divided the instruments of his time into three categories:

- stringed instruments *(tensibilia)*
- wind instruments *(inflatibilia)*
- percussion instruments *(percussibilia)*

As far as is known, none of his contemporaries showed much interest in his work. Apparently, the time was not yet ripe.
The next attempt came two centuries later, in 1511, when the German priest Sebastian Virdung (1460-1515) published a little book entitled book Musica Getutscht und Ausgezoge (Music, Translated and Abbreviated). He wrote it in the form of dialogues, the didactic form adopted by the Renaissance that was a legacy from ancient times. The booklet is not only easy to read, but it also contains numerous woodcuts to illustrate the text. Despite his pronounced aversion to everything that did not reflect a divine purpose, Virdung went about his task with scientific meticulousness. He both described and provided illustrations of carnival instruments, Jew's harps, cow-bells, children's toys, and "rumble pots". Furthermore, the book begins with a classification which is almost the equivalent of that of Johan de Muris:

- instruments blown into by human breath or artificial wind (organs)
- stringed instruments
- instruments made *"von metalle oder ander clingende materien"* ("of metal or other resonant materials") (in Muris: percussion).

Virdung's thorough and didactic approach was copied by others. A short time later, another teaching aid was published in German, the *Musica Instrumentalis*. Based

Harpsichord builder Peter Roovers in his studio.

on vocal technique, it was a method for learning to play different wind instruments and for learning how organs, harps, lutes, viols, and all the stringed instruments should be played, according to the correct tabulature (music scores).
This descriptive title was followed by an actual textbook that contained many jokes to retain the user's attention and it was even written in rhyme to facilitate memorization. It only contained descriptions of instruments, however, without providing any form of classification. The author of the book was church musician Martin Agricola (1486-1556) who lived in Saxony. So popular was *Musica Instrumentalis* that it was reprinted five times. In 1619, the Brunswick choirmaster and composer, Michael Praetorius (1571-1621), published the standard three-volume work covering the complete music theory of his time and entitled *Syntagmatis Musici Michaelis Praetorii C* (better known as *Syntagma Musicum*). The

second volume is devoted to organology. In the book's lengthy subordinate title, Praetorius promised the reader that he would list the names, tuning, and properties of all the ancient, modern, barbaric, foreign, primitive,

The viola de gamba family (Praetorius' *Syntagma Musicum*)

L. 2. 3. Violn de Gamba. 4. Viol Bastarda. 5. Italianische Lyra de bracio.

Combination of wind and percussion instruments (Praetorius' *Syntagma Musicum*)

domestic, familiar, and unfamiliar instruments, and provide illustrations of them. Praetorius' treatise stands out from all earlier works in two ways. Firstly, he used an historical approach, and his theory of music was intended to be not so much didactic as informative for the musicians and instrument-makers of his time.

Because his target group consisted of professionals, Praetorius produced information that was and still is extremely important to later musicologists. His book contains a *tabella universalis*, a table showing the size of all the wind and stringed instruments. He also added a supplement in which all instruments, including those from the sixteenth century, were illustrated against a scale (in Brunswick feet) that could be compared to a life-sized foot on the first page. The instruments were not only illustrated in analogous groups (families), but also in var-

Cover of Mersenne's *Harmonie Universelle*.

Page from the *Harmonie Universelle*, with a bass shawm in the center and a rackett lower left.

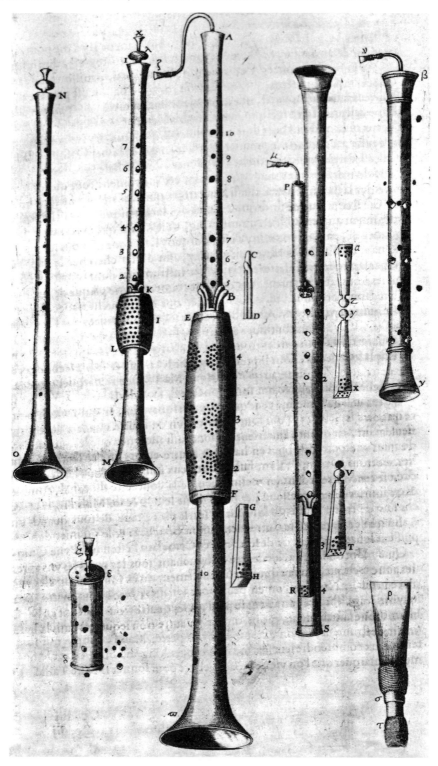

Violins of all types and sizes in a violin-maker's workshop.

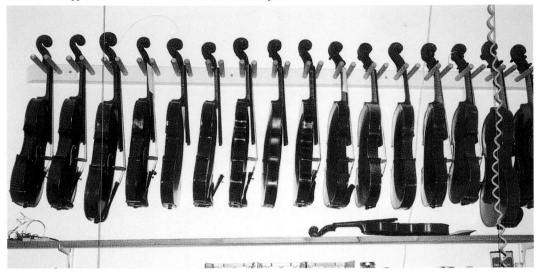

ious forms of ensembles.

In his colossal *Harmonie Universelle* (1637), Father Marin Mersenne (1588-1648), a natural philosopher and mathematician and friend of Descartes, included illustrated descriptions of the mathematics and physics of instrument construction. The instruments were depicted in families, but without systematic classification.

Mersenne focused exclusively on the functional elements of the instrument and ignored a significant characteristic of the Renaissance—the pursuit of esthetic appearance. Musical instruments and paintings from this period show that instrument-makers spared neither expense nor trouble in the construction and finishing of the instruments. Builders strove for harmonic relationships and elegant lines. Most instruments were assembled, lathe-turned, sculpted, and inlaid with care, using expensive materials. Harpsichords were decorated by the finest painters.

In modern scientific organology, which developed in the mid-nineteenth century, the systematic classification of musical instruments was considered to be an essential component of the science, from the outset. The Belgian, François Auguste Gevaert (1828-1908), broke new ground in this field.

His main work, *Traité général d'instrumentation* (1863) provides a classification into four main categories:

- stringed instruments
- wind instruments
- instruments stretched with a membrane
- autophonic instruments.

Gevaert subdivided these categories again into further subcategories, using various criteria. He based the subdivision of stringed and wind instruments on how the sound was produced; for instance, the stringed instruments were subdivided into bowed, plucked, and percussion instruments, and the wind instruments into finger-hole, reed, and mouthpiece instruments. In subdividing autophonic and membranophonic instruments, the resonating material was the criteria. Both categories are divided into instruments with or without a specific pitch. Gevaert's compatriot, Victor-Charles Mahillon (1841-1924), published his authoritative catalogue of the collection in the Museum of the Brussels conservatory—*Catalogue descriptif et analytique du Musée Instrumental du Conservatoire Royal de Musique de Bruxelles*— between 1880 and 1922. This magnum opus consists of five

The violin is in the chordophone category.

Wind instruments are in the aerophone category.

volumes, a total of 2300 pages, Mahillon covered the entire collection of 3300 instruments owned by the Belgian royal conservatory. Mahillon's thorough and systematic classification is based on the acoustic properties of the material, and is similar to the ancient Indian classification. He divided musical instruments into four main categories:

- chordophones (vibrating string), such as guitar, violin, and piano;
- aerophones (vibrating air), such as the flute, oboe, and organ;
- membranophones (vibrating membrane), such as drums (timpani);
- autophones (self-vibrating), such as rattles and cymbals.

These were further subdivided into smaller categories.

From Mahillon's system it was but a small step to the system invented by the German ethnomusicologists, Erich von Hornbostel (1877-1935) and Curt Sachs (1881-1959) who earned their reputation through their research into the history of music which was not confined to Europe. In 1914, they published their *Systematik der Musikinstrumente*, the only classification that is still used very widely today, albeit with some modern revisions.

To avoid misunderstandings, Sachs and Hornbostel replaced the term *autophonic* with the term, *idiophonic*, whose meaning is very similar. They considered that *auto-*

phonic could be construed to mean that autophones played entirely automatically, like music boxes or player pianos.

The work of von Hornbostel and Sachs did not differ materially from that of their predecessors. Their taxonomy was based on three principals. The idiophones and membranophones were subdivided according to the way in which they are played, chordophones by the external appearance of the entire instrument, and aerophones by the appearance of the resonating part.

As in the case of Mahillon, this created a tidy and careful categorization, but it was burdened by a numerical system which was cumbersome to process and which also contained gaps, since combined instruments and those yet to be created were missing; space for an empty category is a necessary condition for a comprehensive system.

Students of Hornbostel and Sachs and international organizations have made attempts at filling the gaps in this system and completing it. It is immediately apparent, however, that there is no category which could accommodate today's electronic instruments. This can be attributed to the date of publication. Since then, this gap has been filled by the inclusion of a fifth category, electrophones. The classification now appears as follows:

- chordophones
- aerophones
- membranophones
- idiophones
- electrophones

In addition to the Hornbostel-Sachs classification system, there is the system devised by the Frenchman André Schaeffner (1895-1973). In 1932, Schaeffner classified instruments by the type of vibratory material of which they were made, a modern, European equivalent of the ancient Chinese system. Schaeffner distinguished two main groups, instruments whose vibrating body consists of a solid material and those whose vibrating body consists of air. These groups were further subdivided according to their other material properties. This system also has its limitations, however.

Newer systems start with a computerized analysis of all the independent acoustic elements into which an instrument can be divided and the relationships between those elements. This results in flow charts that look like radiophonic graphs. These models are still not widely accepted in musicology, however.

It is difficult enough for musicologists to classify the almost 50,000 scientifically described instruments into a comprehensive system. The compilers of this encyclopedia have therefore used a simplified classification system based on the composition of the modern symphony orchestra, with some additions. The following comparison table shows the differences between this system and the Hornbostel-Sachs system.

Sachs/Hornbostel

	chordo	aero	membrano	idio	electro
A Percussion			● (timpani)	● ((cymbals))	
B Wind instruments		●			
C Stringed instruments		●			
D Keyed instruments	● (piano)	● (organ)			
E Electronic instruments					●
F Voice		●			

3. Instruments

Percussion Instruments

Striking—drumming—clattering—stomping, and much more...

Almost every human being is overtaken, at one time or another, by an irresistible urge to rock, clap, or beat a drum along with the music. A human motor response is probably responsible for this phenomenon. Psychologists theorize that our heartbeat is the starting point of our rhythmic expression. This makes it easy to imagine that early man used available materials to express this urge, especially materials such as wood and stone. Subsequently, our remote ancestor seems to have discovered that striking hollow gourds

produced a louder sound, the first instance of amplification. A survey of the number of percussion instruments indicates that percussion is an incredibly varied branch of the family of musical instruments, used in all forms of music—and sometimes even solo. It is especially noteworthy that the most ancient types of many percussion instruments are still being used in their original form.

The various types of percussion instruments have been subdivided here into the following categories:

1. percussion instruments with a drumhead (membranophones), including the tambourine, drum, timpani, bongo, and tabla
2. percussion instruments without a drumhead (idiophones):
   a: non-melodic, including castanets, gong, and cymbals
   b: melodic, including glockenspiel, vibraphone, and marimba

"Nikkelen Nelis," a pedal-operated, one-man-band drum kit, containing drums, cymbals, and bells.

The serouba, an example of a membranophone.

Apinti, another example of a membranophone.

Antique tambourines.

- rubbing
- scraping
- plucking

The percussion instruments are so numerous that they could fill a book by themselves, but the instruments listed here are those most frequently found in classical music, jazz, and world music. The musical examples given are arbitrary, but they are easy for anyone to find in CD catalogues.

In classifying the family of percussion instruments without a drumhead, consideration must be given to the ways in which they are played, or what they rely upon to produce their sound:

- stomping or tapping
- shaking or rattling
- striking

Tambourine.

Tambourine

The tambourine consists of a cylindrical frame about 2½ inches high. There are four or more slots spanned by rods in the circular frame. Attached to each of these rods are one or two loose metal disks that make a jangling sound. Buckskin is stretched over the frame to make the drumhead. It is sometimes nailed to the frame, and sometimes held taut with a wooden or metal hoop and four to six tension screws. The instrument has a diameter of 8½–14 inches.

The tambourine is struck with the fingers, the knuckles, the back of the hand, or the ball of the hand, while being simultaneously shaken back and forth. The various ways of playing the tambourine enable it to produce many different sounds. The tambourine is often used in folk music, especially gypsy music, and can also be found in popular music. Perhaps its most frequent use in modern times is as one of the musical accompaniments to the public meetings of the Salvation Army.

Bodhran

This popular Irish folk instrument belongs to the family of frame drums. It consists of one or two membranes stretched over a frame. In the bodhran, the membrane is stretched over a thin, shallow, circular frame, which means that the sound has little resonance. The bodhran is struck with a small double-headed drumstick known as a *mallet*. The bodhran is also used in modern Irish popular music.

Djembe.

Djembe

The djembe belongs to the family of goblet drums. In most cases, the frame is carved from one piece of wood. It belongs to the African inventory of instruments. The djembe probably originated with the Mandingos, one of the native tribes of Mali. The djembe has been popular ever since Africans brought it from West Africa to Europe and North America. The instrument is 24-39 inches high, and the frame is covered with goat or antelope hide. The skin is stretched taut, using a cord laced around the frame in a very specific pattern. Playing the djembe is a true art. Although mainly rhythmic patterns are played on it, an experienced player is capable of producing a wide range of musical expression. It is claimed that playing the djembe every day has a beneficial effect on the circulation and other organs. Whatever the case, some people get quite a kick out of playing the djembe.

Tabla

The Indian tabla is a double instrument, consisting of a cylindrical drum and a conical drum. Each drum can be played independently, but the drums are frequently attached to each other. The wooden frame is 8-12½ inches high with a 8–10 inch diameter. The frame can also be made of clay,

Tablas.

41

which case the drum is called a *banya*. The drumhead of the tabla is coated with certain substances that enable the player to strike many different nuances of tone. The tabla player plays the instrument with the fingers and hands while squatting, holding the instrument clenched between the legs. The tabla and the banya are tuned differently. The tabla is frequently used to accompany the sitar and is one of the most important instruments in India music.

The Western world became acquainted with the tabla in the 1970s, largely through Indian musicians such as Ravi Shankar, who introduced the sitar and the tabla into Western popular music of the time as well as to classical music, for instance, on an album in which he played a duet with the violinist Yehudi Menuhin.

Conga

The conga is a tall drum with a deep bass tone, which usually has a stubby, tapered base. The drumhead consists of stretched donkey hide or pigskin.

The wooden frame is usually 26-80 inches high, with a diameter of 10-16 inches. The pitch can be tuned by means of adjustable tension screws.

Like the bongo, the conga is played with the fingers and palms, which enables various tones to be produced, for instance, by

Congas.

pressing on the drumhead with the other hand. The player usually holds the instrument between the knees; sometimes the instrument is propped up on a tripod stand. The conga may also have a carrying strap attached.

The conga is played not only singly, but also in pairs, in which case the instruments are tuned differently. There is special form of conga known as the *cocktail drum*.

Tumba

The tumba is an instrument that is closely related to the conga, in terms of size and sound, as well as the way in which it is played. The tumba has a rounded, conical shape and is tuned differently from the conga. The tumba can be retuned from the inside, using a central screw.

Bongo

The bongo drum plays an important role in the Latin American dance orchestra. With its high, crisp, and varied sound, it adds spice to the rhythm section.

The bongo belongs to the family of cylindrical drums with one drumhead. It is approximately 8 inches high with an eight-inch diameter. The original bongo, imported from the Caribbean, had an indefinite pitch. Later forms have tension screws with which the drumhead can be tuned. The tonal range of the bongo ranges from c minor to c sharp. In South American dance orchestras, it is largely played in paired sets. The frames (frequently of unequal height) are attached to each other with a crossbar, and one drum will be tuned high while the other is tuned low. The instrument is usually gripped between the knees. The drumhead is struck with the fingers or the palm, while small variations in pitch are produced by stretching the drumhead with the thumbs.

A bongo can occasionally be found in the modern symphony orchestra because a few composers, mainly South Americans, such

Bongos.

as the Mexican Carlos Chavez (1899-1978), have included the bongo drums in their scores. Bongo drums were also introduced into North American jazz and popular music in the mid-twentieth century.

Timbales

Timbales are closely related to the bongo in a number of respects. For one thing, they are played exclusively in paired sets, but unlike the bongo, the two drums are always at the same height, though they are not of equal size. The frame is usually made of copper or brass and trimmed with chrome or mother-of-pearl. Timbales are set on a stand so that the smaller of the two is to the player's right. The instrument is played using thin, cylindrical drumsticks about 12 inches long, known as timbale sticks. The tone is changed by using different sticks. There is a special way of beating the drum called the "rim shot," in which the stick is allowed to hit the rim and the drumhead at the same time.

Timpani or Kettledrum

The timpani or kettledrum is shaped almost like a hemisphere. The basic material is usually hand-wrought copper, although nowadays other light metals may be used as well. The kettle has a hole in the bottom to

release air pressure and acts as a resonator. The top of the kettle is sealed with an even, thin membrane. This membrane is stretched over a framework consisting of one fixed and one adjustable ring. The kettledrum can be tuned by adjusting the movable ring, turning the six or eight wing nuts by hand, but it can also be tuned by using the follows:
- a rotary mechanism, by which the timpani is rotated, stretching the drumhead from the center;
- a kind of crankshaft, with which the drumhead can be uniformly retuned via a number of tension rods
- a pedal, which makes very reliable and more precise tuning possible using a crown mechanism.

The timpani with the pedal mechanism is the most common type of kettledrum to be found in the modern symphony orchestra. The "classic" timpani, from which no more than three or four notes are required, is also

Timbales with cencerro.

Timpani or kettledrum.

Detail of the adjustment system of the timpani.

used quite frequently nowadays for authentic performances. At least two kettledrums are used in such performances, although there are usually three or more on stage.

A distinction is made between the large timpani with a diameter of ± 28 inches and the small or piccolo timpani with a diameter of 25½ inches. In addition, there are the bass timpani or large D timpani, with a diameter of 32 inches, and a tall timpani with a diameter of 22 inches. The timpani is struck with a range of drumsticks, such as the typical 12-inch kettledrum sticks made of ash whose heads are made of cork or cloth. The timpani is usually struck at a point one quarter of the diameter from the rim. If the striking point is closer to the center, the tone becomes less resonant. Examples of music in which the timpani or

Modern orchestra timpanis.

kettledrum feature are:
- the pedal-tuned timpani: Music for strings, percussion, and celesta (1936) by Bartok;
- the rolling timpani: *With the Roll of the Kettledrum* (1795) by Haydn;
- Beethoven's Sixth Symphony opus 68 *Pastorale* (1807/1808).

The forerunner of the modern Western timpani comes from Arabia. The *naqara* is a small kettledrum that is always played in pairs. The body is ordinarily made of clay or wood and the drumhead is stretched taut with a lacework of cords. By twisting a stick in the lacework, the tension of the drumhead can be raised, thus changing the pitch.

Bass Drum

This imposing instrument can be found under a number of different names in the symphony orchestra. The most common are the Turkish drum, bass drum, and cassa grande. The instrument is most often encountered in its double-headed form, with one drumhead on each side of the frame. The single-headed gong drum is rarer. Its cylinder-shaped frame is usually made of wood laminate, although brass can also be used.

The bass drum appears in different versions. The version usually used to play symphonic music, the frame has a depth of 14–21½ inches and a diameter of 27½–31½ inches. Usually, the instrument stands vertically, but there is a mechanism for rotating it into a horizontal position.

The bass drum used in popular music is somewhat smaller, about 12-16 inches high with a diameter of 18–23½ inches. In the world of marching bands and brass bands, it will ordinarily be 10–18 inches high with a diameter of around 14 inches.

The symphonic version is struck with large cloth-covered sticks, also known as "beaters," and leaves an indelible impression in the concert hall. Countless examples can be found in romantic and 20th-century musical compositions, from Stravinsky's *Sacre du Printemps* to Verdi's *Requiem* and, of course, Bartók's Music for Strings, Percussion, and Celesta.

In popular music, the bass drum stands vertically and is struck with a pedal. The instrument will commonly have only one drumhead. In marching bands, the instrument will

Bass drum with a number of beaters.

Sticks used for beating several percussion instruments, but mostly intended for use with the bass drum.

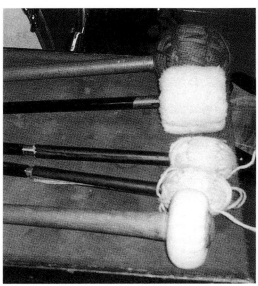

be carried using shoulder straps, and the single drumstick held in the right hand. A fixed cymbal will often be attached to the frame, and it can be struck with a loose cymbal held in the left hand.

The bass drum is also a component of the "one-man band," consisting of a number of percussion instruments which are carried on the back of a street performer which he operated with his feet by means of cords. An accordion is typically used as the melodic instrument.

Snare Drum

The snare drum is an instrument encountered in the symphony orchestra, jazz, and the world of popular music. It belongs to the family of double-headed cylindrical drums. It is also called a "side-drum" or a "military drum." The snare drum has a cylinder-shaped frame, usually made of laminated wood or brass. It comes in various sizes, as follows:

- in symphonic music, the frame is 6-8 inches high and has a diameter of about 14 inches;

Snare drum with drumsticks.

Snare drum with drumsticks.

- in popular music, the diameter is similar but the frame is significantly shallower (about 4 inches)
- in the world of marching bands and brass bands, the snare drum has a height of 6½ inches and a diameter of 15 inches.

The snare drum is carried on the hip on a leather strap. As its name implies, the snare drum includes strings or snares. A number of snares made of gut, nylon, or metal are stretched over the bottom drumhead. The purpose of this is to give extra sharpness to the sound. The snare drum is struck with two thin wooden drumsticks, 15 inches long, which narrow toward the end, finishing in a bullet-shaped tip. The most striking example of the use of the snare drum is in Ravel's *Boléro* (1928).

Tenor Drum

The tenor drum, also known as the "beating drum", is somewhat larger than the snare drum. Its frame is usually made of ash or another type of wood and is between 14 and 23½ inches high. The diameter of the drumhead is 11–16 inches. On the top and bottom, the drumhead is held taut by a framework attached to cords. In the world of marching and brass bands, the tenor drum is secured on a leather carrying-strap.

Tomtom

The tomtom is a drumlike instrument that can come in different sizes. It originates in China and found its way into popular music in the 1920s. The smallest version is flat. The frame bulges outward slightly and is approximately 4 inches high with an eight-inch diameter. The frame is stretched with two drumheads which are immovably fixed. The tomtom can be attached by a grommet to the bass drum of a jazz ensemble and is struck with a drumstick with a felt or leather head. The best-known version consists of a cylindrical frame of wood laminate, about 16½ inches high and 16½ inches across. The instrument stands on three feet.

Two strong pieces of buckskin are stretched on individual frameworks, with which they can each be independently tuned. Unlike

Military drum with sticks that also serve as tuning keys.

Detail of snare drum: sticks for playing and tuning.

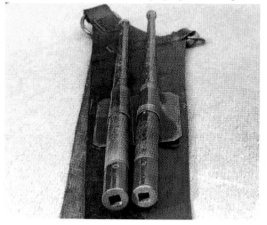

Military drum.

the snare drum, the resonating drumhead on the bottom has no resonating snares. The top drumhead is struck with drumsticks made of various materials. Another version is struck on the bottom drumhead by means

Snare drum and tenor drum, played by two orchestra musicians.

of a pedal, commonly in combination with some sort of damping on the inside. The somewhat smaller version of this last tomtom is played in pairs, commonly attached to the bass drum of the drum set.

Long Drums

All types of drum have lengthened variants. These classify these as long drums. In its simplest form, a long drum is a hollowed-out section of tree trunk over which a drumhead is stretched. There are, of course, much more elaborate forms to be found. In particular, the long drums found on New Guinea are distinguished by the way in which they are finished and by the characteristic hand grips that are carved out of the side of the wooden body. Most long drums are played with the hands, but there are also African versions that are played with sticks.

Goblet Drums and Footed Drums

Single-headed goblet drums are especially important in the Arab world. They are made of unglazed earthenware, wood, and less

Modern orchestra tomtoms.

Long drums, Congo, Kassai region.

frequently, metal. The dimensions vary widely. The drumhead is, in most cases, glued to the frame, though sometimes it is both sewn and glued.

Some familiar representatives of this type of drum are the *darabukka* drums from Islamic countries, but they can also be found in other Mediterranean countries. The same instrument, of Arab origin, is called *tarabuka* in Greece, *darbuk* in the Balkans, and *tof* in Israel. The manner in which all these drums are played is very similar to that of the Arab drum. The instrument rests horizontally on the knees of the squatting player, who plays the drum with both hands and sometimes the fingers. The Mexican *tlalpanhuéhuetl* is currently the best-known example of a footed drum. The feet are carved from the wooden frame, which is often handsomely decorated. The drumhead—sometimes a jaguar hide—is glued to the upper edge of the frame.

Barrel Drums and Hourglass Drums

Barrel-shaped drums and hourglass-shaped drums are important variations on the simpler tubular drums. In both cases, the ends

Darbukkas.

48

Kalungu or "talking drums" from Nigeria.

are of about equal size. There are versions of these drums with one and with two drumheads. Familiar representatives are the *mridanga* from southern India, which is played horizontally with one hand, and the *dhola*. In the case of the latter, pitch variations are produced by moving rings over the tension laces of the drumhead.

The *da-daiko* is a large *gagaku* drum from Japan. It is suspended in a complex framework and is struck with large, lacquered sticks. The *tsuzumi* is used in Japanese Noh theater. It is a small hourglass-shaped drum made of cherry or zelkana wood. The two animal hide drumheads are stretched over metal hoops by means of cords. The *tsuzumi* is played in an unusual way, being held by the cords and played with one hand. The pitch can be varied by loosening or tightening the grip on the cords.

The *O-tzuzumi*, the Japanese bass drum. The hourglass-shape of the body of the drum is made of cherry or quince wood, the drumheads from cowside; the lacing with an extra string around them make the drumheads very taut. The body of the drum is heavily decorated.

Set of bougarabou drums from the Gambia.

The *kalungu* is a "talking" drum, one of a family of African drums that are struck with a crooked stick. Several West African tribes use them to imitate specific features of their language. The pitch of the *kalungu* can be modified by changing the tension on the cords.

Rommelpot or Dutch Foekepot.

Friction Drums

The family of friction drums is very varied. Some have a typical drum shape, but they are also encountered in the form of metal thimbles and cardboard hammers. All of them produce sound in the same way, by vibration of the drumhead when it is rubbed. In some types of friction drum, the vibration are produced by means of a stick, with another a cord is used. A stick can produce sound in one of two ways, by rotation or by being moved back and forth. The *rommelpot* is a simple friction drum that was once popular in several European countries. The construction is very simple, consisting of a pig's bladder is stretched over a jar or pot. The drumhead is pierced with a stick. This instrument was especially popular in December, when it would be "played" by children. The rommelpot is known as the *foekepot* in Dutch.

Kazoo (Mirliton)

The kazoo or mirliton belongs to the family of blown membranophones. In its simplest form, it consists of the familiar pocket comb covered with a piece of tissue paper. The player achieves the typical nasal, buzzing sound by blowing or humming with his lips against the paper.

In the early twentieth century, *zobos* came onto the market. These were toy instruments in all shapes and sizes that were supposed to make the sound of the instruments they imitated as realistically as possible. In the 1950s and 1960s, toy saxophones were also very popular, and they produced sound on the same principle.

In the musical instrument known as a kazoo, a membrane is placed halfway down a small tube. By singing or humming into the end of the tube, the very distinctive kazoo sound is produced at the other end. It was in the 1930s that the kazoo reached an unheard of level of popularity. This was the time for small bands of unusual musical instruments, such as the mandolin and

Mirlitons: A pair of toy instruments and a kazoo.

accordion ensembles appear at that time, but even kazoo orchestras in which the kazoo accounted for the whole musical spectrum, from treble to bass.

Another form of mirliton is the *eunuch flute*, which was all the rage in Europe in the seventeenth and eighteenth centuries. In the eunuch flute, the membrane was set on a turned wooden flute shape without holes, and the end then covered with a cap. Mirliton is a French word, meaning the flattish, pale green member of the gourd family known in English as chayote or chocho, due to the fact that its shape is similar to that of the kazoo.

Stomping or Tapping Sticks

One of the simplest types of all rhythm instruments is the stomping or tapping stick. Arbitrarily chosen wooden sticks, wands, or batons, sometimes decorated, are stomped firmly or tapped lightly on the ground. Vacationers in Bali will have seen the stomping stick in use as a "rhythm stick." In this case it is stomped into a trough of grain. The most recent form is the forerunner of the conductor's baton. The conductor of an orchestra used to hold a baton in his hand which he would tap on the ground, instead of waving it in the air as is done nowadays, to indicate the rhythm.

The most famous example of the use of this technique was by the composer Jean Baptiste Lully (1632-1687), who lost his life when he accidentally stomped the baton into his foot rather than on the ground. The drum major or drum majorette who tosses the heavy baton into the air with a flourish, and the cheerleading baton-twirlers are in the same tradition.

Rhythm Board

Striking a board with a stick is an effective means of producing rhythmical sound. Rhythm boards as an accompaniment to singing and dancing are encountered all over the world. The original form consisted of striking a shield with the aim of frightening the enemy with the noise. The shape of the shield had a decisive influence on the volume and the tone of the rhythm board. The sound effect would be increased even more by laying the rhythm board over a well or a large barrel.

Modern orchestra slit drums or woodblocks.

Native slit drum or krin from Guinea.

Rhythm Pots

Pots, jars, tins, bottles, and other resonant, hollow objects deliver characteristic sounds if struck with a stick. They can also be filled with liquid at various levels to produce various sounds.

Slit Drums

Slit drums come in many shapes and sizes. What they all have in common is that they are made from a hollowed-out object, such as a piece of wood or bamboo. To hollow out the object, there has to be a starting point, and it is frequently a slit which is not closed up again after the work is completed. By making the outer wall of uneven thickness, different notes can be produced. There are slit drums with one or more slits, while X-shaped (Java) and H-shaped (Mexico) slits can also be found. The largest slit drums are found in Assam, India, whether they are assembled separately piece by piece in different buildings.

The slit drum is played in two different ways. Small drums are struck on the outside with a stick, and large drums are scraped on the inside. For better resonance, they can be elevated off the ground. Very large drums are partially buried in the ground for stability.

Anvil

The anvil is mainly to be found in the classical and modern symphony orchestra.

Sometimes genuine smithing anvils are used, but in most cases they are simulated using metal bars or rails fixed to a frame, which are struck with a heavy workbench hammer. Johann Strauss used the anvil for percussion in his polkas. Nowadays, the instrument will turn up here and there in so-called peasant choirs. Mahler called for an anvil in his *Sixth Symphony* (1903-1906). The score also lists a hammer. In modern classical music compositions, the anvil is regularly used by such composers as Cornelis de Bondt in *Bint* (1985).

Rattles

Rattles belong to the family of shaken idiophones. These instruments have played an important role throughout human history in various rituals, mainly to ward off evil spirits. The simplest rattles are nothing more than dried pea pods with their contents intact, or dried gourds filled

Traditional slit drums from China.

Set of maracas.

Orchestra cabaza.

with seeds or pebbles. Other materials employed for the body are clay, reed, metal, and animal hides. The *sistrum* is a special type of rattle, consisting of jingling metal disks strung on metal rods. In the Jewish festival of Purim, that occurs in the spring and celebrates the story of Queen Esther of Persia, rattles are brought into the synagogue and shaken

Cartoon dating from 1907, inspired by the use of unusual instruments, such as the anvil in a performance of Mahler's *Sixth Symphony*.

violently whenever the name of the villain of the story, Haman, is mentioned.

Noisemakers

Turkish Crescent

Noisemakers such as the Turkish crescent consist of a number of small rattling objects such as bells, shells, or chains, which produce very little sound in isolation. A special variety of these are the stick or frame noisemakers, such as the *Turkish crescent*. These instruments appeared frequently in so-called Janissary music of the eighteenth century—as a result of the wars against the Turks—for instance in *Mozart's Il Seraglio*. Although they do not count as true noisemakers, most musicologists would

Traditional (left) and modern orchestra cabaza (right).

Sistrum, a Coptic religious instrument.

Various rattles, including large ones at the back.

Authentic Turkish crescent.

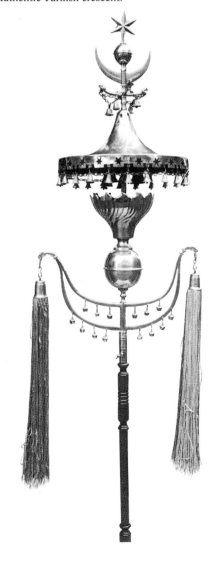

categorize Turkish crescents as aerophones. The most important rattles used in modern music are the bull-roarer and the buzz-disk.

Bull-Roarer

The bull-roarer or whizzer is essentially nothing more than a thin piece of bone or wood tied to a cord. When swung around and over the head, it makes a distinctive sound. The pitch can be modified by varying the speed at which the bull-roarer moves through the air. The bull-roarer had a chiefly ritual function. The roaring sound depicted the voice of the wind, thunder, and other intangible phenomena. The bull-roarer is a very ancient instrument and appears in primitive cultures right back to the Stone Age.

Buzz-Disk

The buzz-disk is closely related to the bull-roarer. The buzz-disk consists of a piece of cord that is twisted up and threaded through a wooden disk. Like a yoyo, the disk begins moving as the twisted cord unwinds. The spinning disk, which may or may not have holes drilled into it, causes the air to vibrate, producing a very characteristic sound. In primitive cultures, buzz-disks are sometimes encountered in fertility rituals. The "modern" variant is our humming-top, in which one or more blades through the axis are made to vibrate by the air stream produced when the top is spun.

Siren

Although the siren is not an instrument in the true sense, it belongs with the noise-makers. A siren is based on a rotating disk with a number of holes drilled into the side. When air stream flows around these spinning holes, a number of eddies are created in the current of air to produce the typical wailing noise. Nowadays, sirens are mechanized and fitted with amplifiers to project the sound further. Sirens are mainly used for alarm purposes but there have been twentieth-century composers who used the siren in their music. The father of modern electronic music, Edgard Varèse

(1883-1965) used the siren in his work *Ionization* (1931) as did George Gershwin (1898-1937) in *An American in Paris* (1928).

Wind Machine

Noisemakers such as the wind machine arose from the need to imitate the sounds of nature. The construction is very simple. A framework of slats is dragged over a canvas. This produces a sound reminiscent of the rushing noise of the wind. Usually, the framework is circular. By attaching a handle, it can be made to move faster or slower over the canvas, to produce "gentle breezes" or "gale-force" winds. In the baroque period,

Siren.

Bull-roarer or whizzer.

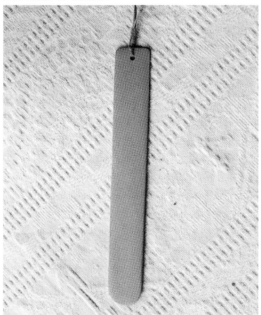

Wind machine .

Jean-Philippe Rameau (1683–1764) made use of the wind machine in his opera *Dardanus (1739) and later*, The German composer, Richard Strauss (1864–1949) employed the wind machine in his composition *Don Quixote (1896-1897)*.

In terms of the way it is used, the thunder machine is related to the wind machine. Thunder is simulated using a large sheet of metal suspended in a framework. When the sheet is struck with a sturdy stick, it oscillates and may even buckle, producing a sound like that of a thunderclap.

Scrapers

The family of scrapers is another large group of percussion instruments first used in prehistoric times. This would most frequently be an instrument that had been prepared from, say, wood or bone, in which notches were cut. A stick would then be scraped over the notches. Other members of this family include the *washboard* (q.v.) and the *ratchet rattle (q.v.)*.

Washboard

The washboard became very popular in Europe in the 1950s during the "skiffle" era, and was played alongside the soapbox with it's single string of twine that served as a double-bass. Before this, the washboard had played a role in the United States in the emergence of jazz and it is still used often used in "jug and washboard bands" and other country music bands. The washboard would at times be "played" with a metal rod, at other times with metal thimbles.

Ratchet Rattle

This instrument consists of a handle to which a gearwheel is attached. The small wooden slab spun around the gearwheel makes the ratcheting sound. In practice, the ratchet rattle is not often heard. Perhaps the best-known example of its use is in *Til Eulenspiegel's Merry Pranks* (1894-1895) by Richard Strauss.

Guiro

In South American music, the *guiro* or gourd is the best-known scraping instrument. The name reveals something of its origin (*guiro* means a gourd). One side of its upper surface is notched, and this is scraped

Modern Rasps.

Large orchestra ratchet rattle.

Guiro (foreground).

with a wooden or metal rod. Nowadays, guiros are usually made of wood or plastic, but a finely-polished cow horn is also frequently used, particularly for the unusual sound it makes.

Clappers

Clappers consist two objects of the same shape, made of wood or another material, that are struck against each other. In ancient Egypt it has been discovered that clappers were used an alternative to hand-claps. Clappers were not exclusive to the land of the pharaohs, however. Indeed, clappers in a wide variety of shapes can be found in all ages and in many parts of the world. The Western, twentieth-century variant consists of two slabs held in a special way between the fingers of one hand, which with a flip of the wrist produce a short, crisp, quickly repeating sound. Clappers have also been to provide the beat for all-girl singing groups. The literature of classical music has at least retained the *Kleppermars*. In the modern symphony orchestra, clappers are known as *claves*.

Hand-Clapping

Rhythmic hand-clapping is the most popular way of providing the beat for music and dance. It can, however, simply be used on its own. Finger-snapping is another manual way of producing a beat, much used in jazz and popular music.

Ratchet rattle.

Various types of clapper.

Claves.

player usually has a pair of castanets in each hand, each with a different pitch. The upper dish is struck with the fingertips in such a way as to strike the lower dish, producing a sharp, crisp sound that can be very rapidly repeated. An experienced player can achieve a wide variety of different effects but this takes a lot of practice. For an easier-to-use variant, the castanets are fastened to a handle. Castanets are always associated with Spain and especially with flamenco music, but they have also been used in many other cultures, including ancient Egyptian and Chinese. Their use in symphonic compositions of the twentieth century is primarily to evoke a Spanish atmosphere. One of the best-known examples of this is Claude Debussy's (1862–1918) suite *Iberia* (1905-1910).

Whip-Crack

The whip crack or slapstick consists of two wooden planks linked by a hinge. If they are forcefully struck against each other, a sound is produced that sounds like the cracking of a whip. The best-known "whip crack" is the one at the beginning of Ravel's *Piano Concert in G* (1929-1931).

Castanets

Castanets are shell-shaped wooden plates. There is a protrusion on each of these containing two holes, through which a string is run to loosely connect both dishes. The most commonly-used material for castanets is ebony or another kind of hardwood. The

Whip crack (slapstick).

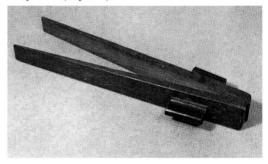

Hand-clapping.

Finger snapping.

Castanets on a handle.

Various antique castanets, of which one specimen has a handle.

Castanets as used in a symphony orchestra.

Flexatone

The flexatone is a very modern instrument although the construction is quite simple. A rectangular metal plate is mounted on a handle made of thick wire. The plate contains a thumb grip and two small mallets with wooden or rubber heads.When the whole instrument is moved, the mallets hit the metal plate, and produce vibrations that make the sound. Using the thumb, the tension on the plate can be increased or decreased, causing a change of pitch. The flexatone is frequently used in modern popular

Whip crack.

music. In classical music, the *Concerto for Piano in D-flat* (1936) by the Russian composer, Aram Khatchaturian, contains a large part for the flexatone.

Tap-Dancing

Stomping the feet on the ground has been always been a simple form of producing rhythm. Sometimes, special footwear is worn for the purpose, usually in combination with a resonating floor. The most familiar form is tap-dancing, in which special footwear, consisting of hard-soled dancing shoes to which small metal plates are attached are used on a wooden dance surface to produce a lively, rhythmic sound.
The clog dance, performed by the clog-wearers of the Netherlands and Lancashire, England is a variation on tap-dancing. Another variant is dancing in bare feet on a board laid over a pit, so that a deep, droning sound is produced by the feet. The American composer Morton Gould wrote a *Concerto for Tap Dance and Orchestra* (1952), that is

Orchestra cymbals ring out when clashed against each other.

Cymbals

Cymbals belong to the family of idiophones: percussion instruments that produce ringing from themselves. The cymbal is slightly

Flexatone.

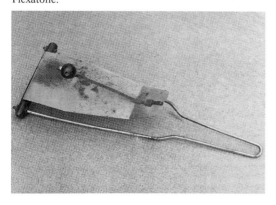

performed, among others, by the Chicago Symphony Orchestra, with the tap dancer Savion Glover as soloist.

convex. There are a number of basic forms of the cymbal, including:

- Turkish: a slightly convex cymbal with a smooth upper surface. Toward the center, the surface bulges into a sort of inverted bowl, in which the hole for hanging the cymbal can be found;
- Chinese: a slightly convex cymbal, arced, in which the edge is turned slightly upward. Toward the center, the cymbal bulges into a kettle-shaped protrusion on which the hanging point is to be found;
- the modern orchestra cymbal is relatively flat, though very slightly convex, and has a diameter of up to 24 inches.

The most frequently used material is bronze. Cymbals are used in pairs as well as singly. The dimensions can vary widely. There are large types, in which one is held in each hand, but there are also miniature cymbals that are worn on the fingers (see *Finger*

Orchestra cymbals being "swept" against each other.

Cymbals). In Western music, the large cymbals are more common in both symphony orchestras and percussion groups, and in brass and marching bands.

The large cymbals can be played in three ways. In one, the cymbals are horizontally clashed against each other, and in another, the cymbals are slid vertically past each other, brushing against each other. Sometimes a single cymbal is struck with a stick.

Cymbals date back to the most ancient times and are found in almost all cultures, for example among the Chinese and the Assyrians. The cymbal (*metsiltayim* for the pair of cymbals and *zilzal* for the single cymbal) is mentioned in the Bible and was played in the Solomon's temple. The Egyptians, Greeks, and Romans knew and used cymbals as well, but chiefly the smaller forms. In modern popular music, the cymbal is a component of the drum set, in which the single cymbal is attached to a stand and struck with sticks of all different shapes and sizes, from hard to soft.

The cymbal can also be struck using brushes of a springy material that the drummer can use in a sweeping or striking motion. *Hi-hat* cymbals are of a special type, consisting of two cymbals mounted on a stand in such a way that one cymbal, that is pedal-operated, is clashed against the other, mounted in a fixed position. The *sizzle cymbals* have small holes in the rim that contain loose rivets. When the cymbals are struck, the rivets produce a high, rushing sound.

In classical orchestra music, cymbals are encountered in some very specific adaptations, such as in Wolfgang Amadeus Mozart's (1756-1791) opera *Il Seraglio* (1782). This is another example of so-called Janissary music, when Turkish themes were very much in vogue. Mozart's "Turkish" opera has a special, excitement-generating role for the cymbals and other percussion instruments. A very different use of the cymbal is the single cymbal clash in the slow third movement of Anton Bruckner's (1824-1896)

Single cymbal on a stand (left) and a hi-hat with foot pedal.

Ceng-ceng; cymbals for a gong/chime ensemble, Bali, Indonesia.

Eighth Symphony (1884-1887) that constitutes the climax of the symphony. The orchestra can play an alternative version, written in 1890, in which the cymbal splash is edited out .

Finger Cymbals

The metal variant of the clapper or castanets has a special name: finger cymbals. These are miniature cymbals, attached to the thumb and index finger are encountered in Spanish and Islamic music. When the thumb and index finger are struck against each other, a short, sharp tone is produced. Another effect can be obtained by sliding the cymbals against each other in a sort of "money-counting" movement.

Cymbales antiques are a related form. They are larger and are played with both hands. When the player strikes the cymbales antiques against each other in a certain way, a

specific note can be struck. The large Indonesian cymbals known as *ceng-ceng* whose name is onomatopoeic, make a distinctive sound.

Leopold Mozart's (1719-1787) divertimento *Die musikalische Schlittenfahrt* (1755), uses a collection of cymbals and sleigh bells of indeterminate pitch to imitate the jingling of carriage bells. Sleigh bells are also used in different pitches for musical purposes. The popular piece of music called *Sleigh Ride (1948)* by Leroy Anderson (1908–1975) is the best-known use of sleigh bells for producing rhythm.

Cymbals of indefinite pitch or sleigh bells.

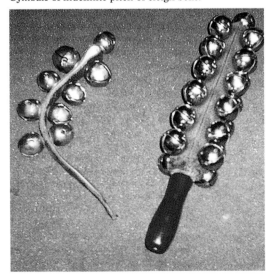

Gong

The gong is a slightly convex, round metal disk, usually made of brass, copper, or bronze, suspended by a cord attached at two points to the wide rim. The pitch depends on the size and weight of the gong. Gongs are to be found with diameters ranging from 8-28 inches. The gong is struck in the center with a stick that may or may not be cloth-tipped. Where required, the tone is dampened with the hand.

Cymbals of specific pitch.

Chromatically-tuned cymbals.

Finger cymbals.

The gong originates from southeast Asia, and in particular from China. The gong gradually found its way to western Europe, not only as an ornament to decorate the walls of well-to-do citizens, but also as an instrument in Western music. The Western gong may alternatively be called a *tamtam*.

Tamtam

Although the tamtam resembles the gong, it is an instrument of indefinite pitch. The slightly convex disk with a diameter of 20–43 inches has a rim that is bent slightly backward. The tamtam is suspended on a framework from this rim and is struck with a wide range of different sticks, varying from thick beaters with felt heads to xylophone mallets. The nature of the sound changes with the type of stick that is used. The echo is particularly important.

The type of sound has been described as "dark and threatening," as in the *Mars* movement of *The Planets* (1914-1916) by the English composer, Gustav Holst (1874–1934).

Gong in a stand of japara woodwork, Java.

Tamtam as used in concert.

equilateral triangle with a gap in one corner. The triangle comes in various sizes, but it is usually about 12 inches long. The instrument is suspended on a strap attached to one of the two continuous corners. The player holds the instrument aloft by the strap and strikes it with a 6-inch steel rod held in the other hand. Average volume levels are attained by striking the uppermost sides and the base is used for loud passages. A jingling sound is made by moving the rod back and forth between two sides.

Triangle

The triangle is a cylindrical metal rod around half an inch thick, bent into an

The gong has an overwhelming and threatening sound.

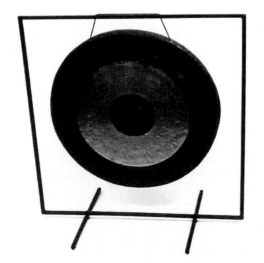

Bells

Although bells truly belong in melodic bell ringing, there are also individual bells of indefinite pitch. There are two basic forms, the clapper bell and the struck bell. The clapper bell is struck on the inside by a clapper hanging from a rope or chain.
The struck bell is struck with a stick on the inside or the outside. Bells may be cast, or wrought from metal that is worked into the appropriate shape.

Cow Bell

The cow bell is an instrument used very occasionally in the symphonies of the late Romantic period, such as in Gustav Mahler's *Sixth* and *Seventh Symphonies*, and in Richard Strauss (*An Alpen Symphony*). The cow bell is 3–10 inches in diameter and is made of copper or brass. The sides are parallel and it has a somewhat

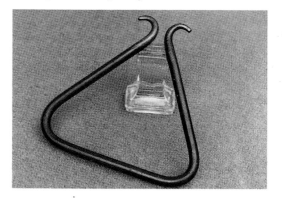

An early 19th-century triangle.

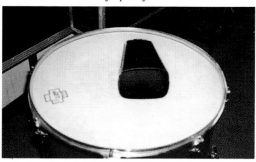

Cow bell as used in a symphony orchestra.

trapezoidal shape. It is held loosely in the hand and struck with a short, thick drumstick. The sound can be varied by striking different places on the instrument. When it is are played together with similar instruments, it is usually mounted on a support on the bass drum. Cow bells can also be found in series, suspended on a frame. In South American music, the cow bell is part of the percussion section under the name *cencerro*.

Modern orchestra triangle.

Tubular Bells

The modern symphony orchestra includes a number of percussion instruments that can be used for playing melodies, and the tubular bells is one of these. In its commonest form, the bells are suspended on a frame. The standard instrument has eighteen tubes with a range of 1½ octaves, but there are also sets containing 25 tubes. The bells are struck with a mallet. To prevent the sound decaying, there is a damping mechanism that is operated with the foot.

The *glockenspiel* is a close relative of the tubular bells, in which the relatively small metal bars lie in a horizontal frame, and are arranged like piano keys. The frame is set in a flat case, which in some respects acts as a resonator. The bars are struck with small metal mallets, creating a rarefied, chiming sound. Sometimes a simple piano keyboard with the necessary machinery is adapted to this. This kind of glockenspiel was much used by the German composer, Carl Orff (1895-1982), in his compositions for school orchestras.

The best-known orchestra part for tubular bells is in the last movement of Berlioz's *Symphonie Fantastique* (1830) but Mike Oldfield's (1954–) best-selling album, simply entitled, *Tubular Bells (1973)*, brought this sound to the attention of popular music lovers. Oldfield continues to perform his own compositions in concert, in which the tubular bells still feature prominently.

Hand bells.

Tubular bells in a rack, as they are used in a modern symphony orchestra.

Celesta

The celesta is a kind of improved form of the orchestral glockenspiel. The instrument was patented by the Frenchman, Auguste Mustel, in 1886. The celeste consists of tuned bars set in a harmonium-like case. These metal bars are struck by felt-covered hammers operated by a simple piano mechanism from a keyboard.

Unlike the orchestral glockenspiel, each bar has its own resonating chamber. Tchaikovsky described the sound produced by the celesta as "heavenly, divine music," as its name implies. Gabriel Fauré (1845–1924) and Gustav Mahler (1860–1911) are among the composers who have given the celesta a prominent role in their music. Another example is Bela Bartók's (1888–1945) *Music for Strings, Percussion, and celesta* (1936) but it is best-known for providing the melody in the *Dance of the Sugar Plum Fairy* in Piotr Ilyich Tchaikovsky's (1840-1893) *Nutcracker Suite (1892)*.

Bell Ringing

The bell as a melodic instrument can be found in many different arrangements and forms, such as the *hand-bell* in bell-ringing ensembles. Each player has a number of bells with different pitches, and these can be rung individually or in combination. In this way, reasonably complex melodies can be produced. Ordinarily, the sound of the individual bells will be allowed to decay naturally, but bells can also be dampened against the chest.

Church Bell

The church bell has been used since the eighth century. Roman Catholic churches tend to favor the carillon, but Protestant, and especially Episcopalian (Anglican) churches favor sounding bells. These bells come in all kinds of shapes and sizes,

Glockenspiel: tuned metal bars on a wooden framework.

Celesta.

used in conjunction with a clock. Sounding bells will frequently have specific names such as wedding bells and the death knell.Individual bells have been given names, such as the Liberty Bell in Philadelphia, Pennsylvania, USA. In England, church bell-ringing has been brought to a fine art, and the various peals have such names as Stedman, Plain Bob, and Grandsire Doubles. English church bells are unlike those in other countries, in that they swing in a complete 360° circle, rather than just swinging back and forth.

Carillon

The carillon was developed in northern Europe in the thirteenth century. It consists of a number of tuned bells, usually hung in a tower, the clappers being operated by a mechanism with ropes and levers. Nowadays, electrical and hydraulically operated

weighing from less than 100 pounds to several tons. The pitch can be specified with reasonable precision when the bell is cast. In its simplest form, the bell is swung back and forth in its "seat" with a rope so that the clapper hits the bell. Nowadays, electric mechanisms can do this, and they may be

Medieval church bells.

Modern orchestra glockenspiel with mallets.

carillons can also be found, sometimes even in conjunction with an automatic "player," that can usually be switched off, so the bells can be played by hand (see also Music-boxes). The best-known mechanism is a stiff piano-style keyboard consisting of sticks that the carillon-player hits with his fists. He operates the heavier bells with foot-pedals. In view of the heaviness of the mechanism, it is amazing how much subtlety a carillon-player can achieve. The electrification of the carillon has made his life easier, however as the piano keyboard can simply be played with the fingers, but true carillon lovers swear by the stick keyboard.

Carillons can be built in two ways—with clappers inside the bells or with hammers outside the bells. In a carillon, the bells hang stationary or "dead." Each bell has its own timbre, producing a melodious sound in harmony with the others.

Carillon.

The range of a true carillon is at least 30 bells and encompasses about 2½ octaves. Smaller constructions are called bell chimes. The best carillons in Europe can be found in Belgium, in the cities of Bruges, Ghent, and Mechelen (Malines). Outside Europe, the Riverside Church in New York also has an outstanding carillon.

Lithophone

Lithophones are melodic percussion instruments, in which, as the name implies, the sound is made by pieces of stone. Stones of different sizes produce different tones when struck with sturdy sticks or with another stone. There are a surprising number of these instruments around the world in places as far apart as Togo, Iceland, and Venezuela. The Chinese *pien ch'ing* is a set of 16 L-shaped tuned stone slabs, suspended on a large frame and struck with wooden mallets or padded sticks. The Vietnamese *dan da* is a very ancient musical instrument since examples were found in 1949 that are about 6,000 years old.

Metallophone

The term "metallophone" actually refers to a whole group of melodic percussion instruments, that are all made of tuned metal bars. Metallophones of diverse shapes and dimensions are to be found in an especially highly-developed form on the islands of the Indonesian archipelago. These instruments, such as the *saron*, the *gansa gambang*, and the *gender*, make up the largest section in the *gamelan* orchestras of southeast Asia. The last of these, the *gender*, distinguishes itself from the other Indonesian metallophones by the presence of individual bamboo resonators. Another difference is in the types of mallet used for striking the keys. Most Indonesian metallophones are played with wooden mallets, but the *gender* is struck with a mallet head covered in cloth.

In the Western world, children make the

Metallophone, Java, 19th century.

acquaintance of the metallophone early on, in the form of the toy xylophone. This instrument is still incorrectly called a *xylophone* (q.v.), despite the fact that it uses metal plates and not wood (Greek: xylos = wood). The world of brass and marching bands contains another variant—the *bell lyre*. This is a metallophone built into a lyre-shaped frame. The instrument is carried on a belt and is played by being held upright, gripped with one hand, while the other plays the instrument with a metal mallet.

In school music, *chime bars* are used. These can be played either one at a time or several at a time. In many modern compositions, as well as jazz, composers use the *vibraphone* (often known in jazz as the *vibes*). This instrument, its bars laid out like a piano keyboard, owes its distinctive sound qualities to an combination of acoustic and electric elements. The tubular resonators are almost entirely sealed by disks that are spun by means of an electric motor, hence the distinctive vibrato effect. The bars are struck with special vibraphone mallets, often covered in felt or rubber.

Bell lyre metalophone.

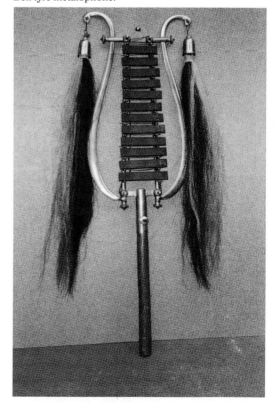

Vibraphone.

Since 1930, the vibraphone has had a pedal to damp the decaying sound. Lionel Hampton (1908–2002) undoubtedly put the vibraphone on the map. The "King of the Vibes" first discovered the instrument in 1930, in its early form that used a clockwork mechanism. It was not until 1936 that the vibraphone was fitted with an electric motor, thus making it possible to control the vibrato.

The best-known contemporary jazz vibraphonist is Gary Burton (1943–), whose 1971 album *Alone at Last*, a solo vibraphone concert recorded at the Montreux Jazz Festival was honored with a Grammy Award.

Steel Drum

The national instrument of the island of Trinidad in the West Indies is the steel drum. This instrument is a positive by-product of the development of the oil industry on the island. The steel drum has also been turned into a musical instrument on the Central American mainland.

The steel drum is a steel oil barrel. To turn it into a musical instrument requires quite a lot of work. First of all, the top of the barrel is pounded concave with a heavy hammer, into a shallow bowl shape. Next, an outline is drawn of where the various tones will eventually be. Hundreds of tiny dents are pounded into the top inside the outlines, using an awl. These hammered-in grooves determine the note produced by each section.

Depending on the desired size of the steel drum, the barrel is sawed off crosswise to a certain depth. The tone segments are then hammered from the inside to make them bulge outward. Next, the drum is tempered in a fire and then dunked in cold water to harden the steel. The last thing to be done is to tune the drum by tapping on each section with a hammer.

There is a whole family of steel drums, from the bass drum with five segments to the pingpong with 25 segments or more. The pingpong is, of course, the shallowest, the barrel being sawn off 5 inches below the rim. In most cases, steel drums are played in a sort of "family relationship", with or without the accompaniment of other instruments such as guitars. Smaller steel drums can be carried on a belt; the larger ones stand on the ground.

The steel drum is struck with two wooden mallets whose tips are covered in hard rubber or of cloth, held in place with rubber bands.

Xylophone

The most basic type of xylophone consists of several wooden bars laid across the legs

The treble of the steel drum family, the kid drum.

70

of the player and struck with sticks. In somewhat less primitive forms, the bars are arranged on a framework. Xylophones are found all over the world. Primitive forms are found in Africa. The xylophone called *aso* or *doso* in Benin is doubtless the largest xylophone in the world. The longest keys are huge, 6-foot beams. The keyboard of the big instrument is divided into two sections, one to the left of the musician and one to the right. He sits between them, resting his legs in the pit dug below the xylophone which acts as a resonator. The keys lie parallel to one another over and across the pit, which is about 28 inches deep and almost 80 inches wide. The musician strikes the left-hand keys (the bass) with a softwood club and the right-hand keys with a heavy crooked mallet made of extremely hard wood. The keyboard of the smaller instrument (*doso kpevi*) is set above another shallower pit. Its role is to provide a melodic and rhythmic ostinato as a cue for the main xylophone which renders the different themes designed to persuade each deity to dance at voodoo ceremonies.

Other ingenious forms are found on the islands of the Indonesian archipelago. The Thai xylophone, or *ranat ek*, stands on a base which was often elaborately decorated and is struck with wooden mallets. In Western music, the xylophone has been extensively developed as a permanent member of the percussion section of the orchestra, though it is also played as a solo instrument. The bars are ordinarily made of a hard wood, such as teak or rosewood, and are usually rectangular in shape; but there are other shapes. They are usually slightly bowed, and somewhat hollowed out on the underside. The smallest is 5½ inches long, the largest measures 15 inches. The modern Western xylophone comes two versions. The classic trapezoidal version has bars arranged in four rows on five rubber strips, but it is less common. The more usual arrangement is in two rows, so that the bars resemble a piano keyboard. The bars are struck with two or more spoon-like wooden mallets. In order to play very softly, mallets can be used whose heads are covered in rubber. The sound is sharp, but to simulate an echo, a player will often play a rapid trill. The best-known example of the xylophone played in a symphony orchestra is in Camille Saint-Saëns' (1835–1931) *Danse Macabre* (1874).

Marimba

The marimba originates in Africa and Central America. Its distinguishing feature is the resonators made of dried gourds that hang from wooden bars. The instrument is closely related to the xylophone, but the three-to-five octave range is somewhat greater.

The *marimbaphone* is derived from the folk marimba and is encountered in almost all forms of music. The wooden bars follow the sequence of a piano keyboard, with a tubular resonator under each of them. Because the marimbaphone is usually played with soft sticks covered in felt, its sound is fuller, yet less precise than that of the xylophone. The Dutch composer, Ton de Leeuw (1926–1996), wrote the solo piece *Midare for the Marimba* (1972).

Thumb Piano

The thumb piano or thumb harp is largely known in the Western world as an instrument for children, but in Africa, where it is known as a *sansa,* the thumb piano is a serious instrument. Sansas are plucked instruments of varying dimensions, on which

Xylophone.

Sansa or thumb piano.

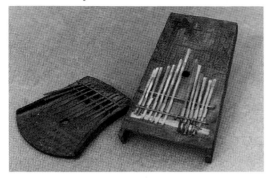

Two Jew's harps of bamboo from the Philippines.

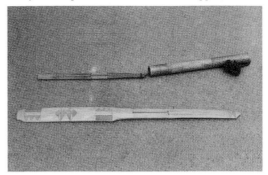

a number of metal tongues or blades are held down by a crossbar over a resonator. Each tongue has one free end that is usually plucked with the fingers. The pitches of the tongues can easily be varied by sliding them forward or backward.

Jew's Harp

The Jew's harp or *gewgaw* consists of an elastic tongue, carved out of or attached to a small frame. The frame is usually made of metal, bamboo, or wood. The player holds the instrument in the mouth, which acts as a resonator. Sound is produced when the player plucks the tongue with the finger. The shape of the mouth cavity determines the tone.

Franz Koch (1761-1831) Karl Eulenstein (1802-1890) were German virtuosos on the Jew's Harp, and the latter composed several pieces of music for it. Eulenstein lived in

Various European Jew's harps of different periods.

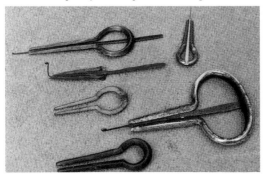

England for some time and played his Jew's harp for King William IV and the Duchess of Kent, the mother of Queen Victoria.

Friction Instruments

One way of producing sound is to rub two of the same type of object against each

Glass harmonica (after Tischbein, The Sanders sisters with a glass harmonica).

72

Musical saws with a bow. A support is attached the one in the foreground.

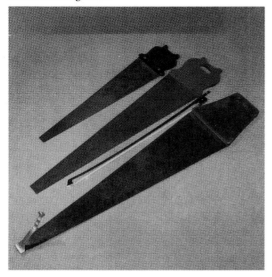

Glass xylophone.

other. They may be bones, pine cones, stones, or sticks. Another way is to rub an object with something different, which could be a bundle of twigs, or even oiled human hands. The most familiar example of this is the "musical saw," which is played with a violin bow. The pitch can be varied according to how hard the saw is bent.

Another well-known form of friction in-

Glass harmonica based on Benjamin Franklin's system, the *armonica* (Germany, early 19th century).

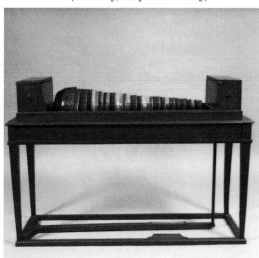

strument is the "glass harmonica," for which even classical composers such as Gluck, Haydn, and Mozart wrote music. The simplest form of this is a glass filled with water that is rubbed with a moistened finger. In 1743, an Irishman named Richard Pockridge created the *angelic organ*, which was a set of tuned wine glasses. This inspired Benjamin Franklin (1706-1790) to invent something he called the *glass armonica*, armonica being the Italian word for "harmony." Benjamin Franklin's *armonica* was a much more sophisticated version. It eliminated the need to tune the glasses by means of water (and thus avoiding the problem of the glasses going out of tune through evaporation) by making each glass of the correct size and thickness to give the desired pitch. The glass disks were nested inside each other to make them more compact, and they were mounted on a spindle that was turned by a foot treadle. The player moistened his fingers in a tray of water before rubbing them round the rims.

Another glass curiosity, is the "glass xylophone," played with mallets (see the illustration above).

Several types of brass musical instruments have been copied in glass, often by glassware manufacturers and glass blowers, as a way of demonstrating their skills. They are very often quite playable but very fragile, of course.

Wind Instruments

Details of the origin and development of wind instruments are largely shrouded in mystery. It is more or less certain, however, that the oldest materials of which wind instruments were fashioned had a decisive influence on their ultimate shape, and most were very similar to modern wind instruments. The different shapes of materials—shellfish, bone, and horn—that could be used to make wind instruments made it possible to create many different types. Thus, whistles would be made from small bones and flutes from longer ones. Tusks, conch shells, and animal horns, on the other hand, were very likely refashioned into horns to be used for signaling, the forerunners of today's horns, klaxons, cornets, and trumpets. The later addition of a mouthpiece (whether artificial or not) contributed to the crafting of primitive musical instruments.

The subsequent discovery of the reed as a musical instrument was a breakthrough that further expanded on the original collection of instruments. It did not matter whether the reed was cut out of the instrument itself or attached to the instrument as an add-on. Archeology has been the main source of knowledge of and insight into

Depiction of the *aulos, a* reed pipe, on a Greek mural. The first wind instruments were made of reeds, bones, and shells.

A clay flute from South America.

Ancient Chinese bas-relief depicting the rhythm of nature. Playing the jade flute connects humans, gods, and birds, according to the poet Li-Tai -Pe.

The *kena*, a carved reed flute.

ancient musical instruments. In the French Lower Pyrenees, near Isturitz, a bone flute has been found that is about 22,000 years old, and on the Danish island of Bornholm a neolithic flute has surfaced from about 10,000 years ago. Signal horns from the

Woodcut print from Praetorius' *Syntagma Musicum* with reed wind instruments.

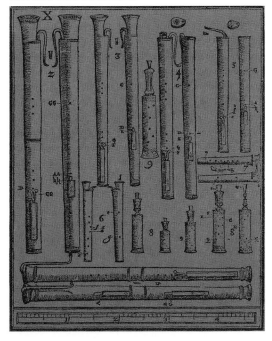

Bronze Age (3500-4000 years old) have been unearthed in Ireland and Denmark. In Egypt, a slate plaque has been unearthed depicting masked flute players. The plaque is about five millennia old.

In addition to discoveries such as these, quite a lot of information is available about the backgrounds of a good portion of the large number of ancient wind instruments discovered. The data derives from a variety of sources—pottery, jewelry, paintings, and sculptures from different countries of the eastern Mediterranean, eastern Europe, and South America. They tell us about scores of wind instruments and the way these instruments were used, starting in about the fourth millennium before the common era. There are even large numbers of texts that provide further information.

Despite their prehistoric origin, it was not until as late as the 16th century that the detailed description of musical instruments became a true science. From that point forward, numerous weighty tomes on the topic have been published. One of the most influential is the authoritative work of Michael Praetorius (1571-1621) entitled *Syntagma Musicum*, written between 1614 and 1620.

Woodwind

Out of the great diversity of flutes, pipes, shawms, and the like, there ultimately arose the group of wooden wind instruments, called woodwind for short. The various types of woodwind are distinguished by virtue of the different ways in which they are blown. For instance, the lips of a flute player serve as the "body in motion," the wind coming from the side of the instrument. The shawm and clarinet, on the other hand, include a reed; the oboe and bassoon have a double reed.

Until sometime in the eighteenth century, the only woodwind instruments included in the orchestra were oboes and bassoons. They were later accompanied by flutes and clarinets.

A group of 17th-century wind instrument players accompanying a singer.

Rushing pipe.

In the nineteenth century, the "family" of woodwinds was further expanded with the piccolo and the alto oboe (incorrectly called the English horn), as well as the basset horn, the bass clarinet, and the contrabassoon. Until sometime in the nineteenth century, only the woodwinds were accorded the same priority as the stringed instruments, and their privileged position in baroque and classical music was a result of this. In "classical" scores, the woodwinds are still located at the top. In continuation of an age-old tradition, the woodwinds would be present in pairs. This may be due to the fact that the oldest instruments, such as the *lur*, have also been found in pairs. The first wind instruments were mostly made of animal horn and were therefore, almost without exception, used in pairs.

From the fifteenth century onward, keys were added to some woodwind instruments that were used to open and close of the tone-holes (or finger-holes). As is still the case with the recorder, the tone-holes of

Bassoon, made by Wijne, in 1725 and oboe, made by Richters, 1720.

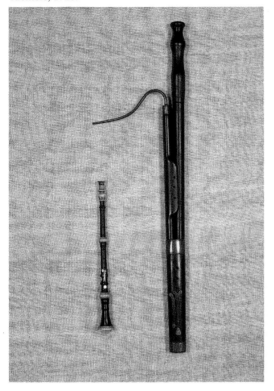

early flutes were always covered and uncovered with the fingertips. This created practical problems and meant that not all the notes could be played. At first, keys served only to open and close those holes that were out of reach of the fingers while playing, thereby increasing the range of the instrument in question. Later on, however, keys were employed to avoid so-called fork fingerings. In the mid-seventeenth century, closed keys appeared. The number of movable keys on the instruments gradually increased, but ca. 1800 there were still more finger-holes than keys on almost all instruments. Problems of intonation resulting from a player having an inadequate hand span were not resolved until 1832, by the German, Theobald Boehm. He rearranged the keys in accordance with the acoustic requirements of the instrument. This had consequences for the placement of the tone-holes. In addition to the simple keys that only corresponded to one hole, there were now existed "ring-keys" that could cover several holes at the same time. Following Boehm's example for the flute, key systems were subsequently developed for other woodwinds. At the same time, valves were introduced for brass wind instruments.

To this day there still exists a somewhat understandable confusion about the saxophone, for instance, which is sometimes classified as a brass instrument. In fact, it belongs among the woodwinds, because the instrument is blown with a reed. The saxophone is, to be sure, made of metal (frequently with a silver alloy), but that is also the case for the flute and other instruments classified as woodwind.

Syrinx

The syrinx (Greek for tube) is a *panpipe* without a mouthpiece, of the type given by the god Hermes to his son Pan, the god of shepherds, according to Greek mythology. The absence of a mouthpiece indicates that,

A collection of panpipes.

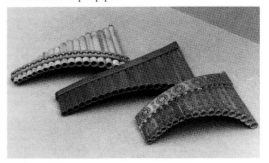

Baroque oboe, copy made by Paul van der Linden after an instrument by Denner from around 1700.

musically speaking, it is a fairly unsophisticated instrument. It is used in folk music, mainly by shepherds. The syrinx was not of great artistic importance. In its double form, with two divergent pipes, this flute was called the *diaulos*, not to be confused with the double *aulos* (q.v.), which is not a flute at all.

Recorder

The recorder is a wooden wind instrument that has been known for over 5000 years. It consists of tube through which an inverted conical hole is bored. The mouthpiece, which is often beak-shaped, consists of a block with a narrow slit in it, to serve as an air channel. Through this slit, the breath of the player hits a sharp edge, at which point the air stream breaks off and sets the air column inside the borehole in motion. The instrument has seven finger-holes along the top and a thumb hole on the underside.

The recorder can be found in almost every country in the world. In western Europe, the instrument has existed for more than 1000 years. The recorder was one of the instruments played in the late Middle Ages, by jugglers and minstrels. It was especially popular in France.

The recorder reached the height of its popularity in the fifteenth and sixteenth centuries. Up until the time of Johann Sebastian Bach (1685-1750) and George Frederick Hndel (1685-1759), it was the recorder that

Medieval recorder, found at the bottom of a well in Dordrecht, Netherlands.

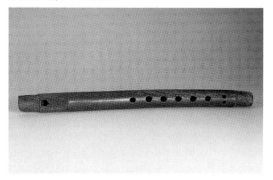

was meant when the "flute" was referred to. The so-called "transverse flute" did not enter Western music until the mid-nineteenth century.

From the Renaissance onward, the recorder was produced "in choruses,"meaning that recorders were available in every key. There were at least nine different formats for the recorder. Nowadays there are, with few exceptions, four "voices," the soprano, contralto, the tenor, and bass recorder.

In 1910 –1920, the recorder experienced a revival, starting in England, owing mainly to the efforts of a French-born musician and musical instrument maker, Arnold Dolmetsch (1858-1940), whose interest in the recorder was part of his enthusiasm for

Alto recorder, copy built after an 18th-century instrument by Dolmetsch.

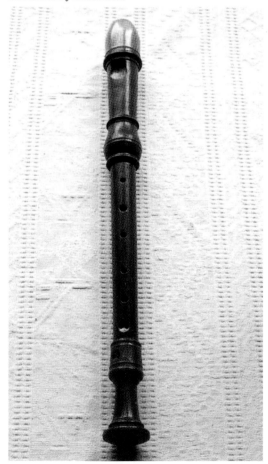

A hand-worked alto recorder from the Baroque.

"early" musical instruments that he re-created in his workshop. Just after World War I, numerous recorders were handmade by Peter Harlan (1898-1966), who changed the position of the tone holes in some instruments, introducing the so-called "German fingering." Nowadays, recorders are largely mass produced, because their easy playability makes them so suitable for beginners and for school ensembles.

A collection of recorders.

There is a very extensive repertoire of music for the recorder, from solo pieces to works A great deal of music was composed for the recorder in the sixteenth, seventeenth, and eighteenth centuries, for example, by Alessandro Scarlatti (1660-1725), Antonio Vivaldi (1678-1741), Hotteterre, Telemann, Bach and Handel. The twentieth century revival saw a new wave of compositions, for instance by the British composer, Benjamin Britten (1913-1976), who wrote the *Alpine Suite* (1955) for recorder trio, the children's opera *Noye's Fludde* (Noah's Flood) (1957) and *A Midsummer Night's Dream* (1960). Another English composer, Malcolm Arnold (1921-), uses it extensively in his work. Kazimierz Serocki (1922-1981), a Polish composer, also used the recorder in his compositions, such as *Arrangements for 1-4 Recorders* (1975-76) and the *Concerto all' Cadenza* (1974), in which he used a new playing technique. The most famous modern recorder player is the Dutchman Frans Brüggen (1934-).

Tin Whistle

This is a very popular copper or brass tubular flute, usually with six tone-holes. The tin whistle, also known as the penny whistle, was a favorite instrument of street musicians in the late nineteenth and early twentieth centuries . Currently, this flute is much heard in bars, especially in Irish pubs. The tin whistle is probably a modern variant of the *flageolet* (q.v.) Nowadays, such whistles are frequently made of plastic.

Shakuhatchi

This is a heavy, vertical Japanese bamboo flute, known since the eighth century. The instrument has a standard length of 20 inches—*shaku* is the Japanese word for a foot in length, and a *hatchi* is 8 inches, which explains the length of the instrument. The tube of the flute is open at both ends and has five holes, of which there are four for the fingers on the front and one for the

Shakuhatchi.

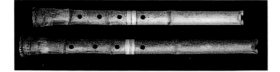

thumb on the back. There are larger and smaller varieties, graduated in half-tones higher or lower than than the basic tuning. Little is known of the origin of the shakuhatchi. It has been established that the instrument made its way from China to Japan in the eighth century and that it has been in use there for a long time. In the late twelfth century, the flute suddenly disappeared, only to reappear a century later among mendicant monks, who possessed extraordinarily decorative flutes. These new versions of the flutes produced many more sounds. In the sixteenth century, a mendicant order was founded that was dedicated to the teachings of an eighth-century Chinese Zen master. The symbol of the order was the shakuhatchi.

Ocarina

The ocarina (Italian for "little goose") is an instrument that works on the principal of the so-called globular flutes, which are normally oval-shaped and have finger-holes and a mouthpiece. The most elementary form of this is the *sifflet*, versions of which can be found all over the world, from Oceania, Asia, the Middle East, and Africa, to the Americas.

The ocarina is often shaped like a shell or a bird, and is made out of earthenware or porcelain.

The modern ocarina was invented by Giuseppe Donati from Budrio, Italy in 1860. It is made of metal and comes with a mouthpiece with a pipe and 8 tone-holes. The instrument has become popular outside of Italy, as well, for its hollow, muffled sound, mainly for playing at home.

A collection of ocarinas.

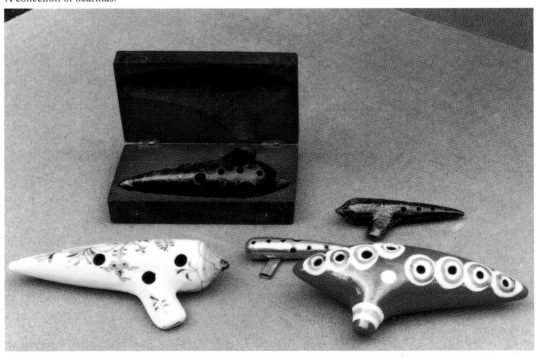

Flageolet

The flageolet is a small recorder also known as the *flauto piccolo*—not to be confused with the *piccolo* (q.v.). From the sixteenth through the nineteenth centuries, the flageolet was ia popular instrument in France and England.

A flageolet, like most other recorders, has six tone-holes, four on the top and two on the underside for the thumbs, except for the English model in which all six holes are on the top.

The flageolet was given keys in the eighteenth century, and in the nineteenth century, it was fitted with the movable rings of the Boehm system (see Transverse Flutes). Originally, flageolets were part of the baroque orchestra (including in works by Bach and Handel), but it wasn't long before they were also being played in chamber music ensembles. In France, they were frequently played to accompany the quadrille and other dances. In the early nineteenth century, a double flageolet was invented in England that was very popular for some

A collection of flageolets ranging from a simple model without keys to models with Boehm-system keywork.

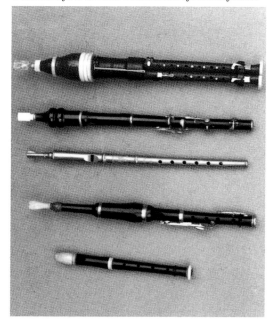

Wooden double flageolet, trimmed with ivory.

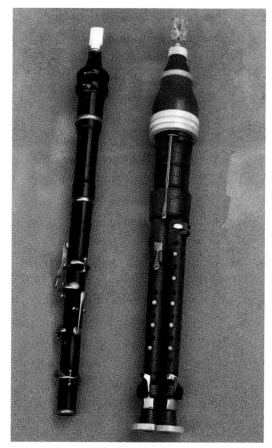

time. It meant that two pipes could be played simultaneously, making it possible to produce parallel thirds. There is also a triple flageolet but this is something of a rarity. Miniature flageolets were even made to encourage caged birds to sing.

Transverse Flutes

The flute is the oldest wind instrument without a reed. The air stream produced by the player's lips is directed toward a sharp edge, where the stream splits and causes the air column in the hollow tube of the instrument to vibrate.

The flute held level or pointing downward, has a "beak" that also gives it the name of *beaked flute*. The most familiar examples of this type of flute are the recorder and the transverse flute. The flute is a woodwind instrument, although it was made of ivory and, for a period in the nineteenth century, entirely from polished glass (above all in Paris). Nowadays, the silver Boehm flute is the most commonly used.

The transverse flute existed three thousand years ago in east Asia. The transverse flute was even played in ancient Egypt, although this type of flute was blown on top into the open end of the tube rather than through a mouthpiece. In Europe, the transverse flute first emerged during the Etruscan period. In the music of central Europe, the transverse flute can be found from the twelfth century. This instrument, which had seven to fourteen tone-holes, was much favored by medieval knights.

The development of the modern transverse flute began in around 1660. At first, a single key was added, and later the cylindrical bore was replaced by a conical bore, an adaptation credited to both the flautists bearing the name of Jean Hotteterre (second half of the seventeenth century). Then a flute was created that could be dismantled into three pieces. The top piece was

Transverse flutes made of various materials: ivory, crystal, rosewood, and brass.

cylindrical while the others had a conical bore. Together with a small, sharp blowing hole, the various elements created a clear, nuanced sound. The fact that this flute could be dismantled meant that a more precise bore was possible, and the tuning could be adjusted by using middle joints of varying sizes. The instrument was first used in France. Jean-Baptiste Lully was the first composer to write the instrument into an orchestral score, in his ballet *Le Triomphe de l'Amour* (The Triumph of Love) (1672). Afterward, the conical transverse flute with one key really began to gain in popularity. J.S. Bach is said to have begun composing for the transverse flute, instead of the recorder, after he had heard the instrument only once, in Dresden, in 1717. All the same, it needed more than the conical bore and the single key to completely eliminate the flaws that this relatively primitive instrument still possessed.

The oboist and (later) flautist Johann Joachim Quantz (1697–1773) not only

The flautist playing a tune on a simple transverse flute. Lithograph by Hieronymus Hess.

added a second key to the transverse flute, but also invented a tuning screw.

In the eighteenth century, the transverse flute become so popular that it displaced the recorder from its predominant position. After 1750, mention of "the flute" was an allusion to the transverse flute. Unlike the recorder, which largely was used in ensembles (from soprano to bass), the transverse flute remained almost exclusively limited to the soprano version. An *alto flute*, pitched a fourth below the regular flute, exists but it is much rarer. The *bass flute*, which occurs as a recorder as well, never gained the importance in music that the soprano flute did.

The number of keys used to open tone-holes has tended to increase. The flautist Theobald Boehm (1794-1881) was responsible for the most important reform, sometime around 1850. He was actually an iron foundry technician, and in 1828, with the technical knowledge he had gained from his occupation, he started a workshop in Munich for making musical instruments. Starting in 1844, Boehm was active also as a court musician in Munich, the capital of Bavaria. Boehm enjoyed an enormous reputation as a flute virtuoso and he also composed many pieces for his own version of the instrument. He made an extremely important musical contribution with his

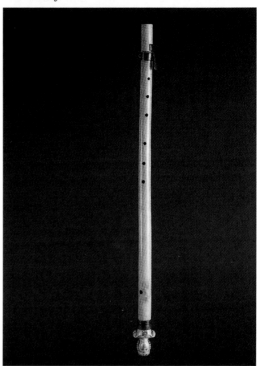

Primitive transverse flute with as yet only one key, 17th century.

system for building woodwind instruments- one that set an entire revolution in motion. Working with the Swiss musical instrument maker William Gordon (1791-1839), Boehm started with the notion that it was not the convenience of the keywork, but rather the acoustic principles of ideal resonance that should dictate where the tone-holes were placed. He therefore first determined the scaling of the flute before he occupied himself with a suitable arrangement for the mechanisms. One of the most important consequences was that he made the very small tone-holes so wide that they could no longer be covered by a fingertip. He also introduced the parabolic head joint and improved the key system. The tone produced by a Boehm flute is indeed very different from older instruments, as it much fuller and rounder.

The Boehm flute was adopted very rapidly in France and England, but opponents of the Boehm system, above all in Germany,

Collection of primitive transverse flutes, from top to bottom: a *lotus flute* or *swanny whistle*, two tin whistles, including a penny whistle manufactured by Clark, a *szakan* (Russian transverse flute), a Yugoslavian *double flute*, and an Irish tin whistle.

Flute with three interchangeable middle joints, built by Borkens.

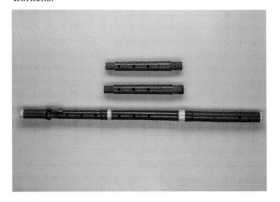

Details of transverse flutes made of wood and ivory from the second half of the 18th century.

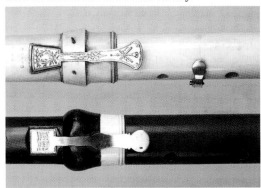

complained of a lack of the distinctive flute sound in his instruments. And so it happened that Maximilian Schwedler constructed a "reformed flute," dubbed a *Schwedler flute*, as a variation on a model that had been designed in 1885.

There are three differences of consequence between the Schwedler flute and the Boehm flute. The bore (which remained conical in the Schwedler flute), the key system (which had a character all its own), and the blowing hole, which was not only oval, but was also raised along the sides (the "reformed mouthpiece.")

The objections to Boehm's instruments could not keep them from being used in modern orchestras. Of the earlier types of flute, only the tiny *piccolo* (q.v.) and the *alto flute* (q.v.) have remained in use.

Boehm expounded his philosophy of flute-making in his book *An Essay On the Construction of Flutes* (1847) which was translated into English and French in 1882, a year after his death. Not long afterward, French and English studies of the Boehm system were published. Johann Joachim Quantz (1697-1773) another accomplished flutist who played at the Bavarian court, wrote a book entitled *The Art of Flute-playing* (1752) that has remained the seminal work on the subject for two and a half centuries. In 1983, a facsimile of the original German version of the book was reissued by the music publisher Bärenreiter,

and since 1992 it has been available in an inexpensive pocket edition. This work stands alone in terms of quality, much as the *Violinschule* (Violin School) written by Mozart's father, Leopold (1719-1787), and the *Klavierschule* (Piano School) by Bach's son, Carl Philipp Emanuel (1714-1788).

In addition to a great deal of chamber music, many concerti featuring the flute as a solo instrument were composed in the eighteenth century by Vivaldi, Telemann, Quantz, C.P. Bach, Stamitz, and Mozart. By the nineteenth century, the popularity of the flute concerto had waned, but flute virtuosi such as François Devienne (1759-1803) frequently performed their own variations and chamber pieces.

It was not until after 1900 that the flute came into its own again as a solo instrument, largely thanks to French composers, such as Claude Debussy and Maurice Ravel, and in the solos and other works by Jacques Ibert (1890-1962), Darius Milhaud (1892-1974), Francis Poulenc (1899-1963), and Olivier Messiaen (1908-1985). Not only did they write original works, but they also developed new playing techniques for the instrument.

Base flute.

Transverse flute.

Richly decorated baroque recorder.

Great flautists of the second half of the twentieth century included the Irishman James Galway, and the Frenchman Jean-Pierre Rampal. Rampal interpreted compositions for his own instrument, and also adapted early music for this relatively modern instrument. He was so impressed by the *Violin Concerto* (1940) by the Armenian composer Aram Khatchaturian (1903-1978), known for his *Saber Dance* from the ballet *Gayane* (1942), that he pleaded with him to write a concerto for flute as well. Khatchaturian suggested to Rampal that he should simply rearrange the *Violin Concerto* for the flute.Thus it was that the *Flute Concerto by Aram Khatchaturian* was written in 1968, but with a new cadence by Rampal (albeit with the solo passage left as intact as possible). Since the flute, unlike the violin,

cannot produce different notes simultaneously, the piece had to be "attacked" sparingly. The Italian flautist Severino Gazzelloni (1919-1992) promoted contemporary music for his instrument, including the music of Petrassi, Berio, Maderna, Henze, Zimmermann, Pierre Boulez, and Edgard Varèse (1883-1965). He performed Varèse's *Densité 21.5*, composed in 1936, having been commissioned by the flautist, Georges Barrère, who wanted to use it to break in a new

Nineteenth-century flutes in their cases.

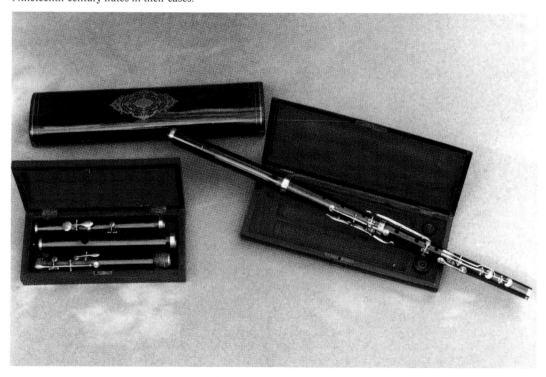

Modern transverse flute.

flute. The first performance was held at a concert
on February 16, 1936, in New York. Varèse's title refers to the specific gravity of platinum, the precious material of which Barrère's flute was made.

In 1975, a version was released by flautist Paul Horn with live recordings in various spaces in the Egyptian pyramids. It consisted of 39 original psalms, of which seven were vocal, eighteen for alto flute, twelve for the C flute, and two for piccolo. The recordings were made in the king's chamber, the queen's chamber of the Cheops pyramid, the grave room of the Chefren pyramid, and the grave room of the Mycerinus pyramid. Paul Horn had already made recordings in the Taj Mahal, and there as

well, the spatial effect contributed significantly to the success of his project. Further recordings were made in other unusually shaped buildings to benefit from their acoustic properties. In 1991, a CD version of the twelve psalms was released.

Piccolo

The piccolo (Italian for "small") is a transverse flute that is about half the size of the regular flute. The range is an octave higher. Without accompaniment, the piccolo does not sound very convincing, but it is certainly capable of being heard in a large orchestra. The piccolo has the highest pitch of any instrument in the classical orchestra. Originally, the "little one" was confined to military bands, but it gradually won a place in the symphonic repertoire, and can be heard in Beethoven's *Sixth Symphony*, the *Pastorale* (1808), and in Berlioz's *Symphonie Fantastique* (1830).
The piccolo may be made of wood, or it may

A number of unusual flutes: three piccolo flutes, specifically a *tierce flute*, a *B flute*, and an *F flute*, an American *A flute* (manufactured by Pond & Firth), a *G flute* (manufactured by Geissler), a German *fife*, a cylindrical military flute in *A* (ca. 1800), and an orchestra *piccolo* in C (manufactured by Buerger, 1880).

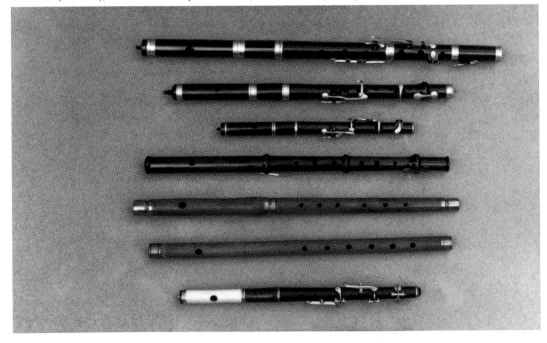

Piccolo.

be silver-plated or made of white metal (alpacca), and nowadays even of plastic. The advantage of this instrument is that it combines so perfectly with the regular flute, such that the impression is created that the listener is hearing only one instrument. *Daphnis et Chloë* (1912) by Ravel is a superb example of this. In one passage, a melodic phrase is first entrusted to the piccolo, then to the regular flute, and subsequently to the alto flute.

It was not until the late eighteenth century that the piccolo gained a place in the orchestra. Beethoven wrote music for the instrument in his *Fifth* and *Sixth Symphonies*, but it was Tchaikovsky who gave the piccolo a prominent role in his *Nutcracker Suite* (1892) and managed to take full·advantage of all of the possibilities of this instrument.

Of the many flute concerti that Vivaldi composed, there is also one for piccolo. The Frenchman Jean Françaix (1912-) wrote a *Suite* (1962) that featured solo passages for the G flute, transverse flute, and piccolo.

Chalumeau

The English word *shawm* and its related terms in French *chalumeau* (calamus=reed) and in German *Schalmei* (calamer=straw) have a tendency to lead to confusion, as all these words are used interchangeably for the instrument that was the forerunner of the oboe.

"Chalumeau" parts were written in the eighteenth century, but it is not certain which instrument they refer to—an oboe, a folk forerunner of the clarinet, or an early form of the clarinet itself. The shawm played an important role in numerous operas and cantatas of the baroque period.

Shortly after 1700, the chalumeau was refashioned into the clarinet. The instrument maker Johann Christoph Denner (1655-1707) from Nuremberg, Germany, did little more, in fact, than add two extra (keyed) tone-holes to the instrument, thus significantly extending the range of the instrument and satisfying the demands that music was increasingly making on the players. By "overblowing," an "extra register" could be created that was dubbed *clarino*, not to be confused with the difficult upper register of the *baroque trumpet* or *clarino (q.v.)*.

A chalumeau is an instrument with a cylindrical bore, equipped with a single reed and therefore a woodwind instrument. It was very popular in in central European folk music during the Renaissance. The lowest register of the modern clarinet is still called the chalumeau.

There exists an extensive repertoire for the chalumeau, written primarily by composers who lived between 1660 and 1780. The best-known pieces are by Georg Philipp Telemann (1681-1767). At the beginning of his career, he played the instrument himself. Some composers, such as Antonio Caldara (1670-1736) and Atillio Ariosti (1666-1740) wrote several parts for the instrument, while others wrote a single concerto or a part for the chalumeau. These composers include Reinhard Keiser (1674-1739),·Johann Adolph Hasse (1699-1783), and Jan Dismas Zelenka (1679-1745).

Chalumeau is also the name for a schalmei-like (4' or 8') reed stop for the organ.

Clarinet

Of all important woodwind instruments in classical music, the clarinet is the youngest.

Chalumeaux of various dimensions were frequently employed in folk music. Just after 1700, the instrument maker Johann Christoph Denner (1655-1707) of Nuremberg, Germany fitted the chalumeau with two extra tone-holes, covered with keys, thereby initiating the development of the clarinet. The instrument was improved several times more in the course of the eighteenth century, including by Mozart's friend Anton Stadler (1753-1812). In 1696, Denner submitted a request to the city of Nuremberg to be recognized as a master woodwind instrument-maker, a profession which was not officially recognized at the time. The request was granted and Denner was able to perfect his new woodwind instrument. The term "clarinet" appears for the first time in the archives of the city of

Three folk clarinets: a *launeddas* from Sardinia (an unusual feature is the bourdon pipe) and two Egyptian *double clarinets*.

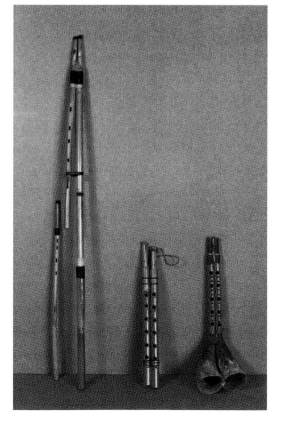

The clarinetist, a lithograph by H. Hess.

Nuremberg in 1710.

At the beginning of the nineteenth century, Iwan Müller (1786-1854) developed an arrangement with thirteen keys, rendering the instrument suitable for virtuoso playing in all keys.

The word clarinet is the diminutive of *clarino* (q.v.). In Bach's time, this was a trumpet without valves, which was played through a very narrow mouthpiece. The clarinet is a woodwind instrument with a single reed and a cylindrical bore. The modern clarinet shape dates from around 1700, but nowadays, the instrument has eighteen tone-holes and 20-22 keys. The clarinet can be tuned to any key, but nowadays the B-flat clarinet is the most popular. There are also compositions for the A clarinet, but hardly any for the E-flat clarinet or the C clarinet.

The clarinet sounds almost "dark" in its low register, exceedingly mild in its middle register, and very penetrating and even raucous

The development of keys on the clarinet, from left to right: B-flat clarinet (Mueller system, made by Mahilon, Belgium, ca. 1840), B-flat clarinet (Mueller system with ring-keys, made by Albert, Belgium, ca. 1840), E-flat clarinet (made by Bertin, France, ca. 1890), clarinet (Boehm-system and Klosé system, made by Godefroy, France, ca. 1870), clarinet (Albert system with closed keys, maker unknown, ca. 1920), clarinet (Albert system, made by Buffet, France, ca. 1920).

Modern clarinet.

in its upper register, which was only exploited for the first time in jazz. Around 1800, a *bass clarinet* was designed and made. It is tuned an octave lower (usually in B-flat). It was through the composers of the Mannheim School—the best-known being Franz Danzi (1763-1826) and Carl Stamitz (1745-1801)—that the clarinet was accepted into the orchestra. One of the first composers to write solos for the instrument was Mozart. The clarinet really flourished when music was written for it by Louis Spohr (1784-1859), Carl Maria von Weber (1786-1826), and Felix Mendelssohn (1809-1847). Richard Wagner perhaps took greater advantage than any other composer of the possibilities of the bass clarinet. Claude Debussy (1862-1918) and Paul Hindemith (1895-1963), like Mozart and Richard Strauss, wrote pieces for clarinet solo and orchestra. In addition to the well-known works, there are various interesting compositions for the solo instrument with a symphony orchestra, chamber ensemble, or

string quartet, of which many are very much worth listening to.

The chamber music clarinet repertoire is also quite extensive, and includes pieces for the clarinet, combined with harpsichord or harp, or the clarinet with strings, with or without piano accompaniment. A splendid example is the three *Clarinet Quartets* by the relatively obscure Swedish composer, Bernard Henrik Crusell (1775-1838), which were released on compact disk in 1993. Crusell was himself a renowned clarinetist, and composed three concerti and various duos, in addition to the three quartets written in 1803, 1804, and 1821. In those days, quartets for clarinet and string trio were very much in vogue, particularly for performance in the home. These quartets are extraordinarily balanced pieces, even though the clarinet dominates on occasion. The influences of Crusell's great idols Mozart and Weber (he met the latter

Historical clarinets, from left to right: clarinet with two keys and a tuning joint (made by Scherer, ca. 1730), a clarinet with five keys (made by Brandt, ca. 1760), clarinet with six keys (maker unknown, ca. 1830), clarinet with six keys (maker unknown, England, ca. 1840), clarinet with six keys (England, ca. 1830, made by Wolf & Co.).

in person in Dresden) are unmistakable. Works have also been written for one or more clarinets without any accompaniment, by Igor Stravinsky (1882-1971) and Francis Poulenc (1899-1963), among others.

Basset Horn

The basset horn is an alto clarinet tuned to the key of F. It is believed to have been invented by Anton Mayrhofer (ca. 1706-1774) in the Bavarian town of Passau. The first musicians to play this instrument were not Bavarian, however, but Bohemian. The instrument that Mayrhofer made himself still exists and can be viewed in the Museum of Hamburg History in Hamburg, Germany.
The basset horn needs an extra-long tube and is therefore bent. Mozart made frequent use of the instrument, for instance, in his unsurpassed *Serenade for Thirteen Wind Instruments* KV 361 (ca. 1780). It is worth nothing that nowadays, this piece is often played by twelve wind instruments and a double-bass, instead of a contrabassoon.
The modern basset horn is of a different shape, as it no longer needs to be bent, and is played notably in the so-called Strauss orchestra. Richard Strauss wrote parts for the instrument in several of his operas, but his example has rarely been followed. The basset horn is now approximately 39 inches long and is generally tuned to the key of F or E-flat.

Saxophone

The saxophone is a modern, single-reed, wind instrument that is made of brass. It is named for its inventor, the Belgian instrument-maker Adolphe Sax (1814-1894). Sax. a close friend of the composer Hector Berlioz, perfected his invention around

Basset horn

Unusual soprano saxophone (make King, model Saxello, built in 1924). This instrument was made famous by the saxophonist Ronald Kirk.

1840, when he was still living in Brussels. In 1846, he registered a patent on his saxophone with a patent agent in Paris. How Sax invented the saxophone is not known, but it is certain that he also contributed to the development of the bass clarinet. While working on improving that instrument, it is highly likely that Sax started experimenting

The unusual bell of the Saxello.

Unusual alto saxophone (make King, model Naked Lady, built in 1914).

Tenor saxophone.

with the clarinet mouthpiece, attaching it to various brass instruments.

The saxophone consists of a wide metal tube that is generally bent at the opposite end to the mouthpiece. The most unusual feature of this instrument is certainly the mouthpiece. The use of different materials for the mouthpiece creates different tone colors. The strength and quality of the reed can also change the timbre. Professionals generally choose a mouthpiece based on their style or on the piece to be played.

Saxophone fingerings are like the oboe's, the mouthpiece is like the clarinet's (blown with a single reed).

The timbre lies somewhere between that of a woodwind instrument and that of a brass instrument, and ranges from the mellowness of a flute to the metallic forcefulness of a cornet.

The most important representative of this family is without any doubt the alto saxophone. Together with the soprano saxophone, the tenor saxophone, and the bass saxophone, the alto saxophone completes the familiar quartet. In addition, some man-

Unusual tenor saxophone (make Buescher, model Aristocrat, built in 1939).

Various modern saxophones.

ufacturers have produced a sopranino saxophone and three larger ones, up to and including the subcontrabass saxophone, which is pitched an octave lower than the double-bass).

Johann Georg (also known as Jean-George Kastner) (1810-1867) was the first composer to introduce the saxophone into one of his scores, in 1844, although Berlioz conducted a concert in the same year, featuring an arrangement of his choral work, *Chant Sacré*, that featured a saxophone. The instrument came into greater use thereafter, mainly in Italy and France. It was accorded an important role not only in military music, but also in opera, in concerti, and in chamber music.

Subsequent improvements were made to the instruments after Sax's own patent expired in 1866. For instance, in 1868, Pierre Louis Gautrot & Co. patented a screw-in pad system and in 1875 the French firm of Goumas patented a saxophone with a fingering system similar to the very popular Boehm system for the clarinet (q.v.).

The Russian, Alexander Glazenov (1865-1936), composed a concerto for alto saxophone and orchestra (1934), as did the Dutchman Tristan Keuris (1946-1996) in 1971. An older compatriot of his, Matthijs Vermeulen (1888-1967), wrote the alto saxophone into his *Seventh Symphony* (1963-1965). Jascha Gurewich (1896–1938) was a player and composer who played in John

Unusual baritone saxophone (make Buescher, model 400, built in 1966).

Modern alto saxophone.

Philip Sousa's (1854-1932) bands. Sousa, born in Washington D.C. and composer of so many rousing marching tunes, of which the best known is probably *The Stars and Stripes*, had an entire saxophone section in his later bands. In Ravel's orchestration of Mussorgsky's *Pictures at an Exhibition*, in 1922, there is also a superb saxophone part. The saxophone may have been invented in the age of classical music, but it really came into its own in the Jazz Age, to such an extent that many people consider it to be an "American" instrument. Yet the first saxophone was not made in America until Gus Buescher's version, based on Sax's patent, manufactured in 1885.

George Gershwin and Aaron Copeland are just a couple of the American composers who have prominently featured the various types of saxophone in their music, Gershwin in *Rhapsody in Blue* (1923) and *An American in Paris* (1928) and Copeland in *Symphony No. 1* (1928).

The saxophone is primarily known as a popular music and jazz instrument. The saxophone was first popularized among the American public by Tom Brown and the Brown Brothers, starting in 1911, with such compositions as *Bullfrog Blues* and *Chicken Walk*.

The great jazz saxophonists include Lester Young (1909–1959), Coleman Hawkins (1904–1969), John Coltrane (1926–1967), Charlie "Bird" Parker (1920–1955, Stan Getz (1927–1991, and Ornette Coleman (1930–), all of them from the United States. Probably the best known jazz composition featuring the saxophone is Paul Desmond's *Take Five*, first recorded on an album by the Dave Brubeck Quartet in 1959.

A North African bagpipe.

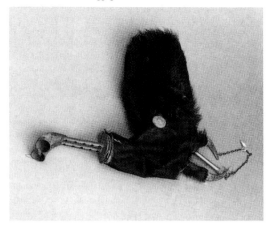

A Northumbrian bagpipe.

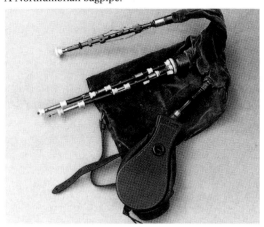

Bagpipe

A Turkish bagpipe.

This instrument takes a variety of forms and names in different languages. In France, it is known as *cornemuse*, the Breton version being known as . *In Scots Gaelic, it is known as pibroch, doedelzak* in Dutch and *Dudelsack* in German). The last two names are derived from the Polish *duda*, meaning "pipe." The bagpipe is an instrument (the pipes) to which an air reservoir (the bag) is attached. The bag is made of tanned animal hide and contains openings for the sounding pipes. These pipes are of varying lengths and are

Musicians with an Italian bagpipe (*zampogna*) and a shawm (*ciaramella*) (hand-colored etching by Alfredo Mueller, 19th century).

each fitted with a single or a double reed. The airbag is held tightly under the arm of the player, and by squeezing the bag, air is pushed out through the pipes. Because the

Two replicas aulos and an original in pieces (5th century BC).

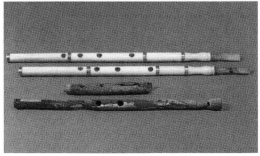

94

pipes are not directly blown by the player, he has no influence on the tone that is ultimately produced. As a result, the instrument has a piercing and inflexible, rather mournful, tone.

The bagpipe has a melody pipe with six tone-holes for the fingerings. One to three drones, which perform the function of a bass line, complete the instrument.

The origin of the bagpipe can only be guessed at, but the idea of an instrument with its own air reservoir can be found among the ancient Greeks. The Roman Suetonius (ca. 70-130 CE) recorded the fact that the Emperor Nero played the *utricularius*—another Roman author calls the instrument *ascaules*. In the Middle Ages, the bagpipe came to be adopted by street musicians and minstrels. Nowadays, the bagpipe, in its various forms, is still played by farmers and shepherds in the mountain regions of central, eastern, and southern Europe. In Scotland, however, especially in the Highlands, it is the national instrument, and is played by bands of bagpipers as well as solo. Highland regiments are traditionally led into battle by a solitary piper, and a piper always performs on solemn occasions, from Burns Night (January 25, the anniversary of the birth of Robert Burns, Scotland's national poet) to the death of a famous person. There is also a Northumbrian variety of bagpipe, that is smaller than the Scottish pipes.

Aulos

The aulos (Greek for "wind") was the most popular wind instrument of the ancient Greeks. It has a cylindrical or conical tube and a double-reed mouthpiece. The aulos was made of rosewood, lotus wood, or boxwood, of bone or ivory, and occasionally even of metal. In the year 700 BCE, the instrument had four round finger-holes. By the Hellenistic period, the number of tone-holes in the aulos had grown to fifteen holes and they had become oval in shape.

The Egyptians were familiar with this instrument some 3500 years ago. Some sources even report that specimens have been discovered in the royal tombs of Ur of the Chaldees, where the biblical patriarch Abraham was born, and which date from the third millennium bce.

The aulos found its way to Greece by way of the Hittites and Assyrians. According to Greek mythology, the aulos was invented by a Lydian king around 1500 BCE, or by the goddess Pallas Athene, or even by Apollo himself.

The Greek philosophers were less taken with the aulos, claiming the instrument was a corrupting influence, but this did nothing to harm its popularity. It was played at weddings, burials, sporting events, and during the intermission in the theater. The player of the instrument was called an *aulet* and the singing that accompanied by this instrument was called *aulodie*. This nomenclature is recalled in the *Aulodie for Oboe and Orchestra* (1960, revised in 1966) by

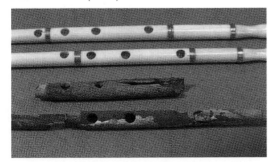

Authentic aulos (detail).

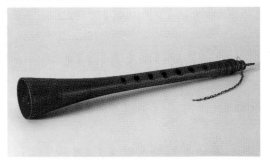

Moroccan shawm.

Orchestra horns.

the German composer Wolfgang Fortner (1907-1987).

Tibia

The Roman counterpart of the aulos, the tibia, was also an import from the east.

Martinshorn (Germany, 19th century).

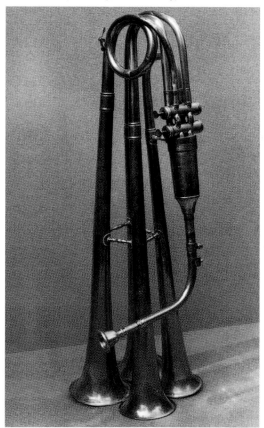

Two folk shawms: the zurla from former Yugoslavia, and the Chinese sona.

It was in widespread use in Phrygia, a kingdom that covered what is now northern Greece and the province of Anatolia in Turkey, and that was called Tibia by the Romans. This type of tibia generally took the form of a double oboe, but in Rome during the Hellenistic period (about 200 years BCE), it was supplanted by the aulos.

The *tibia* was the only instrument permitted to accompany an actor or chorus in the theater. It was also played at funerals and on festive occasions.

Schalmei

The schalmei (calamer = straw) is a double-reeded woodwind instrument with a sharp, piercing tone. Like the *oboe* (q.v.), it has six or seven tone-holes. The schalmei was played by medieval musicians and shepherds in the German-speaking countries. It has much in common with the Greek *aulos (q.v.)* and is the forerunner of the *bombard (q.v.)*, another ancestor of the oboe.

The schalmei originates from the Middle

The bombard, a medieval wind instrument.

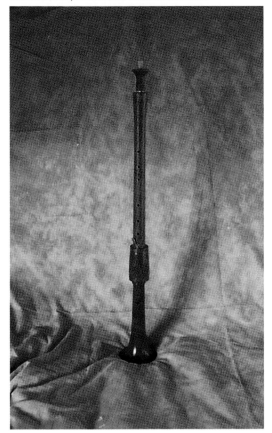

Baroque oboe with three keys (built by Richters).

Bombard

This instrument, also called the *pommer*, is a forerunner of the oboe. it has a narrow, conical bore and a double reed that is held between the lips of the player, as in older schalmeis that had no wind-cap. The bombard has six or seven tone holes.

Various shawms, from left to right: a *musette*, a pastoral oboe, and a bombard.

East and is frequently played there to this day, especially in Egypt. The player lets the reed vibrate freely in the mouth. In Europe, a wind cap was devised, against which the player presses the lips. In Catalonia, the schalmei is still the most important folk instrument, only nowadays it is fitted with modern key mechanisms. The *sardana*, a fast-moving sixteenth-century Catalan folk dance, is always accompanied by two treble and two tenor schalmeis.

A modern variant of the schalmei emerged the nineteenth century . It is called the *martinshorn*, and resembles a brass wind instrument at first glance, but it has a number of schalmei-like tongue mechanisms placed directly in front of the valves. The schalmei is also the name of an organ stop. As a reed-stop it has numerous variants.

The evolution of the oboe: left, a two-keyed oboe from Germany, unknown maker, from ca. 1800 and right, a twelve-keyed oboe from Germany, unknown maker, from ca. 1830, (Selner system).

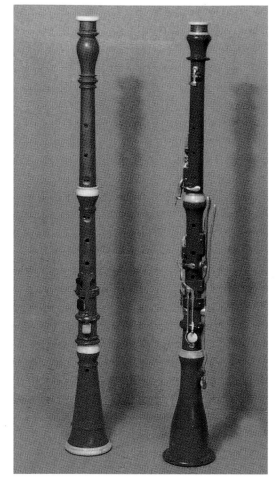

The evolution of the oboe: left, an oboe from ca. 1850, built by Horak, in the center, an oboe from Germany, ca. 1860, maker unknown (Germany), and right, an oboe from ca. 1890, built by Plivric. Note the octave keys on this instrument.

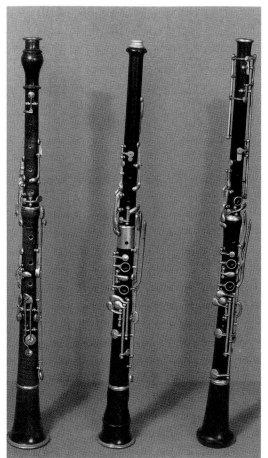

This instrument originally comes from the East and is first recorded as being seen in France in the fourteenth century. The smaller bombard is also called a *schalmei* (q.v.). There were tenor bombards, alto bombards, basset bombards, bass bombards, and double-bass bombards. They lasted until around 1700, but all were ultimately supplanted by the oboe, which gained more and more ground, starting in France.

Nowadays, bombards are again being built for performances of early music. The *pommer* is also the name of an organ stop that is chiefly found in the pedal.

Oboe

The name *oboe* is derived from the French word *hautbois*. It is a wooden wind instrument, slightly conical, with key mechanisms (up to fourteen) and a double reed. Forerunners of the oboe include the *schalmei* (q.v.) and the descant *pommer* or *bombard* (q.v.) An oboe was first built in France around 1650, and in the course of the eighteenth century in Germany, the instrument gained a permanent place in music. Since J.S. Bach used it in his orchestra music, the oboe has gained popularity, as a solo instrument as

The evolution of the oboe: left, an oboe from ca. 1850, built by Horak; in the center, a German oboe from ca. 1860, maker unknown. Right, an oboe with octave keys from ca. 1890, made by Plivric.

instruments are now being built again, thanks to the renewed interest in authentic baroque music, but have no regular place in the modern symphony orchestra, in which only the oboe and the alto oboe are played. The alto oboe is better known as the *English horn*, *cor anglais*, or *corno inglese* although there is, in fact, nothing specifically English about the instrument. The name is probably a corruption of the French *corps anglé* (bent body). In 1839, a straight version of the horn emerged. It has a mellow tone, rather like an English hunting horn.

As an instrument in folk music, the oboe is still quite frequently found in southern Europe, North Africa, and in Asia. where a tapered version is played. Two well-known. oboe-like folk instruments are the Yugoslavian *zurla* and the Chinese *sona*.

Countless composers have written pieces for oboe or alto oboe and orchestra, whether backed by another instrument or not. Jacques Ibert (1890-1962) composed a *Symphonie Concertante* (1948-1949) for orchestra and solo oboe. Mozart, Milhaud, and Telemann also wrote many pieces for the oboe. Antonio Vivaldi wrote no less than 11 concerti for oboe and orchestra. Well-known twentieth-century composers who wrote music for the oboe include Krysztof Penderecki (1933-) and Bernd-Alois Zimmermann (1918-1970).

The oboe is a popular chamber music instrument, whether played solo or accompanied by piano or harpsichord and there is a large repertoire of music for it. The oboe may also be accompanied by strings, with or without piano accompaniment. Much solo music has been written for the alto oboe, notably by Charles Koechlin (1876-1950) and the English composer Benjamin Britten (1913-1976), among others.

well as in an orchestra. Many well-known composers wrote oboe concerti or solos, including Handel, Telemann, Mozart, Schumann, Richard Strauss, and Penderecki. J. S. Bach regularly wrote parts for the *oboe d'amore* or the *oboe da caccia*, which is pitched a fifth lower. Both of these

Oboe D'amore

This instrument is larger than the regular oboe (length around 25 inches), but is pitched a minor third lower. The bell is somewhat pear-shaped, which is intended to

Bassoon.

Oboe da caccia.

make the timbre slightly milder, placing the oboe d'amore somewhere between the regular oboe and the English horn.

The oboe d'amore emerged in the 1720s and was first heard in Hamburg, Germany, in Telemann's opera *Sieg der Schönheit* (first version, 1722). Three years later, the *oboe d'amore* made an appearance in Bach's *Cantata No. 37* (*Wer da glaubet*) and again, a year later, in the opera *Ludwig de Fromme* (1726) by Georg Schürmann (1672-1751). Three decades later, the instrument fell into disuse, but just over a hundred years later, the Belgian Charles Mahillon (1813-1887) reconstructed the oboe d'amore for a performance of Johann Sebastian Bach's *Two Passions and 49 Cantatas*, in which there are parts for this instrument. Nowadays, the oboe d'amore is again being played in authentic performances of the works of Bach, for instance. Bach's *Concerto for Oboe d'Amore and Strings (Keyboard Concerto in A), BWV 1055*, was originally written for the oboe d'amore and later adapted for the harpsichord.

Oboe da Caccia

The oboe da caccia (Italian for *hunting oboe*) was developed during the seventeenth century as one of the improvements made to the alto bombard (q.v.). The oboe da caccia was probably also used as a hunting horn. It is a "transposing"

Heckelphone.

instrument. Around 1850, the oboe da caccia developed into the alto oboe, which was used in opera.

Heckelphone

The heckelphone is a baritone oboe, originally made by Wilhelm Heckel (1856-1909), and first used by Richard Strauss in his opera *Salomé* (1903-1905) and later in *Elektra* (1906-1908) and *Eine Alpensimfonie* (1911-1915). Paul Hindemith (1895-1963) composed a *Trio for Viola, Heckelphone, and Piano* (1928). As an alternative to the heckelphone, which is a rare instrument nowadays, the part can also be played by a tenor saxophone. The instrument is hardly used nor are any built today.

The heckelphone is made of maple, has a length of about 4 foot 6 inches, and a conical bore. The key system resembles that of the oboe and the English horn, and the fingerings are identical. There is a type of heckelphone that is a fourth higher than the oboe and pitched an octave higher than the English horn. Although the heckelphone

The bassoonist (lithograph by H. Hess).

Copy of a three-keyed baroque bassoon made by Dunner.

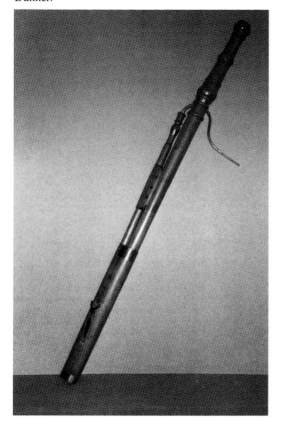

Nine-keyed bassoon from the maker, Simeo (ca. 1825).

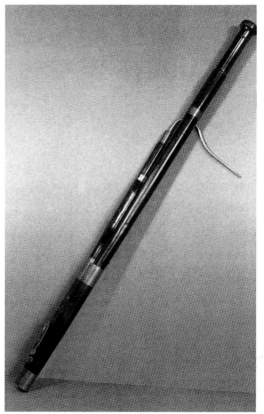

has fallen into disuse, in the clarity of tone, especially in the upper register, it can replace the oboe.

Dulcian

Dulcian (from *dolce* = sweet) is the earlier name of the bassoon. At the beginning of 1600, the dulcian was in use practically everywhere in Europe. However, in France around 1650, it was supplanted by the baroque bassoon that came into fashion at around the same time as the baroque oboe. In German military music, the dulcian was still used until 1720. The instrument-maker, Michael Praetorius, used the names *dulcian* and *fagot* (bassoon) interchangeably. To avoid confusion, the name *dulcian* is used when referring to the instrument played in the Renaissance period, and bassoon when

referring to the baroque and later periods. The dulcian is also a reed stop for the organ.

Bassoon

The bassoon, known as *fagot(t)(o)* in some other languages, meaning "a bundle of twigs" in reference to its appearance, and *basso(o)n* in French and English in reference to its bass sound, is a woodwind instrument with a double reed, like the oboe. The instrument has 24 tone-holes, of which nineteen have keys. The bassoon was originally developed around 1570, but the most significant improvements were made during the nineteenth century by Johann Adam Heckel (1812-1877), for whom the heckelphone (q.v.) was named.

The bassoon is a bass instrument with an extraordinary character because it can

Bass recorder.

Bassoons.

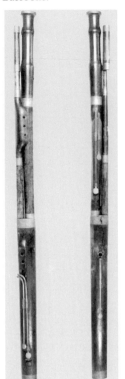

Sarrusophone.

express itself within a range of four octaves in a specific way, varying from solemn up to and including humorous and burlesque. Various composers wrote special solo parts for the bassoon within, or in front of, the orchestra, including Lully, J.S. Bach, Handel, and Rameau, but it was not until sometime in the nineteenth century that the bassoon became a permanent part of the symphony orchestra.

Thirty-eight concerti for bassoon and orchestra have been attributed to Antonio Vivaldi, but it is not certain that he composed them. Less well-known composers who wrote for the bassoon include Marescotti, Maingeneau, and Bourgault-Ducoudray.

Berlioz exploited the dark, sinister elements of the bassoon in his *Symphonie Fantastique* (1830), Stravinsky used the meditative possibilities in *The Firebird* (1909-1910), and Paul Dukas (1865-1935) revealed another side of the bassoon altogether in his *Sorcerer's Apprentice* (1897). One of the most famous and at the same time most popular parts for the bassoon was written by Sergei Prokofiev for *Peter and the Wolf* (1936).

Much chamber music has been written for the bassoon, including pieces with piano, harpsichord, and harp accompaniment. The *contrabassoon* is pitched one octave lower than the regular bassoon.

Sarrusophone

There is some disagreement among scholars about the year in which this instrument was invented, but it was some time between 1856 and 1863. It is certain that a sarrusophone was made in 1863 by the Parisian instrument-maker P.L. Gautrot (1835-1884). The inventor of the instrument was named Sarrus, and he was leader of the military band for the 13th French regiment of the line. The sarrusophone is unique, in that it is a brass instrument with a double reed and eighteen keys. Like the oboe, it is conical in shape, but because the sarrusophone has wider scaling, it has a more powerful tone and is also louder. The fingerings are the same as for the saxophone.

Starting in 1863, Gautrot built sarrusophones in six different sizes, varying from the high descant down to the contrabass. Sarrus had intended his invention to be used exclusively in military bands, to replace oboes and bassoons. The sarrusophone family originally consisted of nine instruments of varying size, all of which (except for the contrabass in C) are transposing instruments with tessitura notated as B-flat/G3. The two smallest instruments, the soprano and sopranino, are straight conical bore instruments while the larger members have tubes that are bent back on each other once or even twice, like a *tuba* (q.v.). The majority of instruments found today are tuned to B-flat and E-flat. The contrabass version can be substituted for the contrabassoon in the symphony orchestra.

Because the instrument had such a mellow sound, and because it was always on the mark in terms of intonation, it was thought to have a great future. Unfortunately, this was not the case. The sarrusophone has fallen almost entirely into disuse since the early twentieth century. Almost all the music written for it was exclusively French, especially "serious music."

Another problem encountered by the sarrusophone is that its legal position was shaky. Almost immediately after the first models were made, Adolphe Sax (see Saxophone) sued Sarrus, claiming that Sarrus was infringing his patent. Sax lost the case but this did not do much for the sarrusophone.

Crumhorn

The crumhorn is a woodwind instrument in the shape of a bent horn with a double reed and a wind cap, which makes "overblowing" impossible, and at the same time limits the range to a ninth. As a result, the crumhorn is built in different keys.

This instrument was mainly popular in France, in the fifteenth and sixteenth centuries, and even as late as the mid-eighteenth century, under the name *tournebout* (meaning "twisted end").

The crumhorn is being made again due to the revived interest in Renaissance music.

There is an organ stop (usually 8') with this name, which produces a rather nasal sound. A *récit de cromorne* will frequently be performed using a *dulcian* (q.v.) if no crumhorn is unavailable.

Racket

This instrument is also called the *ranket*. The name probably comes from the Middle High German word *ranc* (bending). Another name of the racket is *sausage bassoon*. This double-reeded woodwind instrument, which comes in five formats, was played predominantly from the late fifteenth through some time in the seventeenth century. The 12-14 inch long horn is made of wood or ivory. Inside the barrel, there is a

Crumhorn.

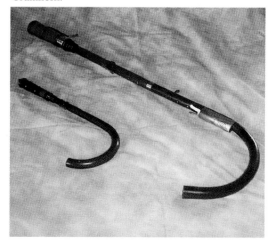

Replica of a *cornu,* a Roman trumpet.

Engraving of *cornett-* and trumpet-players.

long, wrapped pipe, of which the air channel (windpipe) is bent eight or nine times. Eleven hand grips are distributed over the outside of the racket in addition to some tone-holes.

The racket makes a rather muffled sound. According to Michael Praetorius, it sounded "as if one were blowing through a comb." The racket is also the name of an 8' or 16' organ stop with a very distinctive, but somewhat rough-sounding timbre.

Brass Wind Instruments

In theory, the instruments in this category are named after the material they are made of. The group is called "brass" for short. The tones of these instruments are not produced by a "body in motion" or a reed in the mouthpiece instrument, but rather by the lips of the player in the mouthpiece.

The sound of brass is loud and forceful, in some cases even warlike and compelling. That is the reason why armies used to blow signals on brass instruments, to communicate orders to the soldiers, including the order to attack.

At first, brass players could only produce a few fundamental tones, but by overblowing, overtones could be produced as well. Brass players had to live with these limitations for many centuries, but in the course of time two innovations were made that made it possible to blow other notes as well.

The first innovation was lengthening or shortening the tube by sliding the bottom portion of the tube in or out of the rest of the tube. The best example of this device in operation is the trombone. The other innovation was the addition of valves, with which all brass wind instruments could be played fully chromatically.

Until about 1850, the brass section of the orchestra consisted of horns, trumpets, and trombones, with the later addition of the *tuba* (q.v.) or *Wagnerian tuba* (q.v.). Some instruments in the brass section of the symphony orchestra are made partly or entirely of wood and are played with a cup mouthpiece. With these instruments, pitch

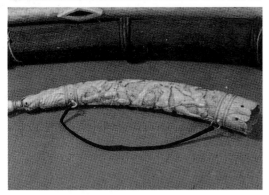

Yemenite shofar. It unusual for the shofar to be carved.

modifications are produced with the help of tone holes or keys. They include the *cornett* (q.v.) and the *ophicleide* (q.v.).

Shofar

The Hebrew word *shofar* means "ram's horn", an unambiguous indication of the material of which the instrument is made. It is a rather rudimentary wind instrument without even a mouthpiece that is blown from the narrow end. In theory, the shofar can produce no more than two or three notes, but the relatively short length of the tube, in fact, make it possible to produce some intermediate notes.

In the Old Testament, the shofar is mentioned in the story of Abraham's sacrifice of Isaac, as a symbol of his redemption. Magical powers were ascribed to the shofar, which were later drawn upon in the battle of Jericho. The Book of Joshua (6:4) recounts: "and seven priests shall bear...seven trumpets of rams' horns..." and in verse 5 of the same chapter: "when they make a long blast with the ram's horn ...", causing the walls of Jericho to crumble and fall.

Originally, the shofar was blown on all Jewish holidays, and this is still the case among Sephardic Jews. Ashkenazic Jews perpetuate the tradition from Temple days, when the levites (priests) blew it to announce the New Moon (and thus the beginning of the month). It is blown on the Jewish New Year

(Rosh Hashana), unless it falls on the sabbath, and it solemnly ends the Day of Atonement (Yom Kippur), a 24-hour fast and the holiest day of the year for all Jews.

Lur

The *lur* is a form of trumpet from the late Nordic Bronze Age. It has a conical tube 2-3 yards long, which consists of various parts joined together, and is bent in a distorted S-shape. At the sound-producing end, there is a bronze disk decorated with geometric figures, considered to be symbols representing the sun. There are *lurs* that have small metal plates on the mouthpiece which come into contact with each other and create a rattling effect.

Numerous perfectly preserved lurs have been dug up in bogs in the Baltic region, predominantly in Denmark and southern Sweden. The most important collection of lurs is housed in the Danish national museum in Copenhagen.

All sorts of theories about Western polyphony have been inspired by the instruments, which were discovered lying next to each other in symmetrical pairs.

The primitive lur is a simple horn, made from the tusk of a mammoth and subsequently decorated with metal. Later on, the instrument was cast in bronze, and later still, furnished with a mouthpiece in the shape of a goblet. In Scandinavia, *lur* is also

Forerunners of modern brass wind instruments, from top to bottom: an African signaling horn, an oliphant (16th-century replica), midwinter horn, alpenhorn.

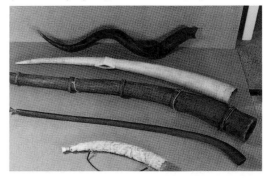

the name for a trumpet made of bark or wood, which was played by shepherds until the late nineteenth century, for chasing away wild animals and keeping the sheep or goats together.

Midwinter Horn

The midwinter horn is an instrument with a strong folk tradition that can be found in the eastern Netherlands, especially in the Twente region, where it is still used in the winter. The midwinter horn-blowing is practiced at twilight. Some local people think that the midwinter horn should only be blown from December 24 until January 6, and others think that the horn-blowing can start at the end of November. Originally, the horn performed the same function as the New Year festivities, namely, to drive away evil spirits. When the horn is blow, the end of the instrument is held over a well, which amplifies the sound significantly. During the rest of the year, when the horn is not being used, it is usually hung inside the well. The reasons for this are shrouded in mystery.

The midwinter horn is usually 4–6 feet long, but longer horns also exist. The instrument is made of two equal, hollow halves of a thick branch of alder wood which are lashed together with strips of willow. Originally, the midwinter horn had no mouthpiece, but nowadays it has a cup mouthpiece, like the French horn (q.v.) and the tuba (q.v.).

A small didgeridoo.

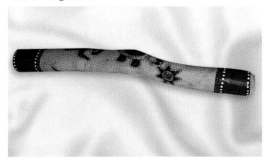

Didgeridoo

The Australian didgeridoo is also a member of the family of wind instruments. It is the most important instrument of the indigenous peoples of Australia, the aborigines. The didgeridoo is made of a slightly conical branch of the eucalyptus tree that has been hollowed out by termites. The instrument varies in length from 3–7 feet long with a mouthpiece consisting of a lip of beeswax. The outside is usually painted with ocher yellow decorations. The playing technique is unique, in that the sound is produced by blowing air through the lips while they are relaxed. This is very different from all other wind instruments, which require tension in the lips. A droning sound is produced which continues uninterruptedly, the result of a very unusual breathing technique called circular breathing, in which the player inhales through the nose while blowing through the mouth. This technique is also used by saxophonists. The didgeridoo is now heard in Western music, especially among street musicians, and there are some players who are not native Australians.

Alpenhorn

The Roman historian Cornelius Tacitus (ca. 50 BCE–116 BCE) wrote that the Germanic tribes possessed a *cornua alpina*. It is possible that this instrument was an ancestor of the alpenhorn. In the Middle Ages, the horn was mostly to be found in Alpine regions, especially in Switzerland where it has been known since at least the sixth century. The alpenhorn is a straight instrument with a length of 6–8 feet and usually ending in a slightly upturned bell. It is generally carved from a tree trunk of a suitable shape, that is then split lengthwise and hollowed out. Afterward, both halves are glued together again and wrapped in strips of tree bark. The horn can only produce a few basic notes.

Johannes Brahms took his inspiration from the alpenhorn, incorporating its booming

Various signaling horns: coach horn (England, end of the 19th century), post horn (Belgium, end of the 19th century), Aïda trumpet (the Netherlands, ca. 1890), tram horn / post horn (ca. 1900).

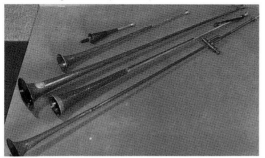

A number of horns: parforce horn (ca. 1800), *trompe de chasse* (France, 19th century), signaling trumpet (Netherlands, 19th century).

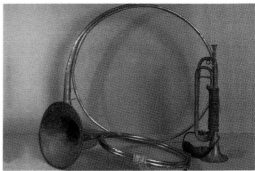

note into the fourth movement of his *First Symphony* (1855-1876). Brahms wrote the passage in musical notation on September 12, 1868, in a letter to Clara Schumann. (He sent her the letter from Switzerland for her birthday.) He provided the passage with the following comment: *"Also blus das Alphorn heute ..."* ("This is how the alpenhorn blew today ...").

Even prior to this, Mozart's father, Leopold (1719-1787), had written the alpenhorn into his *Sinfonia Pastorella*. It is strange, however, that the alpenhorn is not played in the one orchestral work in which one would most expect to find it—*Eine Alpensimfonie* by Richard Strauss.

Horn

The French horn or forest horn is a metal instrument with a cylindrical-conical bore, which possesses a mouthpiece and valves. The original instrument was made out of a conch shell, animal horn, or tusk, and examples have been found dating from prehistoric times. Later, the horn was made of various materials, such as bark, wood, terra cotta, glass, and different metals. The Romans adopted a bronze version of the horn from the Celts.

The horn was first used as a signaling and battle instrument, but before long it was also used while hunting, especially during the Middle Ages. It was initially shaped like a cow's horn, but was made of metal and was carried on the back or on a belt at the hip. It frequently served as an ornament worn by the nobility, and in that function sometimes came in the form of the *oliphant* (q.v.). Later, the instrument was used as a forest horn (*waldhorn*) and a post horn.

The horn is believed to have acquired its circular shape sometime around the

Horn with shanks and crooks in case.

The modern horn.

orchestra (even the trumpets) and so should be played with their bells in the air—in contrast to the customary way of playing, with the bells pointing backward. To obtain the desired effect in the Mahler symphony, most conductors will have the horn-players play the coda standing and will usually use eight horns instead of seven.

The French composer, André Ameller (1912–1990), wrote music for solo brass and orchestra, in this case for a solo horn with orchestral accompaniment. Haydn wrote two concerti plus one concerto for two horns and orchestra, Mozart wrote four horn concerti, and Richard Strauss two. Paul Hindemith and Camille Saint-Saëns composed for the horn as well. Robert Schumann (1810-1856) even composed a *Konzertstück* for four horns and orchestra (1849). Pieces for horn with piano accompaniment were composed by Paul Dukas (who is best known for his *Sorcerer's Apprentice*, 1897), Ameller, Beethoven, and Hindemith. Trios and sonatas (often for four horns) were written by the German Paul Hindemith and another Frenchman, Jean Yves Daniel-Lesur (1908–2002), Mozart, Haydn, Brahms, and Florent Schmitt (1870-1958).

Oliphant

There are divergent opinions about the background of this musical instrument. Some think that the oliphant (made of ivory and richly jeweled) first came to Europe from the Middle East in the tenth century, and that it was mainly used as a status symbol. From the eleventh 11th century onward, oliphants were made more frequently, most commonly by moslem craftsmen working in southern Italy and Sicily.

The French expert on the history of musical instruments, François-René Tranchefort, believes that the first oliphant was offered to Charlemagne by the Caliph Harun al-Rashid, who ruled his empire from Baghdad in the late eighth century. In the Middle Ages, the

middle of the sixteenth century. Only a few basic notes could be blown on it, but when valves were added (two in 1814, then three after 1830), it became possible to play all the intermediate notes of the scale. It was not until the nineteenth century that this form of the horn became more popular.

The symphony orchestra contained two horns in the days of Mozart and Haydn, but Beethoven wanted three for his *Third Symphony*, the *Eroica* (1803-1805). During the Romantic period, the horn quartet gained a permanent place in the orchestra.

Two of the four horns (the first and the third) were pitched high, the other two (the second and the fourth) low, and that is still the case in the symphony orchestra.

Composers of the late Romantic period, such as Anton Bruckner (1824-1896) and Gustav Mahler (1860-1911), regularly wrote for eight horns. Mahler wrote in the coda of his *First Symphony* (*Der Titan*, 1884-1888) that the seven horns that are supposed to be heard above all the other instruments in the

Three descant cornetts.

oliphant was an indispensable accessory for the knights of the higher nobility. It was used for signaling during hunting and in battle. The instrument could produce no more than three or four notes, but according to tradition, their sound was exceptionally powerful. This is how the oliphant is portrayed in the classic French poem *Le Chanson de Roland* (Song of Roland), in which it is claimed that when Roland, the folk hero, blew his horn, it could be heard 30 miles away. This would make the instrument the first European telephone! Anthony Baines writes in *Grove's Dictionary of Musical Instruments* that there is not a shred of proof for the existence of either the oliphant at the time of Charlemagne or even of Roland himself.

Cornett.

Cornett

This instrument is called a *zink* in Dutch and German, derived from the Middle High German word *zinke, meaning* animal horn. Other European languages do not share this word, and use the word cornett, spelled with two T's in English to distinguish it from the *cornet* (see *Cornet à pistons)*.

Cornetts occupy an exceptional place between the woodwinds and the brass section. They make use of a tube that is comparable with the *schalmei* (q.v.) and which also possesses tone-holes—six on the upper side and a seventh on the underside. Cornetts are, however, blown in the same way as brass instruments.

All these different elements come together to create a warm, mellow sound that harmonizes extremely well with other instruments. It is in this that cornetts display an unmistakable family resemblance to the trumpet, although they are made of wood and covered in leather or, less frequently, of ivory. Cornetts are made in various pitches and shapes.

Although the origin of the cornett is not altogether clear, the instrument has been found in Europe since the twelfth century. The cornett reached its zenith in the sixteenth and seventeenth centuries. Until some point during the nineteenth century, it remained in use among city musicians for blowing on special occasions. Cornetts could fill in for the "voice" of violins, and were used as a descant instrument to

Serpent.

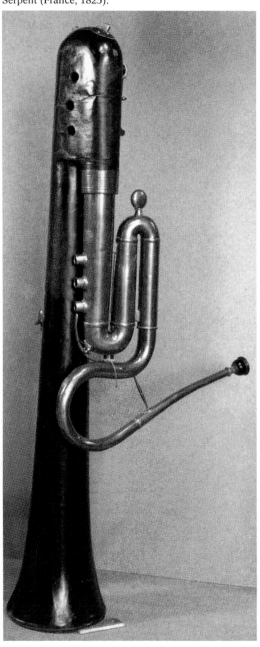

accompany trombones instead of trumpets, which in some cases were only allowed to be played by certain musicians. They could also be used to augment the soprano voices in a chorus, as in Bach's cantatas.

Serpent

The bass version of the cornett is the snake-shaped serpent. The serpent originated around 1590 and was widely used in France in the seventeenth century as a backing for Gregorian chant in the church. In Germany and England, the serpent was much used in military bands to support the bass notes. (this was the case as well in France in the late eighteenth century). It was not until the nineteenth century that the serpent was supplanted by various instruments having a straight shape, such as the *ophicleide (q.v.),* which was in turn supplanted by the *tuba* (q.v.) around 1850.

The serpent had a tube with a conical bore and six tone-holes, arranged in two groups of three. The length of the wavy tube varied from 6–7 feet. The tube was usually made of a piece of wood that had been sliced in half, hollowed out, joined together again, and finally fitted with a brass bell and a mouthpiece. Three keys were added to it in the early nineteenth century. The serpent was then widely used, at the time, in outdoor musical performances.

Ophicleide

This brass wind musical instrument of relatively wide conical bore, the largest of the keyed bugles, was invented in 1817 by Jean-Hilaire Asté of Paris. It had from 8 to 11 keys and a full, loud tone, but it was soon displaced in the orchestra by the bass tuba, which had better intonation. Many composers scored for it before the tuba was invented. The ophicleide is one of the family of large keyed horns that were still common during the first half of the nineteenth century.

The name, which is not very appropriate, derives from the Greek, *ofis* meaning snake and *kleides,* meaning keys, but the ophicleide is not snake-shaped at all, but looks rather like a bass horn or even a bassoon. The most common version of the instrument was the bass (it is actually more of a

The keyed horn family: the ophicleide (made by Guichard, ca. 1840), the serpent (France, ca. 1825), and the keyed horn.

Ophicleides of different sizes.

baritone) in C or in B-flat, with nine to twelve keys. As early as 1819, a part was written for this instrument by the opera composer Gasparo Spontini (1784-1851) in his *Olympia*. The ophicleide also features in the overture to Mendelssohn's *Midsummer Night's Dream* (1826). Although the instrument was replaced by the tuba in the symphony orchestra only decades later, the ophicleide was still in use well into the twentieth century in Italian, French, Spanish, and South American bands, especially in military bands. In a list of instruments used in the Paris Opera orchestra in 1915, one ophicleide is mentioned, but because it is directly preceded by three trombones and

no tuba is listed, it is unclear as to whether this really was an ophicleide and not some other type of keyed bugle (q.v.).

The smaller versions with nine keys tuned to alto and even soprano were not much more successful than the so-called *ophicléide monstre*, built in 1821. The "monster" is a bass instrument, nearly five feet tall, with eleven keys.

The ophicleide is also the name for a reed stop on the organ with clarinet-like intonation. It is located in the manual (8') and in the pedal (16').

Keyed Bugle

The principle of the keyed bugle (known in French as *cornet à pistons*) is analogous to that of the trumpet, although the tube is, to

Keyed bugle (19th century, with Stölzel valves).

be sure, somewhat wider and has a more pronounced conical shape. Furthermore, the mouthpiece is very different in terms of shape and proportions. Around 1825, valves were added to the traditional post horn. This resulted in its becoming enormously popular rather quickly and being built as an instrument in its own right in the 1830s. Some scholars claim that the keyed bugle is not derived from the post horn at all, but rather from the *flügelhorn* (q.v.). A letter written in 1840 by the Italian composer Gasparo Spontini (1774-1851) is used as evidence for this view. He wrote that he had sent ".. numerous keyed bugles, trumpets, or cornets with 2 or 3 pistons or valves (the first that were known in Paris)" from Berlin to Paris between 1823 and 1831. All the same, this letter is not evidence of the origin of the keyed bugle being either in the cornet or the flügelhorn. On closer examination, it turned out that all the old keyed bugles that have been preserved are of French or Belgian manufacture. According to Curt Sachs, a respected authority, there were no German keyed bugles until 1930, and the oldest known instrument (tuned to the key of C and with two valves) is marked with the year 1828 and the name Courtois Frères. Nor does a book about instruments of military music from Berlin that dates from the period mention the existence of the keyed bugle.

At first, the instrument was called a *cornet d'harmonie*. The keyed bugle or cornet was fairly easy to play, which meant that the instrument could be used as a substitute for the trumpet in the nineteenth century. Not only did Berlioz write a part for the keyed bugle in *The Damnation of Faust* (1845-1846) and the *Symphonie Fantastique* (1830), but Giacomo Meyerbeer (1791-1864) wrote a score for the keyed bugle in his opera *L'Africaine* (first performed in 1865). Other composers who made use of it in their work, included Charles Gounod (1818-1893) in his *Faust* (1859), Camille Saint-Saëns (1835-1921) in *Ascanio* (1890), and Giuseppe Verdi (1813-1901) in the opera, *Otello* (1887).

Despite this, the instrument has gradually fallen into disuse, so that the parts that were originally written for it are usually played by trumpets. Nevertheless, there have also been some twentieth-century composers who managed to take advantage of the special features of the keyed bugle. They include Igor Stravinsky who used it in *L'histoire du Soldat* (1914).

The keyed bugle is ordinarily pitched at B-flat or A. Even now, the instrument can still make the transition from one key to the other, provided this is within the range of C, E, E-flat, or A. The instrument's range is more limited than that of the trumpet and it cannot play higher than the key of C. On the other hand, the keyed bugle has an amazing mellowness. The playing technique is the same as for the trumpet. Because the timbre of is less "lofty" than that of the trumpet, the keyed bugle is still specifically called for for effects of caricature, such as in Prokofiev's *Lieutenant Kijé*. The keyed bugle's close relative, the cornet, is used a great deal in brass bands. There is also an organ stop called a cornet. It is an 8' reed stop, as well as a mixture (3-5 strong) consisting of mixed natural tones.

Most works written for the keyed bugle or cornet were intended to give the interpreting musician the chance to show what he was capable of during a competition. Many of the pieces therefore bear the title *Solo de concours* (competition solo). Composers who wrote this type of solo include Jean-Baptiste Arban, a skilled cornetist who was one of those who added improvements to the cornet, and also wrote a book on technique for the instrument. Henri Sauguet (1901-1989) who wrote a *Petite Chanson* for the cornet in 1942.

Bugle

The modern bugle is of German origin. The first bugles had valves and are believed to have been built ca. 1830 in Austria. They were brought to France ten years later. The bugle was modernized by Adolphe Sax and others to the form we know today.

The bugle has a cup mouthpiece and a wide bore. The tube is conical and has a relatively narrow bell. The bugle is less difficult to blow than the trumpet, trombone, or horn, but then again, this instrument does not sound as "radiant" as the others. The bugle has a fierce timbre and is capable of extraordinarily rapid starts.

The name "bugle" was used in England as early as 1750 for an infantry horn. When the bugle was stripped of its valves, however, it inspired the military *clarino* (q.v.).

The bugle is used to this day in brass and marching bands, and is, of course, the instrument used for issuing such commands to the troops as reveille, mealtimes, and "taps", the last post. In symphonic music, the instrument can be heard in Ottorino Respighi's *Pini di Roma* (The Pine Trees of Rome, 1923-1924), where it takes the place of the original *buccina*. Stravinsky also used the bugle in his *Threni* (1957–58).

The large or alto bugle is distinguished from the small or soprano bugle.

Tuba

The Romans already had a musical instrument with the name tuba: a straight trumpet about 4 feet long with a conical tube. It was used by the infantry in the army. According to tradition, this tuba must have had a rather raw sound. The Austrian author and playwright, Franz Grillparzer (1791-1872),

Bugle.

Modern tuba. made by Yamaha.

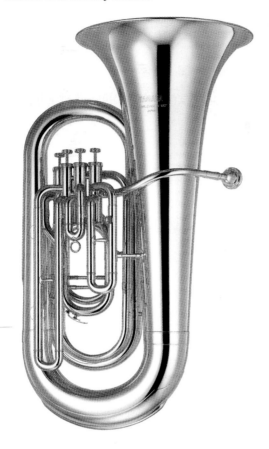

A tuba or baritone horn with rotary valves, Vienna, ca. 1870.

wrote a poem about it.

The modern tuba is a brass wind instrument with a wide bore and three to five valves, which enable it to reach the intermediate notes between the first and second fundamentals (a whole octave) chromatically. The length of the tube requires a large number of windings.

The inventor of the modern contrabass tuba was Wilhelm Friedrich Wieprecht (1802-1872), who was the director of the musical ensembles of the Garde in Berlin. Together with the instrument-maker, J.G. Moritz, he worked on designing the tuba, and by 1835 the first specimen was complete.

This instrument, whose official name is the bass tuba, but which is generally called the tuba for short, is known as the *contrebasse à pistons* in French. It is the most important instrument in the bass wind section, the two other two being the *euphonium* (q.v.) and the *sousaphone (q.v.)*. In military bands, for the convenience of marching musicians, the tuba is given a circular shape called the *helicon* or *bombardon*.

The tuba mostly occurs in the shape that is familiar from today's symphony orchestra. In theory, there are currently four distinct types of tuba, the tenor tuba, the bass tuba, the contrabass tuba, and the Wagnerian tuba. The Wagnerian tuba is, in fact, a horn, having an oval shape and the same mouthpiece as the horn, but the bell is the same as that of a regular tuba. The Wagnerian tuba has four valves.

The tuba is almost always used in the orchestra in two pairs, of which one pair is generally tuned to the key of F and the other pair

to B flat. Thanks to its pleasant, "warm" sound, after 1850 the tuba was increasingly to be found in the classical orchestra, where it was played for symphonic music as well as for opera.

The Wagnerian tuba is so-called because Wagner himself had provided instructions for the way it should be built. The first specimen was completed in 1854. Wagner specifically wrote it into his four-part opera cycle *The Ring of the Nibelung* (*The Rheingold, The Valkyries, Siegfried,* and *Götterdämmerung*). In Germany, the instrument is therefore called the *Rheingold-tuba* or *Ringtuba*.

Anton Bruckner (1824-1896) also included four Wagnerian tubas in his last three symphonies. It is customary for horn players (specifically in the *Second Horn Quartet*, at least when there are eight horn players) to play these instruments. Most medium-sized symphony orchestras do not themselves own Wagernian tubas, which means that their own horn players will have little to no experience with them.

Richard Strauss called for Wagernian tubas in several of his operas, including *Elektra* (1906-1908) and *Die Frau ohne Schatten* (1914-1918), as well as in his *Alpen-simfonie* (1911-1915). Felix Draeseke (1835-1931) wrote them into his

Symphonia Tragica (1885-1886) and Igor Stravinsky in his original version of *The Firebird* (1909-1910) and in *Le Sacre du Printemps* (The Rite of Spring) (1911-1913).

The Anglo-French instrument manufacturer Fontaine-Besson was inspired by the Wagernian tuba and created a whole family of tubas based on the same principle in Paris around 1890, ranging from a soprano version up to and including a contrabass. They were dubbed *cornophones*.

There is not much music for the tuba as a solo instrument in the concerto repertoire. Ameller, Constant, and Lebedev composed pieces for the tuba, but Ralph Vaughan-Williams' (1872-1958) *Concerto for Bass Tuba and Orchestra* (1954) is probably the best-known work. Pieces have also been written for it by less well-known composers. The tuba is an instrument that was played in Hungarian gypsy bands, such as the famous band of Feri Bunkó (1854) which featured two differently tuned tubas . Tuba players in today's gypsy bands always excel in producing mellow sounds and great virtuosity. The Wagernian tuba did much to change the sound of military bands. In 1913, Curt Sachs reported in his *Reallexicon de Musikinstrumente* that the Prussian army band had decided to replace its *waldhorns*

Various trumpets: a natural trumpet in E-flat (19th century), a herald trumpet (early 20th century), a natural trumpet with slide (19th century).

(q.v.) with this type of tuba.

Tuba is also the name of a 16' trumpet organ stop that was particularly popular in the late Romantic period (the mid-nineteenth century).

Trumpet

The origin of the trumpet is more or less the same as that of the horn. It is a metal instrument with a narrow, cylindrical-conical tube, a mouthpiece, and valves.

The trumpet was already being played before the Bronze Age (ca. 1900 BCE), and all the ancient civilizations knew the trumpet in one form or another. The Bible relates that two trumpets, hammered from silver, were used to summon the leaders of the twelve tribes of Israel. In the temple the priests blew sacred trumpet fanfares to announce battle, sacrifices, and for festivals.

The Greek *salphinx* and the Roman *tuba* (not to be confused with the modern *tuba* (q.v.)) of Antiquity were distant ancestors of the modern trumpet. Both these ancient instruments were very long with a straight bore and a narrow tube, like the trumpets found in Tutenkhamun's tomb (ca. 1355-1342 BCE). The Roman *buccina* was a bent instrument, used predominantly by the army, like a bugle (q.v.). Ottorino Respighi (1879-1936) wrote music for this instrument in his *Pini de Roma* (The Pine Trees of Rome, 1923-1924)). A short trumpet was developed in Roman times, similar to another Egyptian trumpet that has been found in tombs dating from 15,000 BCE. These instruments were given a succession of different names, some of which indicated that the instrument was made of metal, although this was frequently not the case.

Over the course of time, the trumpet's functions have been fivefold. It has been used as a signaling instrument, for military use, as an instrument with heroic associations, to be played on solemn occasions, and as a sacred instrument. During the Middle Ages and the Renaissance, the trumpet fulfilled all of these functions, but was rarely used as a musical instrument in ensembles.

In 1607, Claudio Monteverdi (1567-1643) used the high-pitched trumpet (*clarino*) and three other trumpets with mutes in the orchestra for his opera *Orfeo*. The type of mute (*sordino*) that was often used in the seventeenth century fell out of fashion in the course of the eighteenth century, reemerging for the first time in the music of Wagner. After Monteverdi, numerous composers suddenly began writing music for the trumpet, including Jean-Baptiste Lully (1632-1687) in his opera *Alceste* (1674), Giovanni Legrenzi (1626-1690), and Girolamo Frescobaldi (1583-1653). Frescobaldi composed works for trumpet and organ, which he performed himself. Another Italian composer, Girolamo Fantini

(1602–ca. 1675), who was the "trombettiere maggiore" of the Grand Duke of Tuscany, wrote short pieces for one or two trumpets, including a Sonata for trumpet and organ.

In 1690, the English composer, Henry Purcell (1659-1695) wrote an air into his opera, *Diocletian,* that was to be performed as a dialogue between the trumpet and the human voice. Alessandro Scarlatti (1660–1725) and André Campra (1660–1744) also wrote pieces for trumpet and voice. Frederick George Handel (1685–1759) followed suit in his operas *Samson* (1746) and *Alexander's Feast* (1736). Johann Sebastian Bach (1685–1750) and Georg Philipp Telemann (1681–1767) wrote a great deal of music for the trumpet, both in dramatic as well as in religious pieces and instrumental compositions. Probably the best-known trumpet solo of the baroque period is the *Prince of Denmark's March*, better known as the *Trumpet Voluntary* by the English composer, Jeremiah Clarke (1674-1707) (often wrongly attributed to Purcell).

Vivaldi wrote a concerto for two trumpets and orchestra, as did Domenico Cimarosa (1749-1801). Giuseppe Torelli (1658-1709) wrote a whole series of concerti for one or more trumpets and orchestra, as did Weber, Corelli, Joseph and Michael Haydn, the Belgian Joseph Jongen (1873-1953), and

Two trumpets (Nuremberg, ca. 1700).

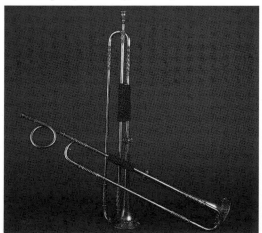

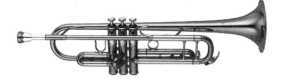

The modern trumpet.

Leopold Mozart.

Since the Middle Ages, the trumpet in Europe has changed in two respects, in terms of length and in terms of register. After many years of research and experimentation, this has resulted in the highly developed solo and orchestral instrument now heard in the concert hall. During the baroque period (ca. 1600–ca. 1750), when the trumpet first became popular as a virtuoso solo instrument, most music for the trumpet was written in the key of D, because most trumpets were tuned to D. The high registers were exceedingly difficult to blow and were almost exclusively the preserve of the so-called clarino-blowers.

Before 1800, the long-stretched "natural trumpet" with only one loop was almost the only trumpet in existence. The valves had yet to be added, so that only natural tones were available (all of them harmonics of the fundamental). This instrument was used by city trumpeters for fanfares as well as for musical recitals.

As composers became more demanding, they pushed for an expansion of the possibilities. Adding a shank (a piece of tubing) could indeed lengthen the tube, thereby changing the tuning of the trumpet, but that was impossible to do in the middle of playing. The desire to be able to insert chromatic intervals demanded another solution. No wonder, then, that woodwinds provided the inspiration for drilling holes in the tube, which could then be opened and closed with a key.

Many attempts made to give the trumpet the correct bend, ultimately resulting in the tube's S-shape. Instruments that have been preserved from the early seventeenth century already have the same shape as the modern trumpet. The Vienna court trumpeter, Anton Weidinger (1767-1852), began in 1770 to make improvements to the trumpet, but it was not until 1795 that he was able to perfect an instrument with four to six keys, each of which could produce a halfnote higher. The player would hold this keyed trumpet horizontally so that the fingers of the left hand could easily wrap around it to reach the holes. Unlike in today's piston or valve system, only one key would be opened at a time on this trumpet, and shanks could be added to it. When valves came into use at the beginning of the nineteenth century, players gained a greater flexibility, but virtuosity in the higher registers remained exceptionally difficult.

Among the classical composers of music for the modern trumpet, Dimitri Shostakovich occupies a prominent place with his famous *Concerto for Piano, Trumpet, and Orchestra* (1933). The Czech composer, Leos Janacek (1854-1928) composed his *Sinfonietta* (1926) to include no fewer than 25 brass instruments, including twelve trumpets and two bass trumpets, a spectacular piece. According to the conductor Charles de Wolff, who has performed this composition twice, there also exists a simplified version, using only nine trumpets.

The Russian-Armenian composer Aram Khatchaturian (1903-1978) wrote his *Symphony No. 3*, better known as the *Symphony-Poem* (1947) for the occasion of the thirtieth anniversary of the October Revolution of 1917. In addition to a large symphony orchestra with three trumpets, the composer wrote in fifteen extra trumpets. Seven weeks after the official première on December 25, 1947, the composition was judged to be "an enemy of the people" by the Central Committee of the Communist Party of the Soviet Union. Khatchaturian subsequently made a public confession of guilt in which he "admitted" that he had failed to respect the correct proportions of musical instruments for the time.

The trumpet plays an important part in jazz, as do all the brass instruments, since this form of music emerged from the marching bands that accompanied funerals in the Deep South of the United States, and such bands were dominated by brass. There have been many famous jazz trumpeters, including William "Bunk" Johnson (1879–1949), Joe "King" Oliver (1885–1938), Leon "Bix" Beiderbecke (1903–1931 (also the greatest jazz cornet-player), Benny Carter (1907–2002), Louis Prima (1911–1978), John Birks "Dizzy" Gillespie (1917–1993). Miles Davis (1926–1991), Chesney "Chet" Baker—and the king of them all, Louis "Satchmo" Armstrong (1898–1971). Although these famous names were interpreters rather than musicians, the improvisational freedom that jazz allows made them far more than mere players of other peoples' compositions. Louis Armstrong is probably the only trumpeter to be commemorated by a statue. His likeness stands in a public square in his home town, New Orleans.

On the organ, the trumpet is an 8' reed stop with inverted, conical pipes.

Clarino.

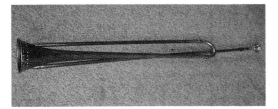

Trombone.

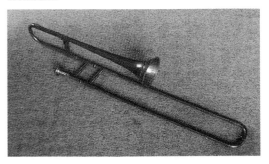

Trombones.

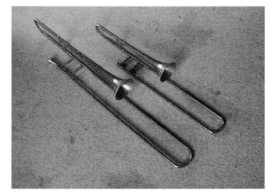

The modern trombone.

A high register of the clarinet, reached by "overblowing," is likewise called a *clarino*.

Trombone

The trumpet and trombone have followed a more or less shared evolutionary path, since ancient times, diverging only when the trombone was given a slide in the fifteenth century, turning it into a bass instrument.

The tube consists of two U-shaped components that can be slid into each other. The main section contains the mouthpiece and bell and the two parallel tubes connected by crossbars, and the other section consists of the slide or movable section, fitted with a water-key.

The fact that the movable section can slide in and out means that the instrument can be smoothly lengthened and shortened during playing. The modern trombone has seven positions or tube segments, with which each natural tone can be lowered six half-steps (up to a whole fifth).

The trombone is believed to have originated around 1450 in Burgundy as the "successor" to the slide-trumpet, because the sound possibilities were thereby deepened.

Clarino

The clarino is a baroque trumpet dating from the time of Johann Sebastian Bach and is also (inaccurately) referred to as a Bach trumpet, because this composer wrote so much music for it.

The clarino has no valves and is a typically solo trumpet. As a consequence of the very narrow mouthpiece, it is possible to play high natural notes. The lower-pitched trumpets, with their larger bores, were frequently called "principals" at the time, to distinguish them from the clarino.

The clarino fell into disuse in the nineteenth century, thanks to the invention of valves. The player no longer had to rely on virtuosity purely of the mouth and he could operate three valves at the same time using the fingers of one hand.

A collection of brass wind instruments, including a pair of valve trombones (late 19th century). One of them has Périnet valves, the other has Belgian valves.

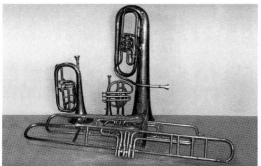

Trumpeter

Henry Purcell (1659-1695).

In the sixteenth century, trombones were made to five different tunings, from descant to contrabass, to produce a complete "family." The most popular was the "regular, straight" trombone that corresponds to the modern tenor trombone.

The descant (soprano) instrument was soon supplanted by the *cornet* (q.v.), *the bugle*, (q.v.), and the trumpet. Nor was the contrabass trombone used for very long, since it was soon displaced by the contrabass tuba. Since the end of the eighteenth century, the orchestra has contained a trombone trio (alto, tenor, and bass) in which the alto can be replaced by a second tenor, and this is often the case in the composition of today's symphony orchestras. Throughout the period of polyphony (the Middle Ages and Renaissance), the trombone continuously played an important role in masses and motets. The ten trombones of the court of King Henry VIII enjoyed enormous renown. Claudio Monteverdi wrote four trombones into his opera *Orfeo* (1607), Jean-Baptiste Lully (1632-1687) used them in his *Te Deum* (1677) and Frederick George Handel (1685-1759) in *Israel in Egypt* (1739). Johann Sebastian Bach

(1685-1759) called upon this instrument now and again, but mainly to follow the voices in his chorales. For a long time, it seemed that the trombone was being neglected by composers, but then Christoph Willibald von Gluck (1714-1787) wrote a significant role for the instrument in his operas *Alceste* (1767) and *Iphegenia in Tauris* (1779). Mozart made use of the trombone in several operas, including *Don Giovanni* (1787) and *The Magic Flute* (1791), and in his *Requiem* (1791).

It is thanks to Ludwig van Beethoven (1770-1827), following in the footsteps of several French symphonic composers of the late eighteenth century, that the trombone again came to occupy a prominent place in the symphony orchestra, especially in his *Fifth*, *Sixth*, and *Ninth Symphonies*.

Of the now three (out of five) members left over from the family of trombones, only the tenor trombone played any significant role until Hector Berlioz (1803-1869) revived the other two (alto and bass) in his *Symphonie Funèbre et Triomphale* (1840). Twenty years later, Richard Wagner (1813-1883) went one further by starting to write music for the contrabass trombone as well. More recently, quite a lot of music has been

Detail from a medieval painting depicting music-making angels.

written for trombone, both in the symphony orchestra, in chamber music and for trombone and string orchestra, as well as with piano accompaniment. Composers include Frank Martin's (1890-1974) *Ballad for Trombone and Orchestra* (1940, and Darius Milhaud's (1892-1974) *A Winter Concertino* (1953), for trombone and string orchestra). The Czech Rudolf Kubin (1909-1973) also composed a *Trombone Concerto* (1937). Baroque composers who wrote for trombone with piano accompaniment include Marc-Antoine Charpentier (1634-1704) and Henry Purcell (1659-1695).

Six compositions for trombone and orchestra are particularly noteworthy. They are three parts from the nine-part *Serenata* (1755) by Leopold Mozart (1719-1787), *Concerto* (1769) by Johann Georg Albrechtsberger (1736-1809), the transcription of a piece for oboe and orchestra by Johann Nepomuk Hummel (1787-1837), and *The Romance, Opus 3* by the Italian Leone Sinigaglia (1868-1944). The opera composer Vincenzo Bellini (1801-1835) wrote a *Concerto for Oboe and Strings* in 1819. The four *Songs without Words* by Felix Mendelssohn have been rearranged for trombone and orchestra and performed by the Yugoslavian trombonist Branimir Slokar (1946-).

In the words of the great jazz critic, Leonard Feather, "over the long haul, the trombone has been the most neglected of the major jazz horns." Many famous jazz musicians, including Benny Goodman, played the trombone while being known for their virtuosity on other instruments (the clarinet, in Goodman's case). The trombone was actually introduced to the jazz band from England, where it featured in the brass bands, that were so popular, especially in the northern cotton- and woollen-mill towns. Many jazz tunes featured the trombone, including *Tiger Rag*, first copyrighted in 1918 by virtuoso trombonist Nick LaRocca and recorded by him and his Original Dixieland Jazz Band, although authorship is claimed by a number of other musicians. Tommy Dorsey first recorded *I'm Getting Sentimental Over You* (1935) written by Ned Washington and George Bashman (1932)

By far the greatest trombone player of all time, who had a unique style but left no imitators, was Jack Teagarden (1905–1964).

The *p'ip'a*, a Chinese short-necked lute.

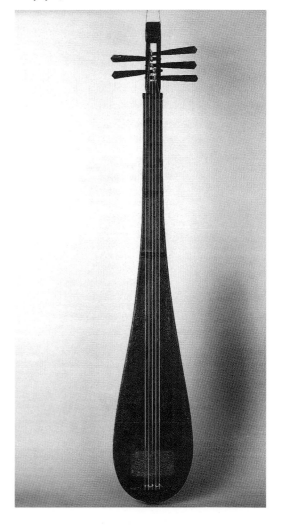

Stringed Instruments

Plucked Instruments

The first plucked instruments must have originated in prehistoric times. A very simple instrument associated with that era is the musical bow. Plucked instruments are both melodic and rhythmic. In classical music, there is the rhythmic accompaniment of the *lute*, (q.v.), *theorbo* (q.v.), and the *vihuela* (q.v.). The guitar, bass guitar, ukelele, banjo, and countless other stringed instruments are of great rhythmic importance all over the world in jazz, folk, and pop music.

A musical bow in its simplest form has no sound-box and therefore produces an un-amplified sound. The pitch varies with the length, thickness, and tension of the string. After a long period of development from the hunting bow, there came the first zithers, plucked instruments without a sound-box. Later zithers were provided with a modest sound box, but it was not very effective.

The berimbau, a Brazilian musical bow which is used in the martial art of capoeira. The player strikes the string with a stick, while modifying the effective length of the string and, thus the pitch, with his other hand.

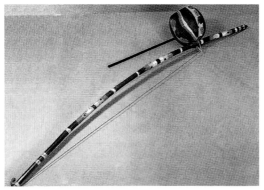

Descendants of the *cittern* (.q.v.)can be found today predominantly in folk music (the *cymbalom*, the *Aeolian harp*, and the *dulcimer*) and sometimes in ancient music (the *psaltery*).

Later, a sound box or resonating chamber was added to the musical bow, in the form of a hollow gourd or pig's bladder, resulting in the ancestors of the *harp*, the *lute*, and the *guitar*. The cittern is a medieval plucked instrument with a pronounced sound box. The harp and the related lyre, have no sound boxes. Both are extremely ancient instruments but were very popular in the Middle Ages, since their soft tones make them very suitable as accompaniments to the human voice.

Musical Bow

The simplest of all the stringed instruments is without a doubt the musical bow. In its simplest form, it is a thin cord tied to both ends of a curved stick. It can safely be assumed that this instrument evolved from the bow that was used for hunting. The musical bow evolved further in the course of history. At some point, several strings were added, and fixed resonators were then included, consisting of halved gourds or coconuts, or even small metal boxes.

Berimbau

An extraordinary example of the musical bow is its use in the Brazilian martial art of capoeira. At these events, a musical bow, called a *berimbau*, is used as the musical accompaniment for the sparring match.

The berimbau is 3-5 feet long and has one metal string stretched taut. A hollow gourd is attached to the bow as a resonator. The instrument is played by rhythmically striking the string with a stick. By pressing the gourd more or less tightly against the body, the player can influence the tone color. The berimbau was brought to Brazil by slaves from Africa.

Biwa

Like many other instruments of the lute family, the Japanese biwa has a resonating body with a rounded back. The strings are stretched over the full length of the body and the neck. This instrument is derived from the Chinese *p'ip'a* (q.v.) and has a relatively shallow, pear-shaped back.ß The wooden table has two half-moon-shaped sound holes. The neck is short and has only four frets. The pegbox is close to the body. The tuning pegs have a distinctive, inverted cone shape. The biwa usually has four silk strings, although there are also instruments with five strings.

The most classic shape of the biwa is the *bugaku biwa*, the lute from the Japanese court orchestra, which adopted its ultimate form in the tenth century. This instrument is just over three feet long and is fairly wide and heavy. It is held upright and tilted by the seated player, who holds it between the legs. The silk strings are struck reasonably

hard with a plectrum. The melody is usually played on the highest string, while the other strings are rarely held down. The distinctive sound is a result of the strings lightly touching the frets. The instrument was originally played much more as a rhythmic accompaniment to the human voice, like the banjo.

Japanese composers, such as Toru Takemitsu (1930-1996) have made use of the biwa in their works. Takemitsu wrote it (along with the *shakuhatchi*) into his *November Steps* (1967), a work commissioned to celebrate the 125th anniversary of the New York Philharmonic Orchestra. Kinshi Tsuruta is famous in Japan as a virtuoso player of the biwa. She has appeared with it in movies and has written music for television dramas, together with shakuhatchi player Katsuya Yokoyama. Takemitsu composed the piece *Eclipse* for both of them, which was performed by them in May, 1966 in the Nissei Theater. It is thanks to Takemitsu and other composers that the biwa has survived. The songs that the instrument is used to accompany are often about the spirit of the samurai. As a result, the biwa was only rarely played in public immediately after World War II. These new compositions gave the old tradition a new lease on life and brought about a revival of traditional Japanese music.

P'ip'a, a Chinese short-necked lute with four silk strings and frets as far down as the sound box.

Hamburg cittern (17th century), Pandurina (Italy, 1651), Pandurina (Italy, 17th century).

Replica cittern, after G. Ga Salo, built by the luthier Gesina Liedmeyer.

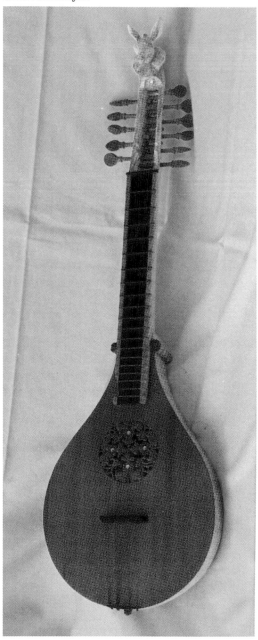

Bandouria, a Spanish folk instrument belonging to the cittern family. It is played frequently in folk bands.

both body and neck. The wooden table has no sound holes, and the four strings are made of silk. The strings are played with the fingers (usually several at a time). The instrument is held vertically, resting on the thighs of the player. Because the fingers touch the strings quickly and repeatedly, a distinctive rolling sound is produced. The unusual thing about the use of the left hand is that it can produce a sort of vibrato effect when used to hold down a string.

Cittern

It is reasonably safe to assume that the cittern is a descendant of the medieval fiddle. The peoples in the countries around the Mediterranean Sea preferred plucked to bowed instruments, and the cittern was a popular example. The instrument takes

P'ip'a

The p'ip'a is the Chinese ancestor of the *biwa*. The instrument has been known for about 2000 years. The body is pear-shaped and relatively shallow and there are frets on

Cittern with the body of a lute (16th century).

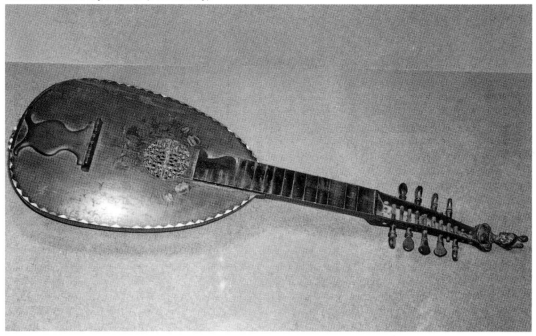

many forms, and the number of different names for it in various European languages attests to its popularity in former times. In German alone, the cittern is known under

Aartcister, Johann Klemm jr., Radeberg, Germany, 1756.

the names of *gittern, zitter, sister, systholle, cytherne,* and *cittharne.* The cittern has a relatively shallow wooden case and a flat back. Over the course of time— from the fifteenth to the eighteenth centuries— the form of the cittern has changed quite substantially. The sound box was originally pear-shaped, but bell-shaped and lyre-shaped instruments were made latterly. The bass instruments were shaped like shells or had other unusual shapes. The table ordinarily has one sound hole. The neck has a distinctive shape, in that the bass side is thinner than the side for the high notes, so that the thumb could do its work more conveniently. There are frets on the neck of the instrument. The metal strings are fastened to the pegbox, which is usually sickle-shaped, by means of side-mounted tuning pegs. The number of strings varies from instrument to instrument. There are four-stringed citterns, but there are also fourteen-stringed citterns, whether or not they are tuned "in families."

Bass citterns, such as the *pandora*, that served as thoroughbass instruments from

A simple Finnish *kantele*.

the early sixteenth century have, in addition to the regular strings, loose bass strings on the fingerboard. As with the *theorbo*, these have a separate pegbox. Another unusual feature can be found in the strangely-shaped *orpharion*, a bass cittern, on which the frets are placed at an angle.

The *citharino* was derived from the cittern and was intended for the descant register. Later on, it can be seen again in the form of the *Hamburg cittern*, a popular instrument with two sets of five strings. Smaller still are the Italian *terzina* and the Spanish *bandouria*. The strings on these instruments are not arranged by pitch, like the strings on the violin and the guitar, so that plucking the strings produces a rather staccato sound.

The piano guitar, built in 1750, was an unusual form of cittern. This misleadingly named instrument had a sort of piano mechanism, in which every string was struck by a piano hammer operated from a key on the sounding board. It was still possible, however, to hold down strings with the left hand.

During the eighteenth century, the cittern was supplanted by the guitar. The reason for this may be that the guitar can produce a greater volume of sound. Its tone stability and convenient way of playing also captured the interest of a larger group of music-lovers, especially those belonging to the upwardly-mobile middle class. The guitar became the favorite instrument for playing at home, having the advantage of being suitable for playing solo, with other instruments, and as an accompaniment to the human voice.

Lyre

The lyre or *lyra* is a stringed instrument with a distinctive shape. It consists of two wooden uprights connected to a sound box at their base and to a crossbar at the top. The strings are strung from the front of the sound box, usually over a bridge, to the crossbar, on which tuning pegs may be mounted. The number of strings ranges from three to ten and they are usually plucked with the fingers or with the nails, or they can be strummed. Sometimes the left hand is used to hold down a string.

The history of the lyre is lost in the mists of time. It existed during the Sumerian civilization and was played by the ancient Egyptians. However, the instrument is most frequently associated with ancient Greece. In the first millennium of western European civilization, the lyre is depicted in illuminated manuscripts, King David being frequently depicted playing the lyre, *kinnor*, instead of the harp (ancient Hebrew used their names interchangeably, although in modern Hebrew, the harp is called *nevel*).

Lyra as played in Ancient Greece.

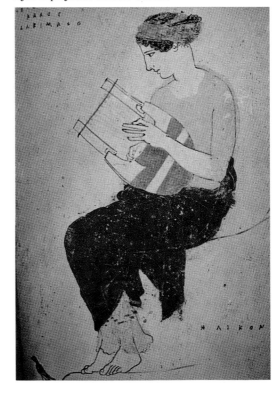

It is known that the lyre occurred in various forms and could be played in any number of ways. The musicologist must unfortunately rely on the depictions encountered in contemporary accounts, and these are not always reliable. It is therefore no wonder that no complete treatise exists that deals with stringed instruments of the Middle Ages.

In Greek antiquity, the lyra was mainly an instrument for the amateur player. According to tradition, the first lyre was made by the god Hermes, the messenger of the gods, from a tortoise shell, to which a framework of sticks was affixed.

The professional musicians of the time preferred to play the *kithara*, a somewhat more complicated instrument. The sound box consisted of a set of small wooden boards. The top and bottom were flat. The kithara had many more strings than the lyre, and there was a primitive way of tuning the strings by means of tiny levers.

The medieval European lyre is much more simply constructed, consisting of a shelf that serves as a sounding board, from which a section of wood is cut. The transition from playing the instrument by plucking to bowing took place around the tenth century. Nowadays, modern plucked lyres can only be found in Africa and some parts of Siberia. Some bowed lyres are still in use.

The *crwth* is a bowed lyre that was especially

The Lute-player, an engraving by Jan Swelinck.

Lute, Agostorelli.

popular in Wales. Its Irish counterpart is called the *cruit*. It has four stopped strings that run over a central fingerboard. The construction of the bridge is unusual, in that it consists of two parts, one of which rests on the top of the sound box, while the other acts as a sort of support and runs through a small sound hole to the bottom of the sound box, to amplify the sounds. There are two bass strings.

In Finland and Estonia, a folk instrument, the *kantele* harp, shares a number of features with a comparable instrument from the valley of the Siberian River Ob. In this form of harp, there is an opening cut from a rough wooden plank. The instrument has three or four strings made of horsehair stretched over it, which are then bowed or plucked with the hand. A somewhat more elegant variant is the Swedish *tallharpa*, which remained popular in the Baltic states until the mid-twentieth century.

Lute

When referring to the lute, the reference is to the short-necked member of the lute fam-

Festively decorated bass lute, great octave (M. Büchenberg, Rome 1613).

Johann Wolfgang von Goethe (1749-1832).

ily. In view of medieval history, it should be no surprise that the name "lute" is derived from the Arabic word "al'ud." In the present day Arab world, there still exists a lute-like instrument with the name "ud."

The lute has taken many different forms. The lute of the early Middle Ages is only known from very unreliable illustrations, and in absence of perspective, it is hard to identify or classify accurately. In the fourteenth century, the lute had an oval shape and in the fifteenth century it had an apple-shaped resonator or body. The most common shape used today is that of the Renaissance lute. This instrument is again being played regularly at authentic performances of medieval music.

The almond-shaped or pear-shaped sounding-board is built up of cut wooden laths, stuck down in layers, joined at the beginning of the neck, and covered with a kind of cap. The top of the body is flat. On the inside there are small support beams that also function as resonators. The lute has a rosette-shaped arrangement of sound holes. The string holder is also located on the top of the body. The neck is rather wide and almost always has metal frets attached to it. They vary in number from five, to eight, or even more frets. The pegbox is usually bent backward, but is sometimes straight. The tuning pegs are mounted laterally on both sides of the pegbox. A lute can be strung in a number of different arrangements from four single or double to more than twenty strings. The most common shape is that in which six double strings are accompanied by one single string, the chanterelle. The chanterelle is used to produce small, subtle ornamental notes. Both strings of a pair are tuned alike, in order to be able to amplify the sound. Originally, catgut was used for the strings, but nowadays nylon strings are used on reconstructions. The lute is plucked with the fingers.

This instrument was not only played by musicians. In his eighth book, the autobiographical *Dichtung und Wahrheit*, Johann Wolfgang von Goethe (1749-1832) wrote

Neopolitan mandolin with a double soundboard (Gelasse, 1913).

about composing music for the lute in his parental home in Frankfurt-on-Main. Like the homes of most wealthy burghers of the time, the house had a special music room. In the sixteenth century, instruments, such as the *viola da gamba (q.v.)*, were built in sets, from soprano to bass. In this way, a whole lute family came into being, from a large octave-bass lute to a small octave lute, the latter having four singular strings. Two lutes were also combined into one instrument, the double-lute.

Mandolin

The mandolin is a double-coursed lute (each string is double), originating from Italy, which used to be strung with steel strings. Unlike the lute, the mandolin has a bridge on its sounding board that raises the strings away from the body slightly in order to make chord-playing easier. The mandolin resembles the guitar, in the shape of the neck, frets, and tuning-post. The steel strings are plucked with a plectrum. The instrument remains popular, especially in Italy, and not least because of the relative ease with which it can be played. As a result of this popularity, the mandolin was subjected to variations, such as the *mandola* (a tenor-mandolin). There is also a bass mandolin that is commonly found in mandolin and accordion-orchestras.

The Portuguese mandolin is a variation of the Italian version. The body of this instrument has a slightly curved base, straight sides. and a flat top, often inlaid with decorative woods, that narrows at the neck.

The mandolin is not a standard instrument in the symphony orchestra, but orchestral works have been written in which the instrument played a part (even though not a prominent one). Gustav Mahler (1860-1911)included the mandolin in his symphonies, such as the *Seventh Symphony* (1904-1905) (which also includes a guitar), in his Eight Symphony (1906) and in his *Song of the Earth* (1908-1909). The last movement of this last work, which includes a contralto or baritone voice (most famously recorded by Kathleen Ferrier (1912–1953), in 1948) the mandolin is not

Mandore (P. Zenatto, Treviso, 1651).

drowned out by other instruments in the orchestra. In the last five bars (64-69) the mandolin accompanies the contralto voice, together with other instruments.

Giuseppe Verdi used the mandolin in his operas *Otello* (1887) and *Falstaff* (1897), to make the music sound even more impressive than usual, with his unparalleled instrumentation. The German composer Hans Pfitzner (1865-1945), a contemporary, colleague and occasional rival of Richard Strauss, described by prominent connoisseurs of music as "the last romantic"—a title later bestowed on the pianist Vladimir Horowitz—also made use of the mandolin in his opera *Palestrina* (1912–1915). Both Arnold Schoenberg (1874–1951) and Igor Stravinsky (1882–1971)incorporated the mandolin into their compositions.

In 1921, the Dutchman Willem Pijper (1894-1947) composed his *Second Symphony* for an enormous orchestra including

Theorbo (M. Tieffenbrucker).

no fewer than six mandolins. The work was premièred the following year, played by the Concertgebouw orchestra conducted by Willem Mengelberg. Pijper later made a simpler version, but this was lost during the bombing of Rotterdam on the May 14, 1940. Karel Mengelberg (1902-1984)—a nephew of the conductor, Pijper's student and well known with the revised version—produced a new arrangement in 1962. This version of the symphony, contining only one mandolin, is the one most frequently performed since then.

Theorbo

The theorbo is an arch lute or bass lute that was produced during the Middle Ages, and was very popular in Europe for a period of 200 years. The instrument was made from the body of a lute with an extra pegbox. This addition made it possible to stretch loose (bass) strings along the neck which, as in the *chitarrone* (.q.v.), tuned for the bass notes, as certain compositions required.

The lute and members of the lute family flourished in the fifteenth century with the

Theorbo (M. Sellon).

rise of polyphonics (music arranged for several voices). The instruments that could play several notes at the same time were given pride of place. The lute family thus played an important role, in addition to that of the keyboard instruments, such as the harpsichord and the clavichord. The lute was a very versatile instrument that could replace almost any other instrument in an ensemble and was the perfect accompaniment for both vocal and instrumental music. Because a variety of music was being published in versions for the lute, the solo role of the lute became very important.

A unique musical notation was developed for the lute in which most fifteenth through eighteenth century music is transcribed. The system, called *tablature*, shows the fingerings for the strings and frets.

The instrument builder and musician Arnold Dolmetsch (1858-1940) has done much to revive lute-playing. Thanks to his interest in building early instruments and the revival of interest in them that he has fostered, the recorder and arch-lute or theorbo again play a role in modern musical performance. His descendants have maintained the tradition.

In the heyday of the lute, almost all composers wrote music for it, of whom three made particularly substantial contributions toward its development. They are the Frenchman Pierre Attaignant (1494?-1552?)—who both wrote and published music—the Englishman John Dowland (1563-1626), and the German Silvius Leopold Weiss (1686-1750).

Long-Necked Lutes

The long-necked lute family is quite extensive outside Europe, but there is only one European version, the *colascione*. In the Balkans there are more such instruments, including the *tambura*, introduced by the Turks during the fourteenth and fifteenth centuries. These lutes are related to the *tamboura* and the *(si)tar*, played throughout western Asia from the Middle East to the

Indian tampura. This is a special stringed instrument that is used for accompaniment in Indian music. Its sound is very soft.

Indian subcontinent. In India, the long-necked lute, or sitar, is mainly used as a bass instrument. It has four strings, but no frets, unlike other lutes.

Sitar

The sitar, a large instrument that is played from a sitting position, is the main member of the family of long-necked lutes that play such an important part in Indian music. The vertical neck of the sitar is slightly crooked. The body is onion-shaped and usually made of wood. Sometimes a calabash or gourd resonator can be found under the neck, against the pegbox. The played strings run via a bridge on the body to the pegbox. Rather high metal frets are attached to the neck that can be repositioned to achieve ,

Left: two tablas. Right: a sitar with player.

the desired note. Bourdon strings, which have been stretched under the frets, can be tuned with slanting pegs. The melody is usually played on one string, by the player's thumb which is fitted with a little plectrum. The sitar suddenly gained fame in the West during the 1970s, thanks to sitar player Ravi Shankar. This was the first time that Indian music had been recognized outside its native land. The then, tolerant and open "flower power" culture made this possible. Thousands enjoyed the literately and figuratively timeless *ragas*, long pieces of music in which the sitar was the primary instrument. There were *ragas* for daytime and *ragas* for nighttime, each with a unique scale and as a result a totally unique color. East-meets-West concerts were held, at which western musicians, such as the violinist Yehudi Menuhin, the flutist Jean-Pierre Rampal, and The Beatles, together with Shankar and his group, improvised on diverse musical themes.

Chitarrone

The chitarrone began to flourish around 1550. The development of the tone spectrum concentrated mainly on the lower tones, which is why lute builders tried to add lower tuned (and thus longer) strings to the instrument. The only limitation was the reach of the left hand on the neck. The construction of the neck could not be widened to more than the left hand span, so the additional bass strings had to be stretched as open strings next to the neck, then joined to a separate pegbox. The musician tuned these bass strings while playing, to achieve the desired notes.

The chitarrone is actually a short-necked lute with a long or very long neck (more than 8 feet). It should in fact be called an arch lute, as it is a kind of bass lute. As with all lutes, the body is rounded, and often built up of wood laminate. The belly has one, or more sound holes. The pegbox for the chittarone strings is straight. There are chitarrones with six and sometimes

Detail of a sitar.

Painting of a woman tuning a chitarrone.

even eight pairs of catgut strings on one key, besides which it has eight bass strings. The chitarrone, like the bass theorbo, played the role of a continuo instrument.

Colascione

Few long-necked lutes have been of importance in European music, the only exception being the colascione (Italian for "sawn wood" or "bad fiddle"). This instrument was especially popular in Italy in the sixteenth and seventeenth centuries. It was a direct descendant of the Persian long-necked lute, the *tanbur*. In Germany, in the seventeenth and eighteenth centuries, it was also played by the continuo player.

The colascione has a small, round, lute-like body with one sound hole. The neck accounts for more than two-thirds of the entire length of the instrument. The colascione usually has three catgut strings that are fastened to the pegbox at the end of the neck with slanted tuning pegs. Between sixteen and twenty-four frets are fitted to the neck.

Balalaika

The balalaika is a member of the cittern family that can be traced back to the Kirgizian *domra*. It is an almost essential instrument in Russian folk music, and there are even complete balalaika orchestras. An instrument from the balalaika family plays all voices in such an ensemble, from piccolo to contrabass.

The instrument has a flat triangular wooden body with a slightly curved base. The sound hole is small and round and, like the rest of the body, beautifully decorated. The neck is slender and attached at the apex of the body. The tuning pegs are slanted in the pegbox. Approximately 24 metal frets cross the relatively narrow bridge. Most balalaikas have three strings that are plucked with a plectrum (seldom with the fingers). Instruments with a higher pitch sometimes are double-strung, as in the mandolin.

Left: a 19th century balalaika; next to it, two tamburisas.

Guitarra Battente, replica built after Sellas by the luthier, Gesina Liedmeyer.

Left: a 19th century balalaika; next to it, two tamburisas.

Guitar

No instrument comes in as many different shapes as the guitar. The classical or Spanish guitar has a characteristic figure-of-eight shape and is approximately 19 inches long. The sound-box is flat with a bridge toward the base in the lower half, and the sound hole is in the top half. The sides are rather deep. The back is sometimes flat, but in most cases slightly curved. The neck is wide, has up to 20 metal frets, and is around two feet long. The pegbox bends slightly backward. The tuning pegs are attached to the side of the pegbox, with three strings on each side in a six-string guitar. Originally, the guitar was strung with catgut, but modern guitars are strung with metal or nylon strings.

In the classical playing position the player is seated, with the instrument held in front of the body, the neck pointing up at an angle, and the left foot hereby resting on a special footrest. The instrument is plucked with the fingers. The vibration length of the strings can be adjusted with a so-called *capo tasto* (a clamp) on the neck.

The guitar is native to the Iberian penin-sula. Originally, the guitar was a folk instrument and the *vihuela de mano* an in-strument played by and for the nobility. The vihuela de mano was a kind of compromise between the guitar and the lute. It had the shape and size of a guitar, but the tuning re-sembled that of the lute, as did the stringing, which consisted of four double-strings. The first compositions for the vihuela de mano were written in the early sixteenth century. Luys Milan (1500-1562) wrote a teaching manual for the instrument, entitled *Libro de musica de vihuela de mano Entitulado El maestro* (1535-1536).

A fifth pair of strings was attached to the

bass side in the course of the seventeenth century. The shape deviated slightly from that of the modern guitar. The sound box was smaller and deeper and the waist less pronounced. The sound hole was covered with a rosette.

In the mid-eighteenth century, the guitar assumed greater importance in music elsewhere in Europe. The reason for this was that the lute had gradually been supplanted by the harpsichord. The unmanageability and fragility of the lute (particularly when it came to tuning) contributed to its decline.

When the stringing was reduced to six, making it suitable for playing by amateur musicians, its popularity rapidly increased. Several early composers, by no means all of them Spanish, wrote music for the guitar. The original accompaniment to Mozart's song, *The Violet,* was the guitar. The new, simplified string arrangement, was accompanied by an enlargement of the sound box, which was changed to its present shape. The rosette over the sound hole disappeared as well. This gave the guitar greater volume, aided by the deep body of the instrument. A solo guitar can be heard clearly everywhere in a large concert hall, while a harpsichord, heard from far away, is usually experienced as a faint tinkling.

Two men were very important for the development of the Spanish guitar, Antonio de Torres Jurado (1817-1892), a guitar-maker who contributed to the shape and sound of the modern instrument, and the guitarist Andrés Segovia (1893-1987) who gave the guitar a new and distinguished place in classical music in the twentieth century. With his virtuoso skill, Segovia rearranged music that had not been written for guitar, by such

Guitar by Riverà.

Two guitars from France, one dating from 1820 and the other from 1850.

A guitar with Gitarron automatic chord player, 1850.

Detail of a Gitarron automatic chord player.

'Remco de Haan and Erik Westerhof, the "Groningen Guitar Duo."

composers as Bach, Scarlatti, and Couperin, for example. He also inspired leading twentieth-century composers, such as the Spanish Manuel de Falla (1876–1946) and the Brazilian Heitor Villa Lobos (1887–1959) to write guitar music for him. The gramophone record also contributed to Segovia's fame.

There are many good classical guitarists in modern Europe who have earned world-wide recognition, such as the Dutch Groningen Guitar Duo.

Chitarra Battente

In the seventeenth and eighteenth century, Italy developed its own guitar shape, the chitarra battente. This guitar has a deep sound box and a strongly curved base. The side and back were assembled from long, narrow ribs. The stringing usually consisted of five double-strings, but sometimes triple stringing was used. They were made of steel and played with a plectrum.

Portuguese or Fado Guitar

Portugal has its own, distinctive guitar culture. The Portuguese guitar is used as accompaniment to *fado* (fate) songs, with their melancholy overtones. In its construction the fado guitar appears to be a mixture of the guitar and the cittern. The pegbox design is very unusual.

Arpeggione

The arpeggione, also called the *guitarre d'amour* (love guitar), is another variation

Portuguese fado guitar.

on the guitar. This large instrument was invented in 1823 by the Viennese instrument-maker Staufer, but did not last long. The arpeggione would have been totally forgotten had not Franz Schubert (1797-1828) written some beautiful music for it. The breath-taking *Sonata for Piano and Arpeggione* (1824) has acquired a permanent place in the chamber music repertoire. The instrument itself is no longer heard in the sonata, unfortunately, because no playable arpeggione survives, so it is replaced by the cello or viola.

Bass Guitar

There are several variations on the classical guitar, tuned to different pitches, one of them being the bass guitar. This hefty instrument has a more strings and two necks. One neck has normal frets on the key, to which six strings have been applied, while the other neck, that has no fret, can have as many as twelve chromatically tuned bass strings.

Rhythm Guitar

The name "Rhythm guitar" is applied to a number of types of guitars that are used as rhythmic accompaniment mainly for jazz, blues and folk music. Rhythm guitars have a larger sound box than the classical guitar and sometimes both the front and back are slightly curved. The shape is not always that of a symmetrical figure-of-eight, because a

Detail of a fado guitar showing the unusual pegbox.

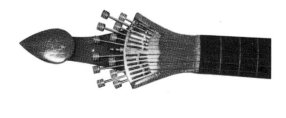

"bite" is often taken out of the neck to facilitate the left hand reaching the furthest frets, which are located on the part of the neck that is attached to the sound box. A so-called pick-guard is often found under this part, which is used to protect the top of the sound box against damage from the plectrum with which the rhythm guitar is always played. Instead of a sound hole there are often two f shaped openings on the top.

Cauquinho or *machete*: a Portuguese instrument, somewhere between a mandolin and a guitar.

The guitar is strung with twelve steel strings in six pairs of two, stretched over a bridge that produces additional vibration.

The *dobro* is a form of rhythm guitar with an unusual shape that was very popular with the early blues singers. Its bridge was mounted on a round metal resonator and the strings were played on the neck with one finger of the left hand on which a kind of thimble was worn. The sliding of the finger over the strings caused a very special effect (see the slide-guitar). The rhythm guitar is mainly played in chords and accompanies vocals. Fingerings have been developed for the rhythm guitar, so even those who can't read music can learn to play it.

Hawaiian Guitar

The Hawaiian guitar is not a Polynesian instrument at all. It is based on the instrument that the Portuguese and American sailors brought with them to the Hawaiian Islands in the latter part of the nineteenth century. Native Hawaiians, notably Joseph Kekuku, James Hoa and Gabriel Davion, made substantial alterations, so that it can be said to be a genuinely Polynesian adaptation of the instrument.

The Hawaiian guitar is played flat, mounted on a tripod. The metal strings, that are always played with a plectrum, are strung higher up the fingerboard than in a classical guitar. The neck is fretless, but has guides on the fingerboard. The left hand holds a metal bar that glides over the strings, to produce the typical "Hawaiian" effect.

Hawaiian music was recorded as early as the 1890s, and became popular in the United States just before World War I, a popularity that continued through the 1920s and 1930s.

Ukulele

The ukulele (the Polynesian word for "flea") is a miniature guitar developed in the nineteenth century from the Portuguese *machete* or *machada*, an instrument that is a cross between a guitar and a mandolin. The ukulele is guitar-shaped and made entirely of wood. It has four strings that are usually played with the fingers. In the blues and folk world, the ukulele has acquired the role of an instrument that is strummed to accompany vocals like the rhythm guitar. The *banjele* is a larger instrument, a cross between the banjo (q.v.) and the ukelele, with more of the characteristics of the former. It enjoyed brief popularity during the Hawaiian music craze that lasted during the inter-war period in the United States and the United Kingdom.

Ukulele.

Samisen

The Japanese samisen is a non-European equivalent of the guitar or banjo (q.v.). Although the samisen is considered to be an instrument played almost exclusively by women, and particularly geishas, it was played in the past by the samurai class, but in all cases as an instrument to accompany the human voice. The samisen is a three stringed banjo-like instrument, the strings of which are plucked with a large bone plectrum.

Electric Guitar

The guitar was one of the first instruments to be electrically amplified. Jazz required a stringed instrument that could be played solo and as rhythm accompaniment. It also needed to have a much louder volume than the standard stringed instrument, because it would have to be heard over the other noisy instruments of the jazz band. An electrode was thus placed under the strings and connected to a loudspeaker with a built-in amplifier. The result was the birth of a new instrument, infinitely louder than the classical guitar, and with an infinite number of new chords. It is through the guitar that electrical amplification first entered music.

During the 1950s, three elements were added, each with its own sound spectrum.

Left: a samisen, a long, three-stringed lute. The front and back of this instrument are made of out of dog skin or cat skin. Right: a three-stringed *kokyuo*, a small samisen. This is the only Japanese stringed instrument that can be bowed.

Electric guitar being built.

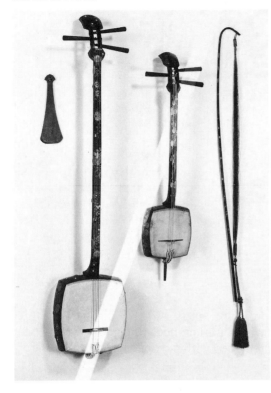

Control knobs, foot pedals, and other operating controls provided for an unprecedented sound spectrum and enhanced volume. By distorting the signal, the volume could be increase, a technique now standard in all types of popular music.

The best-known makes of electric guitar, Gibson and Fender (the famous Stratocruiser), are American. It was Les Paul (1915–), a virtuoso on the electric guitar who contributed substantially to new designs, who first demonstrated that the sound board no longer served a purpose, and the hollow instrument was replaced by a board made to resemble the model of a guitar, the "solid-body guitar." The first real solid body was made by Gibson in 1952, to Les Paul's design. The solid body also exists as a bass guitar, which usually has four metal strings.

These days the guitars are usually connected linked to an amplifier's electronics without a cable, enabling the musicians to move all over the stage.

In view of the advances in digitization, the role of electronics in pop music is one of growing importance. If the Rolling Stones or Tina Turner were to give a pop concert at a race track or in a public park, for instance, the amplification and lighting would consume as much electricity as an average city neighborhood would in a week! The sound level in such cases is very high, yet distortion is negligible, and the clarity exceptional.

The slide *guitar* is a feature of country and western music, which may also have foot- and knee-operated pedals. This guitar usually rests on a tripod and has one or two necks. It is a cross between the classical six-string guitar and a four string bass guitar, but like the Hawaiian guitar, the characteristic slide guitar sound is produced by sliding a metal bar over the strings.

Detail of bass guitar showing tuning knobs.

Banjo

The banjo was an African instrument, brought to the United States through the slave trade. It was one of the first jazz instruments, and is still a feature of Dixieland jazz. The sound board of the banjo is a flat tambour or drum-shape covered with parchment. The neck is proportionally long and fretted, and the back of the neck ends in a pegbox. There are three sizes of banjo, the tenor, bass, and long-necked banjo. Most banjos have four strings, but there are banjos with five strings, the fifth being relatively short. This fifth string is strung on the bass side, and a melody can be played on it with the thumb.

Banjo (Dobson, 19th century).

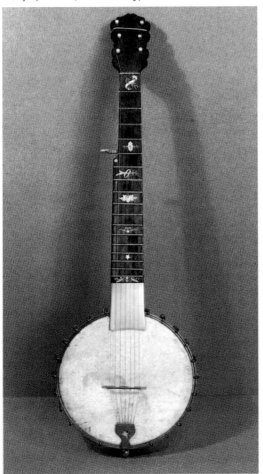

Banjo strings are strummed or plucked, the player often using one or more plectrums attached to the finger tips, the so-called "fingerpicks." The banjo is also played solo or in ensembles to accompany singing.

Zither

The zither family is very large and includes, the dulcimer (q.v.) and the psalter (q.v.). In essence, a zither is a board over which strings have been stretched. The most primitive zithers are bar-shaped or tube-shaped, the strings being stretched over a plank or slat that is sometimes supplied with resonators in the shape of a gourd or calabash. This is a common form of the instrument in Africa and Indonesia. A variation is the dish-zither, on which the strings have been stretched across a shallow dish shape.

A refined shape of the slat-zither is the Indian *vina*. Originally it consisted of a hollow tube resting on two gourds, and the neck was rarely fretted. Later instruments, mainly from southern India, have a much wider, fretted, neck, the gourd having been replaced with a wooden body.

In Europe long zithers or hummels (q.v.) come in many shapes and sizes. The Finnish *kantele*, the Swedish *hummel*, and the Icelandic *langspil* are examples of long zithers used in folk music, some of which are played like a lute or guitar.

In the Far East, the Japanese *koto* is a zither with thirteen silk strings that are plucked

Mi-gyaung, a crocodile-shaped zither (Mandalay, Burma, 9th century).

The vina, an Indian plank zither

Detail of a vina.

Detail of a vina.

with three ivory plectra and stretched over adjustable bridges. In Chinese music, the *qu'qin* is a long, seven-stringed, bridgeless zither. Ivory disks on the soundboard mark the stop positions of the strings. Like the Hawaiian guitar, the *qu'qin* is played flat, in this case on a table. The stopped left hand is used to cause a kind of slide affect.

A more irregular shape is seen in the German folk instrument known as a *scheitholt* or *trumscheit*. This huge, one-stringed instrument, the height of a man, has a long narrow sound box, and stands on a footrest on the ground. The string is stretched over an asymmetrically positioned bridge, attached on one side to the resonance box, so that it can resonate freely on the other side. The instrument can be plucked or strummed.

Another name for this instrument is *tromba marina*, "tromba" because the sound resembles that of a trumpet, but "marina" has

nothing to do with the sea, and is merely a corruption of "from Maria." The instrument is also called a *nonnengeige*, because it was traditionally played in convents instead of the trumpet, which was seen by the nuns as a masculine (warlike) instrument.

The modern, Austrian zither, made famous in the film *The Third Man* (1949) by the *Harry Lime Theme*, composed and played

Below: from left to right, two hommels (Belgium, 1920), an *epinette des Vosges* (20th century), and a home-made hommel, built by E. Verel, 1981.

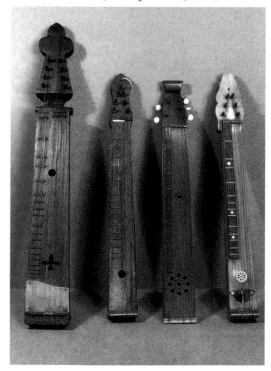

by Anton Karas, is a more or less square sound box arched on one side. The fingerboard has frets and metal strings that are shortened with the fingers of the left hand, and plucked with the thumb of the right hand to which a plectrum is attached. The fingers of the right hand strum the additional accompanying catgut strings.

The *chord-zither* is another variation on the zither. It is strung in such a way that the notes of the desired chords have been grouped together. and is usually used to accompany the human voice. The *autoharp* is a simpler version to which dampers are attached, so that strings not required for the necessary chords are dampened.

The Greek *monochord*, once used as a tuning instrument, was originally a one-stringed plank-zither, this instrument is classified as a type of clavichord or cimbalum, this being the medieval collective name to describe this group of instruments.

Psalter

The psalter or psalterium is closely related to the dulcimer. Illustrations from the early Middle Ages clearly show the difference between a plucked psalterium and a strummed dulcimer. It is generally thought that the plucked psalterium came from the northern Mediterranean countries, and the dulcimer from the eastern Mediterranean and Middle East.

The psalter consists of a flat wooden box with a trapezoid top that functions as a resonator, though there are variations in the

The *ch'in*, a Chinese fretless board zither.

shape. The metal strings are stretched over the resonator or sounding board and are tuned with the aid of tuning keys.

The Arabian *quanan*, still played in Turkish music, is the forerunner to both the psalter and the zither. This instrument has an unusual shape, in that the long sides are of un-equal length and the tuning pegs are attached to a slanted frame between these sides. The instrument reached Europe, where it became known as a *canon* (French) or *kanon* (German), only later acquiring the name *psalter*. This instrument is also the origin of the Russian *gusli* that can have up to thirty-five strings.

It was found that if the psalter was held vertically, the strings could be stretched over

Renaissance etching showing a musician carrying a *tromba marina* on the left.

The koto, a Japanese zither. The instrument has thirteen silk strings, strung over an ivory bridge. By adjusting the position of the bridges, the player can set the desired scale.

both sides of the resonance box, thick brass strings on one side and thin steel strings on the other. This "new" instrument had a considerable range and was called the *wing-harp* or *point harp*.

Due to the increasing interest in medieval music, the psalter is once again being made and used in public performances .

Dulcimer

The origins of the dulcimer family lie in the Near East. In the countries now called Iran and Iraq there is an instrument called the *santir*, a variant on the Greek *psalterion*, and it seems there is also an ancestor of the dulcimer in China, where it is called *yang ch'in*, meaning "foreign zither."

The dulcimer is a shallow wooden box in the shape of a symmetrical trapezium. It can have up to 100 strings, which are tuned by means of screws on the side of the box. Below the strings, there may be bridges that

can be positioned to provide special tonal effects. The strings are struck with soft sticks or mallets.

Cymbalom

The cymbalom or *timpanon* is a dulcimer traditionally played by Hungarian gypsies. At the end of the nineteenth century it was modernized by the Hungarian instrument maker, Schunda. Thus the cymbalom became a predominantly Hungarian instrument, in much the same way that the bagpipes are a typically Scottish musical instrument. The modern cymbalom is mostly played in gypsy bands, but the instrument has also acquired a place in classical music. The Hungarian composer Zoltán Kodaly (1882-1967) used the cymbalom in his orchestral suite *Hary Janos* (1927).

The santoor, an Indian psaltery with sticks.

A *swara mandala*.

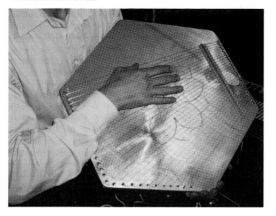

An antique hammered dulcimer.

Aeolian Harp

The Aeolian harp is not actually a harp in the true sense of the word, but rather a zither, with a right-angled body serving as the resonator. The strings are all of equal length and are made to vibrate by wind. Because the strings are of varying thickness and thus of varying pitch, they produce chords when the wind blows through them. The aeolian harp is thus the only musical instrument that plays itself, without any form of human intervention.

The Aeolian harp was said to have been the instrument of Aeolus, the Greek god of wind, and the first of these instruments were made by the ancient Greeks. The modern Aeolian harp dates back to the seventeenth century. The present day instrument is also known as the "wind harp". One type consists of a rectangular sounding board with one hole in the center and a bridge on each end, over which strings are stretched. The number of strings varies from five to twelve and all are tuned to the same pitch.

For the Aeolian harp to play, it must be placed on a windowsill. The harp should be almost as long as the width of the window, and the window should be closed almost to the top of strings. There is usually a spacer or a lid on the harp to keep the window from being closed on the strings. The idea is to concentrate the wind flow on the strings.

A second type of Aeolian harp is one that is designed to remain outdoors. These structures are works of artists, located in public places, where they are meant to catch the eye as well as the breezes.

"Wind chimes" are a variant of the Aeolian harp. They can be made of glass or metal but consist more frequently of a wooden disk from which a number of bamboo tubes are hung. When the wind blows they strike each other giving rise to a sort of plucking noise. They were popular in the 1960s.

Jew's Harp

The Jew's harp consists of a flexible prong, that may be carved out of or attached to a small frame. This little frame is generally metal but is sometimes made of wood or bamboo. The player holds the instrument in

Hammered dulcimer (England, 19th century).

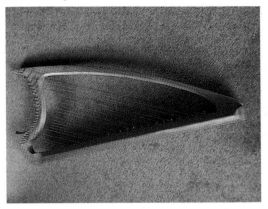
Medieval harp.

the mouth, which then acts as the resonator. The sound is produced by the player plucking the prong with the finger. The shape of the player's mouth cavity defines the sound quality.

The origin of the name is not know but it is believed to a corruption of *jaw's harp*, a name by which the instrument is also known in English. It is also called a *gewgaw*. The instrument has been found throughout Europe, as well as in Asia and the Pacific. Until traded by Europeans, none were found on the African continent, but it is found everywhere in Russia. Bamboo and wooden laminated versions are found in the Pacific, southeast Asia, and in China, except in Northern China where it always made of iron. Through European colonization, the bow-shaped metal Jew's harp was introduced into the Americas, Africa and Australia, mainly by the Dutch and English. In Siberia and Mongolia, the Jew's Harp was a magical instrument, used by shamans to induce trances and to heal the sick.

Thumb Harp

In the West, the thumb harp or thumb piano is usually a child's instrument. In Africa, however, the thumb harp is a folk instrument called the *sansa*. It is a plucked instrument and is found in various sizes. A number of metal or wooden prongs is attached to a resonator by a clamp lying at right angles to them. Each prong has one end free to be plucked by the player, usually with the thumb. The pitch of the prongs can be easily adjusted by pulling it forward or pushing it back.

Harp

The harp is a stringed instrument that is plucked with the fingers. The harp was a popular instrument in Ancient Egypt and in Babylon, as is confirmed by many contemporary illustrations. In the Bible, the story of David, who played the harp to a troubled King Saul, and had some problems with tuning the instrument, is well-known.

The harp came to Europe during the Middle Ages. Minstrels from Scandinavia and troubadours from the France and Spain would accompany themselves on a sort of portable harp. The modern harp developed from the gothic and medieval instrument. The harp was originally tuned to a diatonic scale but during the sixteenth century, the

Aeolian harp.

Clay tablet depicting of a Babylonian harp
(ca. 1900 BCE).

Various pedal harps.

chromatic harp came into being. The first
harp with pedals was built in 1720, significantly different on the underside from the
Renaissance harps that had no pedals, such
as those played in the fifteenth and

Diatonic harp.

Small diatonic harp with four manuals.

sixteenth centuries. Almost a hundred years later, in 1811, Sebastien Erard (1752-1831), a Parisian piano manufacturer who later opened a branch in London (which is still in business today), built a double-action pedal harp similar to those that have been part of the symphony orchestras ever since. This new instrument, with its seven pedals, made it possible for the first time to play in all possible keys.

The harp has undergone a huge metamorphosis during the course of its thirty thousand years of existence, and not just with regard to its shape. The instruments of Antiquity had only five or six strings, nowadays the harp has 46–48. The longest string measures about 60 inches, the shortest about 5 inches. In order to make the strings sound to their greatest potential, the instrument has to be very sturdily built. The sound board regulates the fullness of tone. From it

The Irish harp that once belonged to the famous harpist, Arthur O'Neill (died 1818).

Detailed view of small diatonic harp, the four manuals.

the strings are stretched to the metal "ram" above, where they are attached to metal pegs. Sycamore, a wood that is odorless, tasteless, and very strong, is used throughout for the construction of the modern harp. The longer strings are usually metal and the shorter ones of gut. The lowest note on the harp is C flat. Depressing the pedal to its first position brings this up to C natural and in the second pedal position this becomes C sharp, and so on. The characteristic features of the harp lie primarily in arpeggios. Flageolet notes (harmonics), glissandi, and tremolo-playing are also particular qualities of the instrument.

The harp strings can be played from both

sides. The harp is played with the fingertips, and in earlier times the finger nail was also used. The flat of the palm is used to dampen the sound. It is extremely helpful for the players to prevent them getting lost among so many strings, that the strings are colored in red (for C strings), white, and blue.

Although a lot of music has been written for the harp, from baroque to modern times, one of the most famous pieces, Handel's *Harp Concerto,* was not actually written for the instrument but is an arrangement of one of his organ concertos. The harp was always included in Richard Wagner's opera orchestra, however, and Richard Strauss also used it frequently. The harp played an important role in the orchestra in French music of the late nineteenth century, through composers such as Debussy (*La Mer* and the *Sonata for Flute, Viola and Harp*) and Ravel (*Introduction and Allegro for Harp*

and Orchestra). Even modest symphony orchestras had one or even two harps.

The greatest modern exponent of the harp was undoubtedly the Polish-born harpist, Wanda Landowska (1877-1959).

The Irish or Gaelic harp. a much smaller instrument than the orchestral harp, is one of the symbols of Ireland (and the trademark of Guinness). These harps, which differ from country to country resemble the mediaeval harp in that they are much smaller and played with the instrument balanced on the knees. There is a long tradition of virtuoso Irish harp players, of whom the most famous is the blind harpist and composer Turlogh O'Carolan (1670–1738).

The Triple Harp, with its three rows of strings, is now the classic Welsh harp. The two outer rows are tuned to the diatonic scale and the semitones are in the central row This harp originated in Italy. arriving

A string quartet.

in Wales in the late seventeenth century, where it developed a high head and became larger. Nansi Richards (1888-1979) was a virtuoso harpist and enthusiastic teacher of the technique.

A small Indonesian three-stringed fiddle, probably with a ritual function.

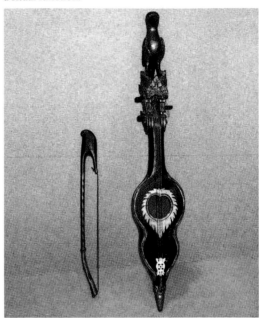

Stringed Instruments

Pre-history

Stringed instruments are defined nowadays as those in which the strings are played with the aid of a bow, although they were around for thousands of years before the bow came on the scene. The earliest stringed instruments were plucked, a technique that is easier on the hand than bowing. The first bow was probably no more than a sort of wooden rubbing-stick. Later shapes are more reminiscent of a hunter's bow.

Not much is known about the origins of string instruments. A stick was first drawn across a string about six thousand years ago, probably in Central Asia. In Europe, stringed instruments have been described and illustrated from the Dark Ages to the Middle Ages, but without bows. The bow is first mentioned by the Arab, Al-Farabi (?-950) who claimed that the bow came from Asia. In the Middle East, some primitive stringed instruments emerged that were stroked with a stick to which a string "or something similar" was attached. The bow

Rebab, a stringed instrument from an Indonesian gamelan ensemble.

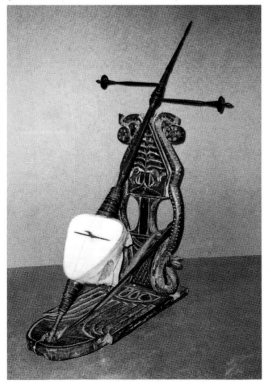

reached Europe by two different routes, from Asia via Constantinople (now Istanbul) and from North Africa by way of southern, Moorish, Spain, around the tenth century, as proved by texts and illustrations. The Asiatic stringed instrument is called the *lura*. In sixth-century Constantinople, it was still a plucked instrument, the bow not coming into use until at least a hundred years later. Around the year 1000, the Arab philosopher Ibn Sina (better known in the West as Avicenna) mentioned the *rebab* as an example of an Arabic stringed instrument. Through the expansion of Islam, stringed reached Europe and Indonesia and secured an important position in Indonesian gamelan orchestras.

In Islamic culture, plucked instruments were held in higher esteem than stringed instruments. Arabic writers described string instruments as imperfect because of their feeble tone and screeching sound. The instruments gradually gained in popularity. . The lura and rebab are viewed as the direct ancestors of the violin.

FROM PLUCKED INSTRUMENT TO VIOLIN: HISTORY

Because string instruments are derived from lute-like plucked instruments, they were described in the Western system of classification as bowed, short-necked lutes. It took from the eleventh through the sixteenth centuries before the bowed plucked instruments developed into string instruments, such as the violin. Initially all sorts of instruments came into being that resembled the lyre and the rebab. The best known of these were the *rubeba* (q.v.) or *rebec* (q.v.)(from the Arabic, *rebab*) and the *viol* (q.v.). The rebec gave rise to a miniature violin that appeared in the fifteenth century only to disappear again in the seventeenth. It was the *dance-master's violin*, also known as the *pocket- or purse-violin*.

A selection of bows.

The viol *(q.v.)* gave rise to instruments named for the manner in which they were played, such as the *lira da braccio* (Italian for "arm lyre") and the *viola da braccio* both of which were held up to the shoulder for playing. The *viola da gamba* (Italian for "leg viol") and the *lira da gambe* (Italian for "legs lyre") rested against the leg or were held between the knees.

Dancing master violin (Germany, ca. 1750).

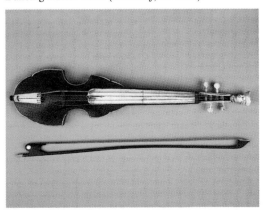

151

Double-bass.

It was no coincidence that the workshops were near the Alps, because the tone quality of a stringed instrument is for the most part defined by the quality of the wood from which the sounding board is made. The wood must have a regular density and homogeneity and such wood is only produced in mountainous areas.

FROM PLUCKED INSTRUMENT TO VIOLIN: CONSTRUCTION

The bowed instruments needed to be constructed differently from plucked instruments in order to achieve the new "ideal" sound. The tension on the strings of plucked instruments did not need to be very great, but bowed strings need to be much more taught and require more room to vibrate. Accordingly they were strung over a separate platform—the bridge, thus transferring the vibration of the string to the sound box.

Medieval stringed instruments originally had a flat bridge, so that all the strings sounded at the same time. This consonance was perfect for early music, in which bourdon effects and parallel movement in the fourths and fifths were intrinsic to the composition. The vaulted bridge came later in response to the desire to be able to play

Shortly after the appearance of the viols a family of them developed, built to various sizes, including the popular *viola da gamba (q.v.)*, a *soprano* or *descant gamba*, an *alto gamba*, *a tenor gamba*, (*gamba,* for short), a large *bass gamba* and a *contrabass gamba* (forerunner of the *double-bass (q.v.*). Various hybrid forms also appeared, such as the *viola bastarda* and the viola d'amore.

In the early sixteenth century, when these instruments were still at the height of popularity, the first violins were made in the area where Italy, Switzerland and Austria meet. The workshops in the foothills of the Alps developed a new instrument from elements of the rebec, the viola da braccio, and the lira da braccio—the violin. By the eighteenth century, this instrument had replaced all these earlier stringed instruments.

The Dutch violin builder, Hein Woldring.

Violin bridge.

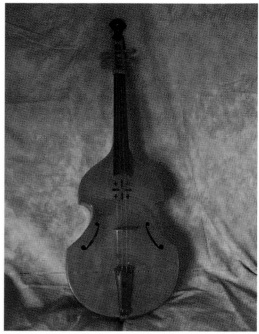
Tenor fiddle.

each string separately. The body of the instrument was then given a "waist" so that the bow had enough room to stroke the outermost strings.

The strings were attached by way of a tailpiece to a substantial knob, or nut, in the sound box. The greater string tension also led to the introduction of two supporting posts under the bridge.

A sounding-beam was the attached to the belly, parallel to the bass strings. This served to transfer the vibration across the whole sounding board. A wooden stake, the sound post, was placed between front and rear plates on the same side as the higher strings, which stiffening the structure and transferred the vibrations to the back. Finally, the increased tension of the strings resulted in the introduction of a vaulted belly. The sound holes in the belly evolved from one round hole to two semi-circular ones and then to the f-shaped slits known today. The f-shape has an important function because, of all the possible shapes, this one causes least interference with the vibration of the belly, resulting in greater projection of the sound in a well-made violin.

From the Middle Ages onward, the bow consisted of a supple stick strung with horse hair. The hairs were rubbed with resin, or rosin, to optimize the friction with the strings. Prior to the eighteenth century, the tension on the hairs was regulated by the thumb and fingers. This changed after the development of the heel with integral tensioning screw. The actual wooden bow

Pochette.

Rebab.

Rebec.

smoothly into the neck, and only two strings.

Rebab

Rebab is the collective name for a group of stringed instruments of various shapes that originated in the Islamic world. The North African rebab, the best-known version, was introduced into Europe in the tenth century and became the direct antecedent of the *European rebec* (q.v). The rebab has existed in Morocco and Tunisia for a thousand years in virtually unchanged form. Nowadays, it appears in Europe beside the rebec in concerts of medieval music and particularly in old Spanish music. The *rebab* has a small, bulbous, pear-shaped body that merges

began with the pronounced arch of the hunting bow but gradually flattened out. The modern bow, in fact, curves slightly inward.

Rebec

The rebec is the European counterpart of the Islamic *rebab* and developed from it in the eleventh century. The two names are obviously similar and when one compares a historical rebec (it disappeared in the seventeenth century) with a contemporary restored rebab from Morocco, the similarities in appearance are also obvious. Both instruments have a small, pear-shaped, bulbous body, narrowing toward the neck. The rebec usually had a few more strings, three to five of them, tuned in fifths. The rebec blossomed in the late Middle Ages. The penetrating, sometimes almost bitter sound, was well suited to religious processions, where it could make itself heard above the wind instruments. Moreover, the rebec was popular in the European courts as an accompaniment to dancing and poetry reading. At the English court of Henry VIII it formed part of the royal orchestra. It was already being depicted in ensembles—and occasionally on its own—in the hands of princes and courtiers who held it vertically on their laps to play it.

The more easily portable dance-master's violin developed from the rebec. This miniature instrument was popular from the fifteenth through the seventeenth centuries, mostly amongst the professional bands who earned their living from music and who gave the instrument both of its names (it was also called the *pocket violin*). The dancing-master would play this lightest of instruments not only to accompany his pupils, but also for demonstration dances. The smallest model, the Italian *sordino*, had a weight of scarcely more than five ounces.

Viol

Confusingly, the Italian name for this instrument is *viola*. Other names include *fiddle, lyra, lira* and, in German, *Geige*. Along with the rebec it was the most popular instrument of the Middle Ages.

The viol is descended partly from the Asiatic *lura* and is mentioned as early as the ninth century in evangelical writings. In contrast to the rebec, the viol has a flat back and the neck is quite distinct from the body. The "waist", introduced to allow more room for the bow, did not appear until the eleventh century.

In the early period, the viol had between three and six strings, seven at the most from the fifteenth century, two of which ran along the neck beside the bridge and acted as resonance or bourdon strings. From illustrations of the time, it seems that the player had two choices of playing position, either resting it against the left shoulder or vertically in front of the body.

The viol is a precursor of the violin by way of the *lira da braccio* and the *viola da braccio* and, looked at this way, the violin is a great-grandchild of the viol.

The original viol fell into disuse in the

Lyra da braccio (Wilhelm Busch). This instrument has five playing strings and two bourdon strings. The pegs sit in a flower-shaped pegbox. This is a Renaissance version.

Detailed view of a Hardanger fiddle, also called Sigrid (1902).

Hurdy-gurdy (Pajeot Jeune, 1887).

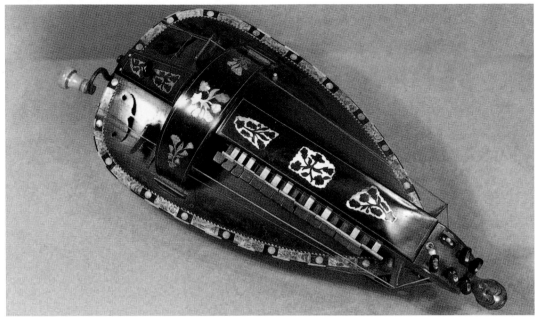

fifteenth century and made way for the lira da braccio, the viola da braccio, and the viola da gamba.

The Hardanger fiddle is a popular Norwegian folk instrument with a somewhat smaller resonating body than the viol. The bridge is lower and the belly and back are curved. Below the melodic strings lie four resonating strings. The instrument is always handsomely finished and is inextricably linked with Norse folk music. Unlike most other folk violins, the Hardanger fiddle is played held against the chin, just like its more refined orchestral relation.

Hurdy-Gurdy

The strings of the hurdy-gurdy are not actually bowed but stroked by a coarse rotating disk. In the Middle Ages, when it was developed, the hurdy-gurdy started off with three strings, but later acquired six. The large version (up to 6 feet high) was called the *organistrum* and was played by two people. The organistrum is, in fact, a sort of poor man's organ, and was played in churches that could not afford an organ to accompany the liturgy. It also came to be played outside churches, becoming one of the favorite instruments of that time.

The hinged tangents (from the Latin, *tangere* = touch), attached along the length of the neck, had the same function as the frets on a guitar. Some examples had a separate melody string; in these cases the other

Nyckelharpa (Stockholm, 1880). The strings are held down by means of keys and are played with a bow. There are twelve resonance strings. This instrument is most common in the Swedish province of Uppland, and is used to accompany dancing.

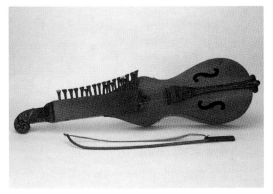

strings were not stroked by the tangents, since they sounded sympathetically, like bourdon strings.

The hurdy-gurdy waned in popularity after the Middle Ages, but it made an unexpected return to popularity in eighteenth-century France (where it is known as the *vielle*), so much so that a real culture of virtuosity built up around the instrument. Even composers like Haydn and Corrette did their bit for its repertoire. In the nineteenth century the hurdy-gurdy fell once more into decline, though it was still played by street musicians. Nowadays the hurdy-gurdy is heard in performances of "world music" and early music.

The Swedish folk instrument called the *nyckelharpa* is a relation of the hurdy-gurdy. This instrument is found mainly in the

Head of Pegasos, a seven-stringed viola da gamba in D, made by the luthier, Liedmeyer.

Viola da gamba.

Viola da gamba (Gaspard Tieffenbrucker, Lyon, ca. 1560).

Swedish province of Uppland. In contrast to the hurdy-gurdy, the strings on this are stroked with a bow. They are foreshortened in the same way as in the hurdy-gurdy.

Viola da Braccio

The viola da braccio is best known as the precursor of the violin family and the direct antecedent of the viola. It is a member of the viol family, supported during playing by the arm (Italian, *braccio*). It forms the continuation in development of the *lira da braccio*. The viola da braccio and its close variant, the lira da braccio, were great favorites of the Italian court poets during the Renaissance, who used them to accompany their songs.

One large and one small member of the viola family, the bass gamba made by Jaye and behind it a viol made by Cuesar.

Viola da Gamba

The viola da gamba (or *gamba* for short) appeared around 1500 CE as a more-or-less "logical" development of the medieval viol. The gamba can be regarded as the equivalent of the bass voice among the viols. As a result of its size, the newcomer could not be played like the arm-fiddle or *viola da braccio* and had to be gripped between the knees, hence *viola da gamba* (knee viol).

Originally, the gamba existed in only one size but it wasn't long before the instrument was made in various sizes. The original model was first called a "bass gamba," but became the "tenor gamba" from the seventeenth century. During the eighteenth century, most of the gamba forms fell into disuse with the exception of the tenor gamba which, as the most distinguished representative of the family, had already made an established name for itself.

The instrument flourished in the sixteenth and seventeenth centuries, primarily in England, where it was very popular with traveling theater companies. The gamba should have retained its popularity well into the eighteenth century but the arrival of the cello put its existence in jeopardy. It remained a very popular solo instrument for

Bass gamba (Paulus Alletsee, Munich, 1726).

Alto gamba, Ventura di Francesco.

Large bass gamba in G after Busch (luthier Liedmeyer)

Mamabear

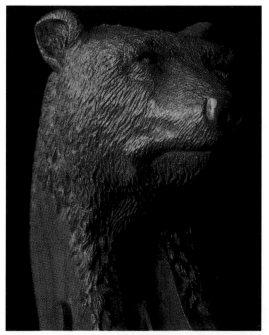

many years. That the cello should gradually have supplanted it was all down to the desire for a "larger" sound.

There has been a renewed interest in the gamba in Europe during the past few decades. This has to do with the pervasive interest in the "authentic" performance of ancient music. In many performances of the Passions, where the gamba had been replaced over the years by the cello, although the parts were originally written for the gamba, the instrument is now making a comeback. To start with. gamba-playing wasn't always immaculate, as the first modern gamba soloists didn't have much of a playing tradition to fall back on. This is illustrated in the following poem, *In the Rests* by Klaas Iwerna (1973):

Jaye descant, a large descant gamba in D after H. Jaye.

Viola da gamba with steel strings (early 20th century).

Viola bastarda (anonymous maker).

Viola d'amore (Astenay Tribaut).

"The cello said
There was something wrong there
That was a gamba
Oh, that was a gamba?
Well that explains it."

The viola da gamba is most closely related in shape to the *violoncello* (the cello)(q.v.), but it has a longer neck and sharply sloping shoulders. The back of the instrument is flat and the sound holes are usually C-shaped. The viola da gamba normally has six strings, but occasionally seven. The scroll is very conspicuous, and is sometimes sculpted in the form of a human or animal head.

Johann Schenck (1660– ca. 1772) was a famous Dutch gamba player and composer from Amsterdam whose complete gamba works are preserved in the library of Durham Cathedral, England. J.S. Bach also wrote many pieces that included the viola da gamba, such as the sonatas (trio and fugues BWV 1021, 1023, 1025, 1026 and 1019a), all for violin and *basso continuo* (pianoforte and viola da gamba). They were issued on CD by Hänssler for the "Bach 2000" project, along with the three Sonatas for viola da gamba and harpsichord, BWV 1027, 1028, and 1029.

The viola d'amore also belongs to the same family. As quite often happens, no one seems completely sure what this instrument looked like, so a lively debate centers around the material of which the strings were made and whether it used sympathetic bourdon strings. A number of seventeenth century sources mention metal under-strings, lying quite close to the belly. Above them there gut strings, which were bowed and strung across a bridge. The under-strings were therefore vibrated by the resonance from the belly. The result was a uniquely characteristic sound with many subtle overtones.

The Viol: History of an Instrument by Annette Otterstedt, goes into detail about the way in which these instruments were fashioned and the cultural history of the viol family, including the viola da gamba, from the late fifteenth century to the present day.

Viola Bastarda

The viola bastarda is a hybrid, a scion of the lira da braccio and the viola da gamba. Just like the baritone, this instrument was born in the seventeenth century from the desire to combine the best qualities of each instrument into one.

The viola bastarda was particularly popular in England in the sixteenth and seventeenth centuries under the name of *lyra viol*. The tuning and playing position correlate with those of the viola da gamba, while the bourdon strings were borrowed from the lira da braccio.

The *viola d'amore* is a variant in the higher, alto register. This instrument is held on the arm, just like the violin, and tuned similarly. In contrast to the viola bastarda, the viola d'amore always sounds delightful, and many composers have been inspired by the sound to write for it. Vivaldi wrote a number of charming concerti for the viola

Baritone (southern Germany, ca. 1800).

d'amore. More recent composers of music for the instrument include Paul Hindemith (1895-1963), who wrote a series of pieces for various solo instruments and orchestra, including one for the viola d'amore (Chamber Music No. 6, Opus 46, no.1). The Swiss-Dutch composer Frank Martin (1890–1974) wrote a beautiful Sonata da Chiesa for viola d'amore and orchestra (1938), following his similarly named work for viola d'amore and organ written in the same year. This work also exists in the form of a Concerto for Flute and Orchestra (1938).

Baritone

The baritone (known in Italian as the *viola di bordone*) is an instrument with six or seven gut strings and from seven through a maximum of forty-four metal resonating or bourdon strings running along the neck. The strings can be plucked with the thumb of the left hand. The baritone was the result of seventeenth-century experimentation, and was developed from the viola bastarda. With one exception thereafter, the continuous sound of the many strings and the complicated playing technique soon became too much for most musicians. The exception was Baron Nicholas Esterhazy, a patron of Joseph Haydn (1732-1809), who played the baritone with taste and verve, a reason for Haydn to write a lengthy series of entertaining baritone trios (the other instruments being the viola and cello).

Various violins wait in the workshop.

Violin

The violin first appeared in the late fifteenth century in the southern foothills of the Alps. Northern Italian murals of the period show the first violins, depicted alongside the lira da braccio, the viola da braccio, and the rebec. The name *violin* is derived from the Italian *violino*, meaning a small viol. From this, it would seem that the Italians regarded the instrument as the successor to the viola da braccio, direct ancestor of the similar sized viola (*bratsche* in German). The *soprano violin* was developed at the same time, so that a whole family was built up around the viola. In the late seventeenth and early eighteenth centuries, the instrument took on its definitive

Violin built by J. Boumeester, Amsterdam, 1683. The neck, fingerboard, and sound post are original, as is the inlay on the fingerboard and the tailpiece. The bottom plate consists of two parts. Boumeester was one of the most important Dutch violin-makers. He was inspired by the Italian Nicolo Amati.

Collection of violins, ranging from one-sixteenth regular size to regular size, by the Dutch violin-maker, Woldring.

shape thanks to the master instrument-makers of Cremona in Italy.

The four strings of the violin were tuned in fifths and made of gut—the G string began to be wound with silver in the eighteenth century, and later this also happened to the A string. On modern instruments, the E string is usually made of steel.

The violin had been around for a long time when the development of the bow started to catch up with it. The present-day shape of the bow is thanks largely to the Frenchman François Tourte (1747-1835) and the Englishman John Dodd (1753-1839), who made the final improvements.

In the sixteenth century, the violin as an accompaniment to the human voice, like so many other stringed instruments. The violin, in its popular form of the fiddle, was appreciated by the common people as an accompaniment for dancing, thanks to its penetrating sound and clearly rhythmical articulation. At that stage, the violin did not enjoy the same prestige as the lute and viola da gamba, which were played exclusively by professionals and aristocratic amateurs.

Although the Amati family of northern Italian violin-makers was already making beautiful violins halfway through the sixteenth century, it was not until the seventeenth

century that the expressive capabilities of the instrument were discovered and further developed. Baroque music required intensely expressive and clearly focused voices and

Page from Leopold Mozart's *Versuch einer gründlichen Violinschule*, a teaching manual (1756).

Monsieur Violonsotini (lithograph).

Violin scroll with tuning pegs.

Violins awaiting an owner.

Various bows.

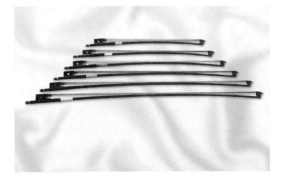

these were the very characteristics that were typical of the violin. From that moment, the violin began its unparalleled rise to fame. The violin family became the core of the baroque ensemble and the classical symphony orchestra.

The violin was also played in chamber music in the seventeenth century. Some of the high points of the violin repertoire are the eighteenth century solo concertos and string quartets for two violins, a viola, and a cello.

The Italian masters of Cremona are considered to be the finest ever violin-makers, whose names—Andrea Amati (1511-1580), Nicolo Amati (1596-1684), his pupil Antonio Stradivari (1644-1737), Andrea Guarneri (c.1626-1698), Giuseppe Guarneri "del Jesu" (1698-1744) and Rugierro Pietro Guarneri (1655-1720)—have gone down in history. Other famous makers include Jakob

Baroque violin.

Eugène Ysaije (1858-1931), a legendary violinist. A competition in Brussels was named for him (now known as the Concours Reine Elisabeth). David Oistrakh was the first winner of this competition. Ysaije was a master of composition but his full virtuosity has never been appreciated.

Stainer (c.1617-1683) from the Tyrol and Matthias Klotz (1653-1743) from Mittenwald. Their instruments were unsurpassed, but by the nineteenth century some had lost their original brilliance, as a result of interference with the stringing to try and produce a bigger tone, using thicker strings, higher string tension, a larger bridge, thicker sound posts, and longer bows.

The violin repertoire is very comprehensive.

Violin.

Solo concertos have been written by Vivaldi, Bach, Mozart, Haydn, Beethoven, Paganini (himself a violin virtuoso), Brahms, Mendelssohn, Bruch, Tchaikowsky, Sibelius, Alban Berg, Arnold Schoenberg, and Serge Prokofiev. The British composers, Edward Elgar (1857–1934) and William Walton (1902-1982) also wrote for the violin. Walton's *Violin Concerto* dates from 1938-39. Benjamin Britten and Paul Hindemith also wrote concertos for the violin in 1939. There are also outstanding violin pieces by Robert Schumann, Alexander Glazunov, Henryk Wieniawski, Dmitri Shostakovich, Samuel Barber, Aram Khachaturian, Sem Dresden, and Hans Kox.

The Dutch Bach specialist Anthon van der Horst (1899–1965) also wrote a work for violin, the *Concerto Espagnola for Violin and Orchestra* (1953). The premier was performed in the 1960s at Groningen by the Netherlands Philharmonic Orchestra under their conductor, Jacques Meyer. Meyer also gave the first post-premier performances in Groningen, The Hague, and on Radio Hilversum of the 1939 *Violin Concerto* by Willem Pijper (1894–1947), who is considered to be the greatest modern Dutch composer.

The reconstructed Bach Concertos, BWV 1052R, 1056R, and 1045, performed by Isabelle Faust, Christoph Poppel, and Muriel Cantoreggi with the Bach-Collegium,

Stuttgart under the direction of Helmuth Rilling, were recently issued on the Hänssler record label. Rilling was also responsible for the whole "BACH 2000" project, under which the entire output of the composer was published on 170 CDs. Faust and Poppel had already issued a recording of the regular versions of the Bach Concertos in 1999, with the same orchestra and conductor.

The most famous collection of solos for the violin repertoire are the sonatas and partitas of Bach, BWV 1001-1006, composed in 1720. Every self-respecting violinist with a solo career, from Yehudi Menuhin to Theo Olof, from Herman Krebbers to Sergiu Lucca, and from Jascha Heifetz to Dimitri Sitkovetski, has wanted to dazzle with these pieces. Sitkovetski recorded the Bach *Sonatas for Violin and Cembalo*, BWV 1014-1019, for Hänssler in 1997, a year before the recording of the sonatas and partitas.

The Belgian violin virtuoso, Eugene Ysaie (1858-1931), never studied composition formally but composed violin music in the post-Romantic style. It has taken a long time for his *Six Sonatas*, Opus 27 (1924), to become well-known. Ysaie also wrote eight violin concertos, several of which he played himself in his younger days. They have remained unpublished for far too long. Amongst his shorter violin works, the

Detail of the bridge of the viocta.

The viocta.

The viocta, an eight-stringed violin, being played by its inventor.

Capriccio (after Saint-Saëns), is a favorite performance piece. For almost the whole of his life, Ysaie played on an instrument made by Guarneri del Jesu. He owned the "Hercules" Stradivarius, which was stolen from his dressing room in 1908 during a tour of Russia. The instrument was to disappear again in 1948.

Viocta

The Dutch musician Willem Wolthuis, (1940–) was a violinist between 1962 and 1990, when he retired from playing. In 1971, he invented an eight-stringed, electric violin that he named the *viocta*. He describes his invention thus: "The neck of this instrument,

a violin, has been widened from one inch to about one-and-a-half inches and then lengthened to accommodate the eight strings. The viocta is provided with eight steel strings, four violin strings and four viola strings. The violin strings are tuned conventionally in G, D, A, and E. The viola strings are tuned to D-flat, A-flat, E-flat, and B-flat—a semi-tone higher than normal. The strings on the viocta lie in the following order from left to right; D-flat-G/ A-flat-D, E-flat-A and B-flat-E, so that they can be bowed two-at-a-time when normal violin fingerings are used.

"This gives rise to the possibility of playing eight-part chords or clusters. The string pairings of G-A-flat/ D-E-flat and A-B-flat can be bowed, allowing for the creation of very

Five-stringed violin, a combination of a violin and a viola. An unusual feature is the "swept-away" tailpiece.

special tone colors, for example, going halfway toward meeting the demands made from time to time by contemporary orchestral music. Four-part harmonics also become a possibility.

"The shape of the bridge is very important. The viola strings lie a fraction lower than the violin strings. In this way, the violin strings can be bowed on their own. Due to the large number of strings, the instrument is subject to a lot of strain, so we have substituted an aluminum tailpiece (aluminum, because it's so light). It is therefore possible to alter the tuning very quickly, so that D-flat becomes D, A-flat becomes A, E-flat becomes E and B-flat becomes B. Then the instrument is tuned in perfect fourths and is exceptionally well-suited to jazz.

"Moreover, with other tuning schemes it is possible to play various types of music. The viocta has acquired quite an individual timbre as a result of the increased tension on the belly. With the addition of a contact microphone and a foot-pedal, the sound becomes absolutely unique. It makes for almost endless possibilities of producing even more abstract sound effects."

Viola

The viola is of similar construction and tuning (fifths) to the violin, but is somewhat longer (about 18 inches body length). The German name *bratsche* betrays its Italian origins, it being about the same size as its predecessor, the *viola da braccio*. It is the oldest member of the violin family.

In general terms, the viola makes a less spectacular sound than its smaller relative,

Tromba marina.

The pickup element of the tromba marina.

simply don't make much of an impact. Carl Stamitz (1745-1801) wrote a *Concerto for Viola* and Wolfgang Amadeus Mozart (1756-1791) gave both the violin and viola solo parts in his *Sinfonia Concertante* KV 364 (1779). In the nineteenth

the violin. Instruments that play in the middle registers are, by their very nature, less conspicuous. Even the cello has inspired more composers than this somewhat awkward instrument, plagued as it is with an unfavorable compass. The highest notes

The Violist, a copper engraving from Johann Christoph Weigel's, *Musicalisches Theatrum*, 1722).

The trumpet violin, an early 20th instrument. The sound is produced via a mechanical pickup element and is amplified by a trumpet bell. This violin became especially popular during the period when phonograph records were still being recorded acoustically.

Viola by the Dutch violin-maker, Woldring.

Bridge of the *violoncello piccolo*.

century Hector Berlioz (1803-1869) wrote the symphony *Harold in Italy*, which is actually a viola concerto in disguise, and in the twentieth century, Bela Bartok (1881-1945) wrote a viola concerto while Paul Hindemith (1895-1963) and Dmitri Shostakovich (1906-1975) also wrote pieces for the viola. An underestimated and therefore seldom-played concerto for viola and orchestra was written by the English composer William Walton (1902-1982). It was originally composed in 1928-29 and revised in 1961. Walton was much influenced by fellow composer Edward Elgar.

A recent example of delightful music for this instrument can be found on a Hänssler CD in collaboration with South-west German Radio, brought out in the fall of 2000. The violist Tabea Zimmerman, with pianist Jascha Nemtsov, plays Jewish chamber music by Alexander Weprik (1899-1958), (including *Kaddish* (prayer for the dead) and *Songs for the Dead*, Alexander Krein's (1883-1951) *Ornaments*, Michail Gnesin (1883-1957) *Minstrel Songs* and *Marianne's Song*, Grigory Gamburg's (1900-1967) *From the Song of Songs*, and Ernst Bloch's (1880-1959) *Suite for Viola and Piano* (1919).

Violoncello

The violoncello, or cello, is usually tuned an octave lower than the viola, so it is not really a tenor violin but more of a bass violin. In the seventeenth century, it generally had five or six strings and formed part of the continuo group of the time, but it slowly but surely took over the role of the viola

da gamba. During the eighteenth century, it became steadily more of a solo instrument than the viola da gamba, as the latter fell out of favor. Johann Sebastian Bach (1685-1750) composed six solo *Suites* for the cello, of which *Number Six* is intended for the smaller *violoncello piccolo*, which probably had an extra E-string. In the eighteenth century, this instrument was made especially for the interpretation of solo parts in ensemble music. The experts do not agree, however, on what the instrument looked like or how it was played.

The cello excelled as the bass voice in chamber music from the eighteenth century onward, and a solo repertoire soon developed for it.

Among the composers who wrote for the cello are Carl Philipp Emanuel (C.P.E.) Bach (1714-1788), Vivaldi, Haydn,

170

Drawing of a cellist (anonymous, 18th century). Note the specific playing position.

Five-stringed *violoncello piccolo*, inspired by the violoncello piccolo (*viola pomposa*) made by Hoffmann, Brussels, no. 1445.

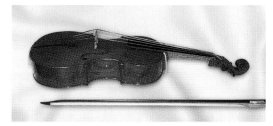

Luigi Boccherini (1743-1805), Schumann, Saint-Saëns, Tchaikovsky (*the Rococo Variations*, 1876), Dvorak, Elgar, and Shostakovich wrote concertos for the cello. The English composer Benjamin Britten wrote his *Cello Symphony*, *Opus 68*, in 1963, commissioned and performed by Mstislav Rostropovich. Rostropovich also performed the two *Cello Suites* by the same composer, *Opus 72* (1963) and *Opus 80* (1967). Five years later, Jean Perrin (1920-1989) wrote a *Cello Concerto* that has had

Various cellos.

The *violoncello piccolo*, played on the shoulder (*a spalda*) by Lambert Smit, an advocate of this manner of playing.

Cellist Yo Yo Ma.

Two double-basses.

far too little international attention, but which has now been recorded by the cellist Alexandra Gutu on a Claves CD.

The standard six-part work for this instrument is the set of *Six Suites* by J.S. Bach(1720), BWV 1007-1012. A number of

Cellos wait in the store for their new owners.

outstanding cellists performed these magnificent pieces as part of their repertoire, particularly after World War II, including

Double-bassist, H. Hess.

double-bass: hand-worked backplate.

Pegbox mechanism of a double-bass.

from the heyday of excess in the nineteenth century, sometimes reached a height of 13 feet! To play it, one bass-player would bow, while a second would press the strings against the neck while trying to maintain his balance on a ladder!

The double-bass is the sole instrument retaining the pointed shoulders of its ancestor, the viola da gamba. The tuning, in fourths, is also a hangover from the gamba. The primary role of the double-bass is as an orchestral instrument because little scope was found for it in eighteenth-century.chamber music for strings.

There are more solo passages for double-bass than one might be imagined. In Gustav Mahler's *First Symphony* (1884-1888), the double-bass plays a conspicuous role in the third movement, the funeral march. In the twentieth century, the double-bass came back into fashion, for example, in two compositions by Benjamin Britten (1913-1976), *The Young Person's Guide to the orchestra* (1946), and *A Midsummer Night's Dream* (1960). The double-bass part in Ravel's 1922 orchestration of Mussorgsky's *Pictures at an Exhibition* is quite striking. The Russian-born conductor and composer Serge Koussevitsky (1874-1951) wrote a *Concerto for Double-bass and Orchestra* in 1905. The double-bass has long been valued in chamber music and small ensembles, for which music was written by Mozart, Beethoven, Schubert (*The Trout, Quintet in A*, D.667, for piano, violin, viola, cello, and double-bass), Louis Spohr, Dvorak, and Prokofiev (Quintet opus 39 for oboe, clarinet, violin, viola, and double-bass).

Pablo Casals, Pierre Fournier, Paul Tortelier, Heinrich Schiff, and Yo Yo Ma. There are also several Dutch virtuoso cellists, including Tibor de Machula, Anner Bylsma, and Pieter Wispelwey.

Double-bass

The elephant of the violin family was actually employed by the French composer Camille Saint-Saëns to depict the elephant in his *Carnival of the Animals* (1886). The body of the instrument normally measures about three-and-a half feet long, but it can be even longer. The largest double-bass, the subcontra bass,

Sheng, the ancestor of the harmonica.

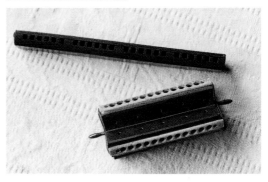

Two historical harmonicas.

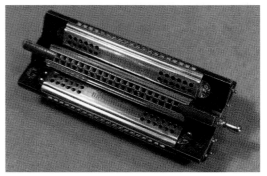

Star-shaped harmonica.

This type of mouth organ was quite common in South-east Asia.

Mouth-organs and Harmonicas

The accordion and its relations belong to the family of wind instruments with basic flat or raised reeds.

Sheng

According to tradition these simple reed mechanisms were first put to use about 5,000 years ago in China in a sort of ancestor of the mouth organ called the sheng.
The sheng consisted of a wooden or ivory wind-box blown into by the player. Bamboo pipes were attached to the box, and a simple reed was placed inside each pipe. Below this reed, a hole was bored into the pipe. The reed vibrated when the hole in the pipe was closed by the player's finger, allowing the air to pass through the reed at pressure.

Mouth-organ

These flat reed instruments were first developed in the West in the late eighteenth century. A Danish physicist named Christian Gottlieb Kratzenstein, had experimented with the mechanism in St. Petersburg, albeit using conventional organ pipes. An agreeable, gentle tone would require further experimentation. In 1818, Anton Häckl of Vienna, built pipeless organs with blown reeds suitable for playing by the general public. They had such eloquent names as the "aelodicon," the "aeoline," the "melodicon," and the "terpodion." It wasn't until the later development of the *harmonium* (q.v.), again using raised reeds, that the necessary air-stream was generated, using bellows operated by foot pedals. The German instrument maker, Christian Friedrich

Modern versions of the harmonica: the *clavietta* (Italy, ca. 1910), the *harmonicor* (France, ca. 1880), and the *fluta* (manufactured by Hohner, Germany, 1907).

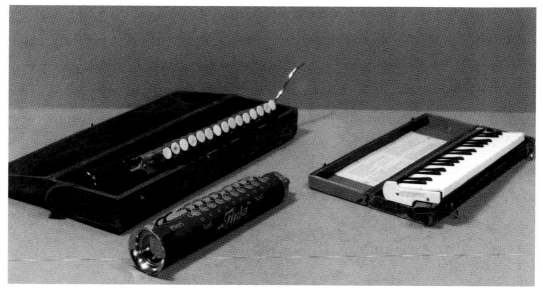

Buschmann, built not only the first mouth-organ (in 1821, at the age of sixteen!) but also the first accordion.

Matthias Hohner, founder of the Hohner factory, was a former clock-maker who made some improvements to harmonica design and opened a factory to make the instrument in 1857 and improvements. An outstanding businessman, Hohner also developed an industrial production method and judicious advertising ("It's fun to own a Hohner"). By 1887, the Hohner factory was producing more than one million harmonicas a year.

Present-day instruments of the flat reed family generally use steel or brass reeds that can vibrate freely on both sides, held inside a metallic voice-plate. The free play between the reed and the opening in the voice-plate must be as small as possible to avoid the unnecessary escape of air and consequent difficulties in producing sound.

The harmonica originally had a wooden frame but nowadays the frame is made of plastic. There are two rows of small square holes, attached to a voice-plate to which are riveted small reeds or tongues of varying lengths, tuned to the desired pitch. The rows of reeds have curved metal covers attached above and below them. The mouth-organ is an instrument than can be tuned to various keys, and sucking and blowing produce different notes. It is usually impossible to play a chromatic scale, however, as most mouth-organs are diatonically tuned, but the chromatic scale can be played if a slider is fitted to the instrument. In the 1930s there were some complete mouth-organ or harmonica orchestras in which all parts, including the bass, were played on harmonicas. It was an impressive sight (and sound!) as the higher voices played their instruments in a star formation. Most players played from memory, even in harmonica ensembles.

The *Concerto for Harmonica and Orchestra* (1954) by the English composer Malcolm Arnold (1921–) was written for the harmonica virtuoso, Larry Adler (1914–2002). The American Sonny Terry and the Belgian Toots Tielemans popularized the jazz harmonica. In the field of light music, the Hotcha Trio brought the harmonica to an international audience, as did Tommy Riley, in his recording of the theme tune of the film *Genevieve* (1953).

A pair of concertinas (Hohner).

Bandonion.

Hohner produces 90 models of harmonica, including the *melodica*, a modern version of the mouth-organ. This instrument has a series of chromatic buttons or piano-style keys that provide the desired notes.

THE ACCORDION AND ITS FAMILY

In 1822, the instrument maker Friedrich Buschmann combined his "mouth aeoline" with a cardboard-and-linen bellows. The result was the "hand aeoline" to which the Viennese instrument maker Demian added a bass extension. He called the final result the "accordeon." A distinction can be made between instruments like the harmonica or mouth-organ, that produces different sounds depending on whether you puff or blow the wind supply and those, like the accordion, that produce the same notes irrespective of the direction of wind movement.

Concertina

In 1829–30, Charles Wheatstone (1802-1875), an English inventor, built a chromatic hand harmonica and called it a "concertina." Many improvements followed. Many variations on his invention were built but the standard concertina has 128 notes, 36 descant buttons, and 28 bass buttons. Each button produces two notes. The box is sometimes hexagonal in section, sometimes square. Chords are produced by depressing more than one button at the same time, giving the instrument special harmonic capabilities. It can also be played in polyphony as a result of individual notes being played on the bass side. Nowadays the concertina, known as the "squeezebox" in slang, is usually employed as an accompaniment to folk music.

Bandonion

Around 1840, the concertina was developed further by Heinrich Band, who called his instrument the *bandonion*. Its 72 keys produced 144 notes and it was this particular octave doubling that gave the bandonion its special tonal character. The bandonion became popular primarily to accompany the tango, a dance, originally from Argentina, that reached its zenith in the dance-halls of Buenos Aires in the early part of the twentieth century. The music for the tango was provided by Spanish and Italian immigrants in which the bandonion played an important part. Both the tango and the bandonion experienced a revival in the 1980s, especially in Europe. A real cult grew up around tango music, thanks to the composer and bandonion player, Astor Piazzola, and such musicians as the violinist Gidon Kremer and the Kronos Quartet. The Sextetto Caniengo is an internationally renowned tango ensemble, in which the bandonion features prominently. The bandonion also accompanies folk music.

Accordion

Demian's *accordeon* underwent several modifications until it evolved into the modern accordion. The bellows themselves

Modern button accordion (Fantini).

remain; only the shape (square) and the format of the instrument are different, and its capabilities have been expanded. Accordions have piano keys and/or push-buttons. Unlike the concertina family, where the player sits the instrument held loosely on the knees, the accordionist hangs the instrument from a belted sling and holds it to the body, which makes it easy to play standing up. The right hand plays the melody keys or buttons. On slightly larger instruments, all sorts of tone combinations can be obtained through register stop-keys that introduce a whole bank of tonal effects, including a tremolo. The button accordion has three rows of descant buttons. Models with five rows do not have a wider compass. The extra rows are duplicates, to facilitate ease of playing. Depending on the

Modern piano accordion (Fantini).

instrument, the bass side has between 24 and 140 bass notes. Only the first rows have individual notes, the remainder being chord keys or buttons, such as for major thirds, minor thirds, and sevenths. On the larger instruments, special tone combinations are available.

The accordion became very popular in Russia. An instrument called the *bayan*, with its own unique keyboard layout, was developed from it, for which various Russian composers have written music.

Quite a few twentieth century composers have written music for the accordion, including Paul Dessau, Serge Prokofiev, Virgil Thomson, Roberto Gerhardt, and Frans Vuursteen. The Dutchman, Harry Mooten, is a virtuoso accordionist who plays Bach arrangements as well as light music.

Harmonium

The harmonium or reed-organ, "the poor man's pipe-organ," belongs to the same family of instruments as the mouth-organs and other accordion-type instruments. It has freely moving reeds (as well as rising reeds) on which a patent was taken out in 1840 by the French instrument maker, Alexandre Debain. It became an extremely popular instrument in the United States and Europe in the second half of the nineteenth

Harmonium "style 4405" (Mason & Hamlin, Boston, 1908).

Harmonium (France, 19th century, 1-row blown-air phisharmonica).

century, used mainly for accompanying the voice in the home and in church, since it had the tone of a pipe-organ without the bulk or the enormous expense.

The harmonium has a piano-like body, often elaborately carved in the fashion of the day. It has two foot–pedals connected to two bellows that provide the air supply. The keyboard has a range of five octaves. Below the keyboard, on the more elaborate instruments, there are two siphon paddles operated by the player's knees. One initiates a sort of swell mechanism while the other is used for musical emphasis like a general crescendo.

Some harmoniums push the air and others use suction. The European instruments tend to use pressure, the suction instruments were developed in the United States. In each case, the keyboard is divided into bass and descant sections. Registers are available through "coupling" in just the same way as on pipe-organs. Simple harmoniums have only one register but the larger and more elaborate instruments have up to eleven.

The role of the harmonium was usurped to some extent by the electric organ in the second half of the twentieth century, though not for religious music.

The gentle and ethereal tone of the harmonium was specifically well suited to the Romantic period. Composers such as Rossini (*Petite Messe Solennelle*) and Erik Satie (*Messe des Pauvres*), both used the

A harmonic harmonium with two manuals by Theophil Kotykiewicz, Vienna, 1895. The lower manual has two temperament possibilities. The stop-knob offers a choice between equal temperament and Pythagorean temperament...

Harmonophone (Koestler & Co, Germany, ca. 1960). This instrument uses a fan as the source of wind.

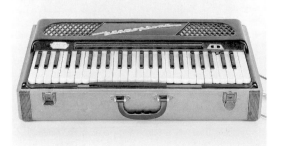

harmonium in their religious music. Other composers of the period who wrote music for the harmonium include César Franck (1822–1890) Franz Liszt (1811–188), and Sigfrid Karg-Elert (1877–1933).

Barrel-organ and Fairground Organs

The mechanical organ was first invented in Renaissance times, but came into its own as an instrument for Church music, in the early nineteenth century. Major makers of church barrel-organs were the London firm of Flight and Robson. Such barrel-organs were fitted with selections of tunes (or hymns) which were reproduced by turning the handle, but could also be played manually, if an organist were available.

The barrel-organ is primarily remembered as the favorite instrument of street musicians, from the late nineteenth century until World War II. The organ-grinder would often have a pet monkey who was trained to collect contributions from bystanders.

There are a number of variations on the barrel-organ, including the *caliope* or fairground organ, which is bigger than the barrel-organ and extravagantly decorated. The chest that contains the barrel mechanism and organ pipes, stands on its own wheels or is on a horse-drawn waggon. The fascia is decorated, with a central opening for the organ pipes. The driving wheel for the barrel mechanism is usually at the back.

The organ-grinder turns the barrel by means

De Stolwijker barrel organ

Serinette, a bird-organ.

of a handle at varying speeds, setting off the pneumatic mechanism that simultaneously blows air through the pipes and also selects which pipes get the air and for how long, thus dictating the music to be played. The mechanism "reads" the information from a punched-out score, a cardboard book that unfolds as it plays. Book and mechanism are, in fact, musician and keyboard for the barrel organ. This ingenious combination was invented by the Italian Anselmo Gavioli, who lived in Paris, in 1880. Many Gavioli-built organs are still in use.

The speed at which the wheel is turned decides the tempo, so that on hand-cranked organs there can be a real "performance." The powerful sounding pipes are made of wood. The open pipes have quite a strident character, and the stopped melodic pipes are often set up in pairs and somewhat approximately tuned so that you get a kind of vibrato effect. Additional effects are produced with drums, castanets, bird-whistles, and other percussion instrument attachments, operated by the same mechanism.

Barrel–organs and fairground organs are so attractive that several museums boast

collections. In 1957, the Barrel Organ Museum opened in Utrecht, covering everything from the music-box to the street- organ. There are also museums in La Salvia, Argentina, and in Wookey Hole, Somerset, England. Barrel-organs are still made in the Netherlands, and a maker called Geert Jacobs has produced one made entirely of ceramic that has a mellow tone.

The music roll of a small barrel organ

Musical Clock

This clockwork musical instrument sounds like a flute and is usually attached to an upright or wall-mounted clock. A rank of organ pipes, primarily labial pipes, is activated in just the same way as a musical bow, by means of a rotating cylinder set with pins.

The was a favorite drawing-room instrument in the late eighteenth century and remained so for many years. Many composers wrote music for this instrument. Haydn wrote *Thirty-two Pieces* (1789-93), Mozart and Allegro and Andante for "a little dance on a little organ" KV 608 (1791) and Beethoven wrote *Five Pieces*.

The *Serinette* is a bird-song organ, a delightful instrument invented in the ninth century. Leo Philosophicus, for instance, built two mechanical instruments with artificial perches and singing birds for the Byzantine Emperor Theophilus. Similar instruments were also produced in the thirteenth century. The mystic, Athanasius Kircher, wrote in 1650 about an "automatic organ that produces animal noises and even bird-song." None of these instruments has survived, unfortunately. The *serinette* was used in eighteenth-century France to teach snatches of song to caged pet songbirds. Marie Antoinette owned a canary organ made by a Parisian horologist. Bédos de Celles described the construction of the serinette In 1778.

Music-boxes

These mechanical instruments were invented in the thirteenth century, originally for bellringers' guilds. They were not developed in a compact form until the eighteenth century, but really came into their own during the nineteenth-century Industrial Revolution, with advances in mechanics.

The smallest and simplest type, the cylinder music–box, consists a case (often lavishly engraved) containing a metal cylinder with a number of pins on its outer surface. Alongside the cylinder and running its length is a metal comb with tuned prongs or tines. When the cylinder is turned, the pins strike the tines following the pattern in which they are spaced on the cylinder. This pattern thus dictates which tines are struck or, to put it another way, they play the tune. The melody may have a chord accompaniment if the appropriate tines are struck at the same time. All notes are of the same duration and the tempo of the music is governed by the turning speed of the cylinder. It can either be turned by hand, using a crank-handle, or by a clockwork movement. The first cylinder music-boxes were introduced in the late eighteenth century by Swiss watchmakers. They were designed for mass production and, beginning in the early nineteenth century, they were made in large numbers by Swiss companies. This set up a monopoly position that the Swiss enjoyed for almost a hundred years.

In the disk music-box, the cylinder is replaced by a rotating metal disk, something like a long-playing record, with the pins protruding so they can strike the tines of the comb hanging above the disk. The advantage of the disk over the cylinder is the fact that the disk can be changed easily, with a consequent increase in the repertoire. Disk music-boxes appeared on the market in huge numbers in the late nineteenth century and included the patented Symphonion and the Polyphon.

Later still, even bigger examples were made that had unforeseen capabilities. The comb, the original sound source for music boxes, was replaced by an ingenious relay mechanism that could select all sorts of sounds, including bells, drums, organ-pipes, and strings). This mechanism was still controlled by the cylinder or disk but was furnished with longer and shorter pins or slots that made the lengths of notes variable. In the late nineteenth century, these mechanisms were provided with moving punched tapes that replaced the disk and cylinder, thus anticipating the barrel organ. The Orchestrion, containing all the strings, flutes, horns, and bells necessary to imitate a large orchestra was an example of this type of music-box.

The principle of the cylinder music-box has been applied to the carillon (q.v.) since the thirteenth century. The carillon was originally entirely mechanical; the carilloneur only came on the scene in the sixteenth century. In the carillon, a cylindrical drum covered with pins is set in motion. The pins pull wires that run up to hammers on the outside of the bells. The thirteenth-century carillon was a part of the clock tower mechanism. In Holland, there is hardly a town without a carillon in either a church tower or a city hall tower. In strictly musical terms, the actual music played was not important but all that changed in the sixteenth century, when manually operated carillons appeared that could be "played" with the aid of a piano-type keyboard. The profession of carilloneur imposed ever higher musical demands. Nowadays a skilled carilloneur (such as the famous Arie Abbenes, for example) can perform complete sonatas or even symphonies. As soon as clock springs were invented, they were built into music boxes. In the Black Forest of Germany, cheap wooden clock mechanisms were manufactured with between eight and sixteen little glass bells that could play a short folk tune. Later on clocks were made with built-in miniature carillons.

Portative, a small portable organ.

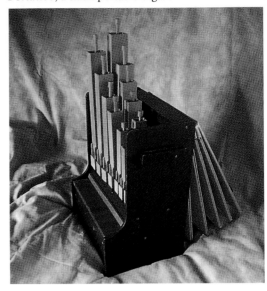

Organ

The organ, or pipe-organ to distinguish it from lesser types of organ, is a keyboard instrument with a mechanism that pressurizes air, collects it in a reservoir and blows sound through one or more pipes, controlled by keys. The name of the instrument is derived from the Greek *organon*, meaning instrument or tool. The organ has a long history and exists in many different forms, but nowadays it is used mostly in churches and cathedrals, where some have been built to huge proportions. In all cases, the organ consists of the following components:

A *regal* with windbag

182

Operating the pedal on early organs required a rather athletic body. Here, the bellows are being pumped with the feet and the "organ blower" is holding onto a bar. To give himself more freedom of movement, he has tucked his tunic into his belt.

– A wind engine that regulates the flow of air. In former times, the air was forced in by the pressure of hand- or foot-operated bellows, but nowadays the air pressure is governed by an electric motor. The air is collected in a wind-chest and flows from there into the pipes.
– One or more keyboards that control the channeling of air to the pipes, through the intervention of other mechanisms. A row of pedals that works like a keyboard played by the feet is a typical adjunct to many organs.
– Pipes, tuned to the tonic solfa. There are many sorts of pipes, each with its own sound.

Organist Charles de Wolff at the console of a Schnitger/Ahrend-orgel

Bellows, Theophilusorgel, a replica of a medieval organ, built by organ builder Wijnand van Putten.

A complete row of pipes of one type is called a register. As a rule, an organ usually has several registers that can be selected or decoupled at will. The pitch of a register is indicated by the pipe length in feet, with the 8' being the standard. A 4' register sounds one octave

Keys, *Theophilusorgel*, with weights attachd to make bourdon tones possible.

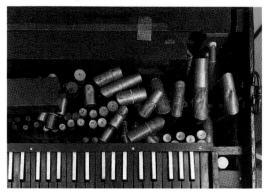
The inside of a positive, Poland ca. 1630.

higher, a 2' register another octave higher still; 16' and 32' registers sound, respectively, one octave or two octaves below the 8' pipes.

Organ pipes are divided into two fundamentally different types, labial or flue pipes (labials), and reed pipes (linguals). A labial pipe consists of two parts, of which the lower part (the pipe foot) is separated from the upper part (the pipe body) by a narrow slot. When the air gets blown into the pipe

Interior pipework of organ, Poitiers cathedral, France

foot, it escapes at the slot, blows against the upper side of it (the labium), and starts to swirl. This swirling of the air makes the air in the pipe vibrate and this, in turn, produces the sound. The pitch is directly related to the length of the pipe body (not the pipe foot). In principle, a pipe that is twice as its predecessor long produces a sound one octave lower. There are also pipes that are blocked at the top. Strangely enough, these pipes also produce a note that is one octave lower than that of an open pipe of the same length. The material from which the pipe is made (metal or wood), the cross-section, and the shape (straight or tapering) are the most important factors in determining the tone color. Registers of labials include prestants, gambas, and various flutes. In reed pipes, there is a metal plate (reed) held in place by a spring against the "float," a small tube open at the side or top, so that the underside of the reed stands slightly proud of the side-opening in the float. Reed and float are both set into a pipe foot, the stem. The pipe body, the sounding-pipe, stands above the float. When the air flows into the stem, it hunts out an escape route in the slit between reed and float, which makes the reed vibrate. The pitch depends on the length of the reed and not the length of the sounding-pipe. The only purpose of the sounding-pipe is to give the sound color and resonance. As a result of their somewhat nasal sound, reed registers have often been given names that refer to such ancient reed instruments as the crumhorn, chalumeau, racket, and dulcian. Other reed registers have names such as oboe, trumpet, regal, and vox humana (Latin for "human voice").

HISTORY

The invention of the organ is attributed to the Alexandrian mechanical engineer Csetibius who lived in the third century BCE. Csetibius placed a row of *auloi* (not the plural of *aulos*, another musical instrument (q.v.) but meaning "pipes" in this

Two Roman arena musicians: organist and horn player in the amphitheater. The musician has a 29-pipe water organ, with an airpump attached to each side, each of which has to be operated by one person; the second musician is a horn player with an instrument that looks like a forest horn. (Floor mosaic, ca. 235 BC, Villa Neumig near Trier, Germany)

probably an earlier invention as a less expensive alternative to the costly waterpipes. After the fall of the Roman Empire, the organ also fell into decline in Western Europe. In the East, it remained in use, particularly in the imperial court of Byzantium where it fulfilled an important role at all sorts of ceremonial and public events. There were also organs in the Arab world, for example in Baghdad. Covered in gold and richly

Depiction of an angel playing a *positive* (Hubert and Jan van Eyck, 1432)

context) beside each other. These *auloi* were blown by a mechanism consisting of two vessels placed one inside the other and filled with water. A piston pump that created an air-lock in the middle vessel. He named this instrument *hydraulos* (water aulos). Although the mechanism was more of a technical achievement than a musical instrument, this type of organ became very popular in the Hellenistic world. In Delphi, an inscription dating from around 90 BCE records that a certain Antipatros had won a glorious victory in an organ-playing contest. The Romans learned of the organ from the Greeks. At the beginning of the common era, Vitruvius described a water-organ that was worked by two hydraulic pumps and had several registers. The emperor Nero appears to have been a lover of the organ. There are also indications that theater performances and gladiatorial games were heralded by organ music, perhaps in combination with brass instruments. By then, organs had bellows to pump air into them,

A regal with beautifully painted cover. The bellows are pedal-operated.

decorated, these instruments were, above all, symbols of wealth and power.

The organ returned to western Europe around 757 CE. In that year, the Emperor Constantine Copronymos of Byzantium made a gift of an organ to Pépin the Short, King of the Franks and father of Charlemagne. This instrument not only made a big impression as a Wonder of the Orient, but also aroused feelings of jealousy. In 826, the Venetian priest Gregorius petitioned the Court at Aix-la-Chapelle (Aachen) to make a copy of this instrument "in the Greek style," that is, in the style of the Eastern Roman Empire, with bellows and several registers. The ruler of the day, Ludovic de Vrome, did not count the cost and was especially proud of the results. From that moment on, the instrument was definitely back on the map in the West.

Northern Europe became the center for organ-building, thanks to the teachings of Gregorius. The instrument was a showpiece in palaces, and used in ceremonies and for open-air parades; it was not a church instrument at that stage. Slowly, the organ came to be seen as more of a typical church instrument. It was probably the Benedictines, a wealthy and enterprising order of monks, who had a hand in this. By ca. 1300, many of the larger town and monastery chapels were in possession of an organ. Little is known about the shape and size of medieval organs, nor about how they were used in divine worship. They were probably only played on feast days.

From the thirteenth through the fifteenth centuries there were some important inventions that played a significant part in the development of the present-day organ:

– The roller-board. The ancient medieval organs had no keyboards. The induction of air into each pipe took place at the pipe itself, where the "keys" were positioned, in the form of a slider or button. The keys could be far apart from each other so that, in larger instruments, several players were needed simultaneously to cover the full compass. The roller-board, a fourteenth century

Positive in an oak case.

Front of the Schnitger-Ahrend organ in the Martini Church, Groningen, Netherlands, restored in 1984, the best example of a neo-baroque organ in northern Europe.

invention, is a mechanism that connects the valve that lets air into the pipe with the keyboard, and remains unchanged to this day;
– The pedal-board. Early examples of the organ had a few special bass pipes inserted, connected by separate valves on the side. The first pedals were used to shift these valves from below. The series was extended in the fourteenth century. In the first instance, the pedals were linked up to the keys (dependant pedals), although organs existed at the time with free pedals and their own pedal registers, played independently of the keyboards.
– Several manuals. In the Middle Ages, a church would normally have a large organ, fixed in one place, and a smaller one that was used to accompany the choir. The latter was not bolted down and could therefore be moved. These smaller organs were called "positive organs" (from the Latin,

ponere = to place). In the fifteenth century, the positive was sometimes also fixed in position, usually at the organist's back, and connected to the wind-chest of the main organ. The keyboard of the positive (by then called the *anterior*) was subsequently brought round, to be fitted below the keyboard of the main organ, so that the instrument now had two manuals. Later organs were given even more manuals, sticking to the accessibility principle whereby each keyboard should control its own registers;
– Registration. Although the ancient organs had several registers that could be sounded separately or together, as the organist chose, the know-how for this technique had been lost. On organs of the early Middle Ages, the registers could only be played all at once (mixture organs). From the fourteenth century onward, attempts were made to find out how to be able to play the registers separately. In the first instance, separate keyboards were required, but registers were designed subsequently that could be linked or decoupled, singly or in multiples, by means of sliders. This development was an important advance in the quest for all sorts of registers with individual tone colors and, consequently, towards an instrument with a far greater range.
In the centuries that followed, the organ grew steadily larger and more complicated. It was often fitted with a heavily ornamented case with pipes on view at the front that were sometimes no more than decoration. The choice of registers was dictated by the taste of the times. In the nineteenth century, some old organs were converted into "romantic" instruments. In the meantime, the air supply had been regulated mechanically and there were many other mechanical developments, both large and small.
Nowadays, nearly all the ancient organs are the result of "improvements" made to them over the course of the centuries. The current trend is to try to restore pipe-organs to their original condition. The old registers may have disappeared or been irretrievably altered, but sometimes later alterations

Front pipes of the organ of the Church of St. Thomas in Strasbourg, France.

The Bach organ in Arnstadt.

Empty organ case of an organ awaiting restoration.

seem to have been really worthwhile. The choices that have to be made during the course of restoration—which, as a rule, is a very costly exercise—nearly always lead to heated debate amongst the experts.

ORGANS AND KEYBOARD INSTRUMENTS

From the eighth through the fourteenth centuries, organ music was primarily used as an accompaniment for religious services, order to inspire the congregation. Later, however, secular music came to be written for the instrument. The first compositions were preludes and variations on Gregorian chant and transcriptions of songs. Specific music for the pieces originated mostly in Italy, an these include the *ricercare, toccata, canzone,* and *fugue.* The relevant composers are Girolamo Frescobaldi (1583-1642), Andrea Gabrieli (1510-1586), and the

Small organ with one piano and pedal.

Console of an organ awaiting restoration.

Dutchman Adriaan Willaert (c.1490-1562). Paul Hofhaimer (1497-1537) was the first Dutch master organist. His Spanish counterpart was Antonio de Cabézon (c.1500-1566). The Dutchman Jan Pieterszoon Sweelinck played a significant part in the education and development of the organ among his fellow countrymen. The first real blossoming of Dutch organ music began with Dietrich Buxtehude (1637-1707) and Vincent Lubeck (1654-1740) in the north, and with Johann Pachelbel (1653-1706) and Johann Jakob Froberger (1616-1667) in the south. Organ music reached an absolute pinnacle in the compositions of Johann Sebastian Bach (1685-1750).

During the Romantic period, the popularity of this kind diminished considerably. Apart from Felix Mendelssohn (1809-1847) and Franz Liszt (1811-1886) no one was writing organ music during this period. César Franck (1822-1890) and Max Reger (1873-1916) re-awakened an interest in the instrument with work based on the works of

Bach. In the twentieth century, Paul Hindemith (1895-1963) and Hugo Distler (1908-1942) in Germany and Olivier Messiaen (1908-1992) in France wrote completely new pieces of organ music.

Bach's Works for the Organ

Almost all of Bach's works for the organ have been performed and recorded by leading organists. In addition to Albert Schweitzer (1875-1965), the blind organist Helmut Walcha (1907-1991) had already made a name for himself as a Bach interpreter in the 1950s. Many others followed including the Frenchwoman Marie-Claire Alain and Englishman Lionel Rogg who recorded the complete organ works, as did the Dutch organist Ewald Kooiman in the 1980s. Kooiman hunted Europe for organs that best suited particular sections of Bach's output, to produce a delightful record of the instruments and of his own virtuosity. The complete output of the master was issued

Franz Liszt (1803-1886) wrote a great deal of music for the organ.

Seal of Johann Sebastian Bach (1685-1750).

under the auspices of the *Bach 2000* project, on 170 CDs, on Hänssler, a German label. Others who have recorded the complete works of Bach for the organ include the Germans Kay Johannsen, Wolfgang Zerer, Gerhard Gnann, and Martin Lücker, the Dane Bine Katrine Bryndorf, the Italian Andrea Marcon, and the Dutchman Peter van Dijk.

Monochord

The word *monochord* literally means "one string(ed)." Euclid (c.365-c.300 B.C.) wrote about this instrument. Pythagoras (c.570-500) seems to have brought the instrument to Greece, but he probably adapted it from the original Egyptian version.

The monochord consists of a sound-box with one gut or metal string running its whole length that can be "stopped" with one or more moveable bridges. There was a scale from which the fingerings of the various notes could be read. The desired note was plucked with a metal plectrum.

The monochord has been used throughout the ages as an accompaniment for singing lessons and music theory teaching. As recently as the nineteenth century, the instrument was an aid in the manufacture of organ

pipes and the tuning of carillon bells.

The multi-stringed *polychord* developed from the monochord in the Middle Ages making it possible to sound two notes

The pipes of a medieval organ.

190

together. This instrument itself later developed into the *clavichord* (q.v.).

Polychord

Polychord means "many strings" or "many stringed." It is the modern name for a variant of the fourteenth-century monochord. The name itself indicates that the instrument had more than one string.

Polychord is also the name for a type of violin with eight to ten strings on which simple chord-playing is made possible. The instrument was built in 1799 by Friedrich Hiller in Leipzig (see *Viocta*).

The third meaning of polychord is for an electronic home- and church-organ with two manuals and pedals. The polychord organ, which has more than eighteen tone color registers, was built by Harald Bode (1909–) as a development of his Bode-organ and produced by the Bavarian Engineering Works in the 1950s. The sound was produced by means of oscillators.

Clavichord

The clavichord, the first true keyboard instrument with strings introduced in the Middle Ages, was developed from the monochord. From the eighteenth century onward, it became an elegant item of furniture with a case and legs, although previously it had been a table-top instrument. The clavichord is regarded as the forerunner of the piano.

The instrument first appeared in the early fifteenth century but it may have existed previously. A very early description of the clavichord dates from the second half of the fifteenth century.

From the fourteenth through the eighteenth century, the clavichord was the most widely played keyboard instrument apart from the organ and the harpsichord. In Germany, this continued to be the position until the early part of the nineteenth century. The clavichord was gradually improved and enlarged by students of the harpsichord and organ. This was thanks in no small measure to the fact that the clavichord—unlike the harpsichord and the piano—could be made quite inexpensively. Moreover, the maintenance was straightforward and it had a very soft tone, all of which made it very suitable for domestic use.

The clavichord, unlike the harpsichord and the organ, can be regarded as the true forerunner of the pianoforte, as the player can vary the dynamics of each individual note.

A spatulate metal pin, usually of brass, called the *tangent*, sits at the far end of the key and makes the string sound on both sides of the spot at which it is plucked. The shorter part of the string is dampened by a

Clavichord (ca. 1700).

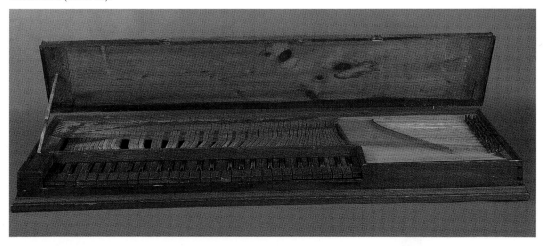

felt ribbon intertwined through the strings. As soon as the key is released, the remaining length of the string is also dampened.

On a "regulated clavichord," one string can be struck by two or three different keys at different places along its length, producing different notes depending on the length involved. Far fewer strings than keys are required in the construction, so that the instrument can be contained within a relatively small case.

The sound production of the clavichord is absolutely unique. As the volume of sound is so tiny, the clavichord can not really be played with other instruments. Only people in the immediate vicinity of the instrument can even hear it and, as a result, its function has been confined to that of a solo instrument for home use.

Harpsichord

The name of this instrument in its alternate form, *clavicembalo*, derives from the Latin word *clavis*, meaning "key" and the Greek *kembalon*, meaning "the hollow of a vessel". The harpsichord is a keyboard instrument with a wing-shaped plan that has enjoyed as much popularity as the clavichord since the sixteenth century. As soon as a key is depressed, a small jack rises up inside a casing inside the "works", and at the same time a "tongue" with a goose- or

Clavichord (credited to J.H. Silbermann, Strasbourg, 1780). This instrument, has double, unfretted strings.

Clavichord, credited to J.A. Stein, Augsburg, 1787; it is unfretted with single strings.

raven-feather quill plucks sound from the string. The tongue is then put through a quarter turn so that it does not strike the string again. Immediately the string is released, it is dampened by a felt damper. A piece of hide, usually buffalo, is sometimes used instead of the quill to pluck the strings. The strings of the harpsichord lie in the same direction as the keys, giving rise to the triangular body shape. Because the strings are plucked with a quill, the sound ebbs away very quickly. Therefore the repertoire for this this instrument therefore contains few prolonged notes, but there are lots of trills and runs, designed to fill in the gaps. As the sound cannot be influenced by the "touch," at some stage, couplers were introduced to connect one keyboard to another. The instrument can also be provided with a pedal board.

The harpsichord was in existence by 1400, when the *psalterion* (q.v.) gained a keyboard (that had only been available hitherto for the organ) as well as a plucking mechanism. A harpsichord was described for the first time in the early 1500s, and about 30 years later a treatise called it the *clavisimbalum*. The oldest known depiction of a harpsichord (c.1425), which was at one time part of the altar of Minden Cathedral, is in the Staatliches Museum, Berlin. According to musicologists, only about 700 signed keyboard instruments—including spinets and virginals—remain from the harpsichord's heyday that lasted about

Harpsichord with two keyboards and 2x 8-foot body, after a German model by Christian Zell (ca. 1740).

Harpsichord, credited to Giovanni Soffenelli, 1827.

Klavecimbel with two keyboards (credited to Petrus Johannes Couchet, Antwerpen 1669)

three-and-a-half centuries and only waned with the increasing use of the piano. The oldest extant instrument dates from 1521 and was built by Hieronymus Bononiensis. It is now in the Victoria and Albert Museum in London, England.

The harpsichord was used not only as a solo instrument but also in the orchestra and, since the time of J.S. Bach, as a solo instrument with orchestral accompaniment. For some time, the harpsichord had to suffer as a member of larger ensembles in which its voice was completely drowned out. Newer models were louder, however (later still they were electronically amplified, by the firm of Neupert, for example, in the late 1960s), so they again came into use as solo instruments.

Examples of music written for the harpsichord include the *Concerto for Harpsichord (or Piano), Flute, Oboe, Clarinet,*

Harpsichord; 1 keyboard, 2x8, GG-d3.

Harpsichord by Andreas Ruckers, Antwerp 1639.

Violin and Cello (1923–26) by Manuel de Falla (1876-1946), and the *Petite Symphonie Concertante for Harpsichord, Piano and Double String Orchestra* by the Swiss composer Frank Martin (1890-1974). Very few composers, however, have accepted commissions for the harpsichord in a classical style.

Sound-hole of a clavicytherium (Albert Delin, ca. 1760).

Clavicytherium

The term *clavicytherium* originates from a combination of Latin and Greek roots. It was originally given to a vertical harpsichord as demonstrated by the Italian and French names—*cembalo verticale* and *clavecin vertical*, respectively.

The instrument has taut strings. The striking impact is rather harder than on a horizontal instrument (and less sensitive as a result) because the movement of the quills is vertical in horizontal instruments, whereas here they can't return to their resting position under their own weight without the need for wire springs.

The clavicytherium offers some advantages over the harpsichord, because it takes up less floor space and the sound is more direct due to the vertical orientation.

P. Paulirinus, of Prague, in a treatise on musical instruments dated ca. 1460, described a vertical harpsichord combined with a positive organ, played by one manual. Some examples can still be seen in museums, such as the Vienna Museum, where there is a late seventeenth-century clavicytherium built by M. Kaiser . The instrument has a richly decorated, pyramid-shaped case about 8 feet tall. The longest strings lie in the center. The oldest clavicytherium still in existence—and perhaps also the oldest known keyboard instrument— is estimated to have been built in Ulm around 1480. This instrument was owned by Leopold I and is now housed in the Royal College of Music in London.

Spinet

Although it is claimed that the name "spinet" is derived from that the keyboard builder Johannes Spinetus (Venice, c. 1500), there is a more plausible explanation. In fact the name actually derives from the Italian word *spina*, meaning "thorn," "pin," or "jack." The musicologist and organist–composer Michael Praetorius (c.1570-1621) used the name "instrument" around 1600 to refer to both the spinet and the virginal. The spinet was relatively prominent between the sixteenth and eighteenth centuries.

The spinet has single strings for each note lying parallel to the keyboard, like those of the virginal. The tuning pegs are on the righthand side and the lowest sounding-strings are directly behind the keyboard. The mechanical principle of the spinet is, in essence, identical to that of the harpsichord,

which is to say that the strings are plucked by quills.

The sound of the instrument is sensitive, and expressive, comparable to that of the Italian harpsichord. The Italian spinet is either rectangular or hexagonal in shape with a protruding keyboard on the wide side, that is often accommodated in a separate "drawer." The spinet is smaller than the harpsichord and was easier to carry around. It was often placed on a stand.

The oldest known spinet was built by Francesco de Portalupi (Verona, 1523) and is now in the Paris Conservatoire.

Virginal

The virginal is a variant of the spinet, but it is square in shape. The strings lie crosswise, at right angles to the keys.

The virginal's mechanism corresponds pretty much to that of the spinet. The bass strings lie directly behind the keyboard and the tuning-board is sideways or diagonal in relation to the keys. The two bridges that define the tuning are fixed onto the soundboard. There is only one manual, just like the spinet. The instrument was built in various formats.

The virginal was particularly popular at the English court in the sixteenth and seventeenth centuries. Composers who qualified as virginalists, such as William Byrd (1543-1623) and Orlando Gibbons (1583-1625), wrote for both virginal and harpsichord, and Queen Elizabeth I herself was said to be something of a virtuoso on the instrument.

Travel spinet by Rijk van Arkel (Gouda, the Netherlands, 1768)

Bent spinet (credited to J.H. Silbermann, Strasbourg, 1765).

Hexagonal spinet by Johannes Celestini in a rectangular case (Venice, 1859).

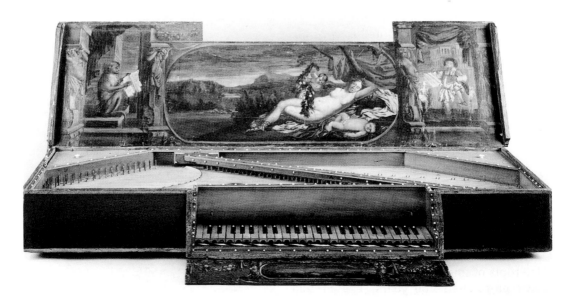

Spinettino by Aloysius Ventura.

Virginal (anonymous builder, Italy, first half of the 17th century).

It was not until the eighteenth century that a clear distinction was made between harpsichord and virginal. The expression "virginal" was used at the time for the rectangular, flat, box-shaped spinet with the keyboard on the left, in the center, or on the right of one of the long sides.

The small compass of the virginal meant that it could be easily transported and placed on a table top. Later on, virginals became articles of furniture on legs, always keeping up with the latest fashions. The double virginal was supplied with a smaller second instrument, usually kept in its own drawer under the main keyboard.

It was common for the lid and case of the virginal to be richly decorated, like those of many spinets, often with mosaic work and with keys inlaid with rare woods. The instrument's name probably doesn't derive from the Latin *virgo*, meaning maiden, but from *virga* meaning a wooden staff, in the sense of a key.

Pianola

Although the pianola, or player-piano, is a member of the piano family, it has also inherited the legacy of all sorts of mechanical instruments from the music-box onward. The roots of this "improper" instrument go back more than 200 years. The French

engineer De Vaucanson made a perforated cylinder that operated like a sort of crank, that did not require the player's hands to turn it. The instrument might properly be called the *phonola*, *pianola* being a trade name registered in various parts of the

Sounding-board of a harpsichord.

Detail of a grand piano.

Steinway grand piano made in 1897. The Steinway label appears on the sound-board.

music is coded into holes on a roll of paper. This roll travels over a row of little slots, corresponding to the twelve notes in the octave of the tuning system. Whenever the openings coincide, the resulting airflow produces a note. The power for the mechanism comes from pedals.

The instrument, produced in various shapes and sizes, looked just like a piano. It arrived on the scene in the late 1800s in the U.S.A., invented by Edwin Scott Votey, in 1895, and flourished for a good number of years. From 1902, the instrument was built and marketed by the Aeolian Company of New York. In the early 1920s, half a million were made inside two years, production reaching a peak in 1923, but the instrument's popularity dwindled quickly in the Depression years, especially with competition from other forms of entertainment like the radio and phonograph. The restricted repertoire also contributed to the drop in popularity.

In the ten years following World War I, this "automaton" was greatly admired by Igor Stravinsky (1882-1971). In 1914, he had attended a pianola demonstration given by the Aeolian Company, and cherished the hope of being able to make authentic performances of his works on this piano. For a while, he took the view that the ideal "interpreter" was a bell–ringer who had nothing else to do than clang the clappers mechanically. In this way, he hoped to be able to restrict what he saw as the "notorious"

Virginal by Celestini.

world and thus coming into widespread usage. The name *pianola* has now come into general use, even for instruments by other makers.

Inside the pianola, there is a cylinder covered with pins and set in motion by a crank. The strings are struck by a row of hammers that are moved in turn by air pressure. The

liberties taken by musical directors and other performers with his music. "This equipment allows me to establish the exact tempo relationships and nuances, as I want them, once and for all," he wrote in his memoirs.

Stravinky's *Etude for Pianola*, opus 7, no.1 (1917) was later used as the fourth of his *Four Studies for Orchestra* (1928; the first three were written between 1914 and 1918). In the 1920s, Stravinsky made piano roll arrangements of his own works for the Pleyel firm in Paris and for Duo Art (Aeolian) in London. The three early ballet scores, *Firebird*, *Petrushka*, and *The Rite of Spring*, were amongst these recordings. These were never published as scores, but the piano rolls were reissued in 1967.

Although leading composers wrote for the pianola, including Ernst Toch (1887-1964), Paul Hindemith (1895-1963), and Gian Francesco Malipieri (1882-1973), the greatest composer for the instrument was Conlon Nancarrow (1912-1997), who created his own pianola rolls, including some dazzling *Studies* that demonstrate the previously unheard capabilities of the pianola. He dreamed up the simultaneous speeding up and slowing down of the tempo in the different "hands" and rhythms, which would be utterly impossible for a human pianist to play.

Upright Piano(forte)

The piano is a keyboard instrument derived from the grand piano, whose origins date back as far as the *psalterion* (q.v.). The piano is roughly the shape of the clavicytherium (q.v.) and has a vertical soundboard with strings laid out across it. Christoph Schröter (1699-1782) built his first *hammerklavier* in 1709, inspired by Pantoleon Hebenstreit (1667-1750), who played an extended dulcimer. Bartolomeo Cristophori (1655-1731) of Padua. who was living in Florence, had done some development work on the instrument. In Germany, his model was imitated by Gottfried Silbermann (1683-1753).

Pianola.

Johann Andreas Stein (1728-1792), one of Silbermann's pupils, rapidly improved the hammerklavier mechanism. English builders followed suit. The Viennese model, actually German in origin, the so-called "Mozart Grand," was different from the English model so greatly preferred by Beethoven. The action of the Viennese model had a very light touch and therefore a greater flexibility; in contrast, the English model went for a fuller sound. The modern grand piano developed from the English model. These pianos have crossed strings, a repetitive action introduced by Sebastien Erard (1752-1831) in 1823 that enabled rapid repetition of notes, and a cast-iron frame (adapted for the first time in 1825 by Alpheus Babcock in Massachusetts) superseding the older wooden frame. From 1855 onward, the grand piano was built by the Steinway

Modern piano, Yamaha U3.

Piano (Erard, Parijs, 1847).

Pianoforte (John Bradwood & Sons, Londen, 1825)

Company. English craftsmen also contributed to the invention of the cast-iron frame. This allowed the string tension to be increased, resulting in the fuller sound that was typical of the English model.

The piano mechanism consists of a keyboard, strings, hammers, dampers, and pedals. The key throws a hammer against one string or a group of two or three strings, tuned to the same note, a technique that had existed in primitive form since the fifteenth century. Of the two or three pedals attached to the instrument, the right-hand one lifts the dampers away from the strings so they can resonate freely. The left-hand pedal halts the movement of the hammer just short of the strings, so that the contact is softer (indicated by the expression *una corda*, meaning one string). On grand pianos, the left-hand pedal actually moves the hammers slightly sideways so that they do not hit the whole set of strings, but just one out of two or two out of three. The third pedal, not always fitted, allows just one note to be sustained.

The square table-piano arrived later in the nineteenth century and the upright piano toward the late 1800s. The baby piano is a *pianino*, a little instrument that has been available—though not widely so—since 1828, with a low body and slightly more restricted sound than the standard piano. It was made possible by, amongst other things, sloping the bass strings diagonally across the frame. Johann Heinrich Pape (1789-1875), a pupil of Ignatz Pleyel (1757-1831), a seller and later maker of pianos in Paris, built this instrument under the name of "console piano." The giraffe piano was built as a vertically standing grand piano, with the strings struck from below. As the strings are placed above the level of the keyboard the instrument is unusually tall. It is also conspicuously asymmetrical, being much taller on the left-hand side. This instrument enjoyed moderate popularity in the mid-eighteenth century, and again in the early nineteenth century.

Virtually all the great composers have

Pianoforte (Erard).

written for the *klavier*, the *fortepiano*, or the pianoforte. Beethoven created a standard work without equal in his thirty-two *Sonatas*, central to the repertoire of all the greatest pianists such as Emil Gilels, Sviatoslav Richter, and Alfred Brendel.
From the 1850s through the 1950s, works of great originality were written for this instrument, for example by Béla Bartok (1881-1945), Guillaume Lekeu (1870-

1894), and Isaac Albéniz (1860-1909).
A splendid version of the piano works of Albéniz is to be found on the Claves label, played by Ricardo Requejo. Geza Anda (1921–1976) was a brilliant exponent of the works of Bartok, a fellow Hungarian.

Grand Piano

This is the name given, in principle, to every

Table piano (Jan Hendrik Hermanus Traut, The Hague, the Netherlands, ca. 1855)

Giraffe piano (Johannes van Raay, Amsterdam, 1830)

piano whose strings run horizontally and all, or nearly all, in line with the keys (as opposed to the upright and baby pianos) and therefore have cases in the shape of a bird's wing. This shape first appeared in 1521 in a harpsichord made by Heironymus Bononiensis (also known as Geronimo) who was working in Bologna. This instrument is the oldest harpsichord extant and is preserved in the Victoria and Albert Museum in London, England.

Grand pianos come in different models up to a length of nearly 11 feet. The concert grand, the largest of them all, has crossed strings, a repeat action and a cast iron frame rather than the older wooden type. There is also a reduced size version known as a

"baby grand."

Beethoven's piano from Pleyel

Small modern piano, Yamaha.

Electronic Instruments

Grand piano built by Muzio Clementi (London, ca. 1827).

It has begun.......but the end is nowhere in sight

When Kurt Sachs and Erich von Kornbostel published their classification system of musical instruments in 1914, some primitive electro-acoustic and electronic instruments were already in existence. Although they came across these instruments in the pages of the trade press, they decided not to include them in their publication. They considered them to be of no significance and thus missed out on the ancestors of the most important

Grand piano built by Conrad Graf, ca. 1830.

Mozart grand piano, ca. 1785.

Grand Piano by Pleyel.

instrumental innovations of the twentieth century.

The electronic oscillator (tone source), developed soon afterward, was the first new type of sound produced since pre-historic times! Nowadays, more electronic than acoustic instruments are manufactured and marketed, certainly if you include chiming clocks, computers, mobile phones, and games machines. Whatever you may think of the sound quality of digital synthesizers and microcomputers, they are undeniably here to stay in the world of music. The advanced electronics behind them doesn't make them more expensive, in fact they are much cheaper than acoustic instruments, with all the craftsmanship that is required to fashion them. The

Left: 71-inch. grand piano (Steinway & Sons, London, 1825).

Grand piano, built by Ignace Pleyel, 1815.

main electronic component, the microchip, is very inexpensive, since the raw material for the silicone used in their manufacture is just sand.

Since the Moog synthesizer was first introduced 1960s, its popularity has reached astonishing heights. In the last ten years of the twentieth century, only the microcomputer outsold the electronic keyboard.

Synthesizers are used mostly in light and popular music but they are receiving ever greater attention from modern composers. An increasing number of concertos are being written that combine synthesizers with acoustic in-

struments. Bands that play electronically generated music are getting air time and there are even "live" performances of electronic music. Only in the symphony orchestra is there still resistance toward electronic music.

There is no such resistance in the case of light music (easy listening), where session musicians are content to use whatever instruments are available, just as they did when only acoustic instruments were used.

The synthesizer has conquered the world. It is extremely popular in Japan, that has a real synthesizer culture, and in India it is much used for the incidental music for Bollywood films. In South Africa, Afrikaans pop music has taken the synthesizer to its heart.

Many instruments that have been developed over the past century, thanks to electronics and the development is still in full flow.

AN OVERVIEW

Some electro-acoustic instruments have hardly any components that require an external power source. Most of them look very much like their acoustic predecessors — pianos, harmoniums, carillons, guitars, and stringed instruments. The number of electro-acoustic instruments is thus quite extensive, as can be shown by some examples. Electro-acoustic keyboard instruments include the electric piano, the electric harpsichord, and an electric clavichord (known as the *clavinet*). They have been in use for over thirty years in jazz and pop music from The Beatles to Miles Davis. Most of these instruments were originally developed as long ago as pre-World War II.

The Neo-Bechstein, built in 1935, was a particularly futuristic instrument. Bechstein the piano maker, Siemens the electro-technical manufacturers, and the Nobel Prize-winner, the physicist and chemist, Hermann Walther Nernst (1864-1941) all got together to make this spectacular product. The Neo-Bechstein was a variation on the "music-plus" concept, a combination of electronically amplified strings, a radio, and a phonograph. The advertisements for it claimed: "This way you can play for hours on end, at any time of day or night, without upsetting the neighbors, and meanwhile drop in on the latest news bulletins, or capture a performance by Lamond of a Beethoven sonata so you can immediately try and play along with him." Yet the Neo-Bechstein was not a great success. Nor were the electronic harmoniums and electrically operated keyed percussion (vibraphone and glockenspiel). The development of an electro-acoustic carillon, in the United States, was a hit, however. This carillon was the first to use electro-magnetic sensors that

were touch-sensitive. These sensors are used nowadays in the electronic striking mechanism used for playing drum-pads.

The experiments that led to the construction of the electric guitar started in the 1920s. They were fueled by a desire for a greater volume of sound in jazz and dance bands. In the 1930s, the American Rickenbacker company was one of the manufacturers building electric guitars, and in 1941, Les Paul built the first electric guitar with a solid body, which went into production through the Gibson Company. Effects pedals came out in the 1960s. Pedals such as the wah-wah pedal and the fuzz-pedal altered the electrical impulses between guitar and amplifier, thus distorting the sound in the desired fashion.

The next development came with Everett Chapman's invention of The Stick in 1973.

Neo-Bechstein grand piano. The sound is produced by means of electro-magnetic vibration sensors. There is a cordless connection to the amplifier and speakers, and the register can be extended using micro-hammers.

A Chapman Stick is quite an incredible instrument. It has 10 strings, the range of a piano, and it is played by hammer-ons only. No picking! The Stick made it possible to play a melody or rhythm separately with each hand.

Other types of electro-acoustic stringed instruments have been around since the 1920s, mostly made by the makers of the first electric guitars. More than anything, the demand from modern pop and jazz musicians was for the speedy development of violins without bodies—a sort of "stick violin." Such violins now come equipped with MIDI (Musical Instrument Digital Interface, 1983), so you can couple instruments together so one of them completely controls the other.

Electro-acoustic instruments still need resonating elements but that is not the case with electronic instruments. There are still some moving parts, however, so it could be said that there is still a certain amount of mechanical vibration. An example of this sort of instrument is the gigantic *telharmonium* invented around 1900 by the American, Thaddeus Cahill. Three keyboards were played by two musicians at once, while the electro-mechanical section took up a whole "machine-room" of its own. Two examples were set up in special rooms in New York City. People subscribed to a service, via a sort of telephone line to their own homes with a loudspeaker on the receiving end, so they could listen to the recitals. The project died a quiet death.

Thirty years later, the Hammond Organ appeared, in which the same principles were applied, albeit on a much smaller scale (motor-driven alternators were used as sound generators) so that it was suitable for home use. The Hammond became an overwhelming success. Automobile magnate Henry

Electric bass guitar.

Amplifiers and loudspeakers, accessories for the electric guitar.

Ford and composer George Gershwin were amongst the early owners. In 1937, a delighted Sir Thomas Beecham (the English orchestra conductor) wrote a letter to Laurence Hammond about a brand new Hammond Organ that had been installed in the Royal Opera House in London. He predicted a great future for the instrument, a prediction that certainly came true. Another success story, but on a smaller scale, was the *mellotron*, an analog precursor of the modern recording studio sampling machines. Previously recorded sounds, from drumbeat to birdsong, were replayed or integrated into a recording. The Beatles, perhaps the greatest experimenters in the history of pop music, made use of the mellotron from 1966 onward. The Moody Blues also included the instrument in some of their numbers.

Electronic instruments no longer contain any mechanical parts in the sound source.

Hammond A tone wheel organ (London, 1937), with two manuals and a 25-note pedal. The amplifier and loudspeaker are built in.

The oscillator is completely electronic. This category can be subdivided between monophonic (one-voiced) and polyphonic (many-voiced) instruments. There are relatively few monophonic electronic instruments, but the *theremin*, the *ondes martenot*, and the early synthesizers fall into this category, in which the array of sound color and articulation were often outstanding. The theremin, invented in 1920 by the Russian Lev Termen (Léon Theremin in his adopted France), was the first successful electronic instrument. The American company RCA put the Theremin into production from 1929. In the 1950s, Robert Moog brought out five different models before producing the synthesizer he designed himself. The playing of the theremin, significantly enough called the *Etherphone* in its early days, had indeed something of the look of a spiritual séance about it. The player controlled the pitch by moving his right hand over or along a vertical antenna, and controlled the volume by similar movements of the left hand in relation to a sort of hoop-shaped aerial. The result in terms of sound was a smoothly gliding scale.

The ondes martenot was developed and built in 1928 by Frenchman Maurice Martenot. His first model was played by pulling and then releasing a string with the right hand. On a later version there was a string with a ring round it that moved up and down the string. In the 1930s, the instrument was provided with a conventional keyboard.

Avant-garde composers of the time used both instruments in their works. Since those days, avant-garde composers have conscientiously kept up with developments in electronic media. When magnetic tape first became available, around 1950, it quickly led to the establishment of the first electronic music studio, opened in Cologne by Herbert Eimert (studio WDR, 1952), who was succeeded by Karlheinz Stockhausen. Stockhausen is the most famous pioneer of electronic music and also exerted an influence on jazz and pop music. In 1953, Milan

Léon Theremin (his original Russian name is Lev Termen) with his instrument, the Theremin.

became the second city to have an electronic studio, run by Luciano Berio and Bruno Maderna. Pierre Boulez took the initiative in Paris (IRCAM, 1975). In the United States, Milton Babbitt pioneered concerts of electronic music from 1952 and important centers were established in New York and New Jersey.

The category of polyphonic instruments includes pianos, organs, string synthesizers, and many analog and digital synthesizers.

Karlheinz Stockhausen

The portable *philicorda* is an old favorite, a small electronic organ produced by Philips in the 1960s. This company maintained an electronic studio in those days, in which composers such the Dutch composer Henk Badings (1907-87) and Edgar Varèse (1883-1965) worked. The philicorda was a product of that studio. The single manual four-octave models could easily be used in a domestic setting while the two-manual and pedal version was common in churches.

The *casiotone* is a handheld, home keyboard instrument developed in the 1980s by Casio, the Japanese electronics firm. The compact Casiotone is clearly a product of the microchip era. Within a short space of time, thirty different mass-produced models had been introduced on the market, the smallest of which were monophonic. They were designed for children but, of course, they could be played by adults too. Even professional jazz and pop musicians added the casiotone to their electronic armory. The instrument, of which millions have been sold, includes a computer, rhythm section, memory, and a digital display, all of them integrated (linked together).

The forerunner of the modern synthesizer (to "synthesize" just means to "assemble") is Canadian Hugh le Caine's rather ugly looking "electronic sackbut." The instrument dates from as long ago as the 1940s but even then it possessed a number of the elements of the classic synthesizer, including a touch-sensitive keyboard, a portamento slide-strip, and modulators for regulating the

The IRCAM in Paris

Philips Philicorda electronic organ. This reasonably successful instrument was on the market from 1964 until 1971. This instrument is polyphonous and works with twelve oscillators. It also has a swell pedal.

Moog synthesizer.

Casio VLtone (1980), a monophonous children's instrument based on a digital synthesizer. There is also a digital calculator and a 100-note memory built in.

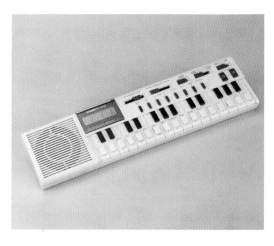

tone color and vibrato. The classic synthesizer is an instrument with the power to synthesize all sorts of sounds. It is built of frequency generators, white noise generators, modulators, various filters, and a mixing mechanism. It can be run from a DC stepdown motor, as discovered by Robert Moog who built his first synthesizer in 1964.

The classic analog synthesizer is also an ingeniously complicated sound builder, in which various modules have to be physically attached to each other in order to achieve the desired result, so it is equipment for experts. The best-known makes are Roland, Moog, and Arp.

The digital synthesizer, dreamed up by John Chowning in 1973, started a revolution. The analog direct current power supply, and the linked modules were done away with. Frequency modulation made its appearance, controlled by software and therefore digital. This turned the computer into a synthesizer.

Frequency modulation (FM) even exists in the animal world, for example in the echolocation system used by bats and whales. The principle of FM was developed further in post-War Germany, in connection with radio research. It was, as it were, just waiting for a creative application to come along. The digital synthesizer can also be played by people without any technical background. The Yamaha DX7 is a digital synthesizer originally created in 1983. It is played from a keyboard and controlled by a couple of buttons and slides but also by using MIDI, a digital communication program for electronic or electro-acoustic instruments. The Yamaha was equipped with the first MIDI software. Since 1983, electronic instruments have been able to communicate with each other. Each input on such an instrument is encoded and can be passed to another instrument or stored in a computer

Yamaha DX7 synthesizer, 1983. This instrument is a 16-voiced polyphonous digital piano synthesizer with pressure-sensitive keys. It can optionally be controlled with MIDI software.

for later reproduction.

ELECTRONIC SOUND EQUIPMENT

Increasing storage density in recording media.
Development of the audio disk:
- 1877 Phonograph
- 1887 Flat disk
- 1950 33⅓ rpm long-playing record (LP)
- 1958 Stereo LP
- 1982 Compact Disk
- 1995 Digital Versatile Disk (DVD)

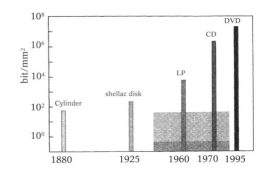

With the advent of radio, the pick-up phonograph, the tape-recorder, and similar devices from the 1930s onward, electronic sound equipment has made a significant incursion into the home as a passive musical instrument. In contrast to mechanical sound equipment designed to create music, the primary function of electronic sound equipment is to reproduce music in the most natural form possible.

MUSICAL EQUIPMENT AND SOUND SYSTEMS FOR THE HOME

Besides actually playing music, the citizen of today has many opportunities to listen to music. The concert hall and other halls where music is performed live still bring him closest to the music. The arrival of the phonograph record in the early twentieth century and all the electronic media that followed it have turned the living-room into a new sort of concert hall, in which music from any age and any part of the world can be played. At the same time, there has been a movement toward sound reproduction in the home environment that is as faithful as possible to the original. The name given to this quest for natural reproduction of music is High Fidelity (hi-fi).

At this point, the authors would like to give you some reliable quality guidelines for the purchase of a sound system for the home. Our preference for choosing the components individually may be described as arbitrary because, of course, there are also good all-in-one systems available. Individual components give you the opportunity for customizing the system, however. Custom building is necessary because your room is bound to be different from that of your neighbor, as are your musical preferences, and the way in which you listen. Furthermore, the argument that a defective component can be replaced is quite persuasive. For example, you should easily expect a minimum lifespan of 15 years from a good amplifier and loudspeaker. You have to realize that every chain is only as strong as its weakest link. One weak link in your music system can result in music reproduction going no further than producing a noise and your musical pleasure will deteriorate into irritation inside of ten minutes. We would strongly advise you to get in touch with a local, specialist dealer rather than visit a chain store. Your local dealer will be a trained expert who will help you achieve exactly what you want in the field of domestic sound reproduction.

The phonograph by Charles Gros

213

A good example of a high-quality all-in-one system

THE MOST IMPORTANT LINK:
YOUR OWN ROOM

The domestic setting is still the most underestimated link in the chain. Along with the loudspeakers, it is responsible for more than ninety percent of the reproduction quality. The phenomenon of acoustics, the behavior of sound waves inside a room, is the defining factor. Acoustics can never reasonably be predicted. The design, contents, shape, reverberation, and damping within the room are all essential elements. In every case, a rigid arrangement of furniture will spell disaster for sound reproduction. Whenever you have a large, empty room with wood flooring and bare walls, a leather couch, shades over the windows, and one large houseplant, then the chances of having a pleasurable and enjoyable musical experience are slim. The other extreme is the heavily damped living room with deep-pile fitted carpet, heavy velvet curtains, and lots of upholstered, plush soft furnishings. Music reproduction has no chance here—everything will sound dead. The golden mean lies somewhere in between. Sometimes a rug and a pair of curtains will work

wonders. If the space still sounds "hard," then position the loudspeakers too far from where you normally sit to listen.

The Resources

The availability, range, and pricing have determined the success of all music media. The oldest medium, the phonograph record, put a wide sector of the public in touch with all sorts of music. The same applies to music cassettes, which took over the role of domestic recording and reproduction medium from tape. Above all, let's not forget the role of radio. Although the sound quality of radio was not so hot originally, it developed into a high-quality medium with the advent of FM, and now there is digital radio which will provide even better quality sound. The arrival of the compact disk (CD) ushered in a whole new era with the time-honored analog technology being replaced by a new digital world with hitherto unknown capabilities both in quality and quantity.

The living room

Record Player

The market in vinyl is still a strong one with a lively trade at swap meets, yard sales, and specialist stores, to say nothing of Internet auctions. The good old phonograph record still enjoys a genuine following. To play records, you need the apparatus that will transform the miniscule movements in the grooved surface into electrical signals. We call this apparatus the record player, previously known as the "pick-up," and prior to that, the phonograph. A record player consists of the following components:

– The turntable. The disk has to turn at a constant speed of 33⅓ revolutions per minute (there are also 45 rpm and 78 rpm records). A good turntable has a heavy balanced platen, weighing over two pounds, a precise but, above all silent, bearing, and a motor that doesn't contribute to the musical output by producing deviations in speed. Most turntables available nowadays use a belt drive. Previously, gear drives were very common, although rumble from the motor could scarcely be avoided in the lighter, cheaper models. Besides these, direct-drive turntables are used in professional contexts, of most interest to those looking for a turntable that starts instantly, such as disk-jockeys. You can also recognize a good turntable by the quality of the base or chassis. A turntable with one corner

A high-end turntable

that you can easily push down, while the others stay in place, should make you suspicious. The motto should be, the simpler and heavier, the better.

– The arm. The arm carries the cartridge over the upper surface of the record and regulates the weight of the needle or stylus. This would appear to be the simplest of tasks but appearances can be deceptive. The arm must be light as well as rigid and non-resonant. The bearing must be vibration-free but have no free play. The construction of a good arm depends on trying to square the circle, so this component is an expensive one. Be on the lookout for cheap, "sloppy" manufacture. A good turntable has adjustments for stylus pressure and lateral compensation. The end of the arm should have a wide, flat surface on which to mount the cartridge.

– The cartridge. This consists of a diamond needle attached to a small box, the

A source: pickup in the record groove

A heavy turntable platter

cantilever, to which an electric generator is linked that translates the movement of the needle into electrical frequencies. The standard type of cartridge delivered with most turntables is magneto-dynamic. These usually have elliptical needles that can easily be replaced. You should expect a reasonable reproduction quality from this sort of cartridge. You can do better, however. Don't economize on the cartridge. Replace the existing cartridge on your turntable with a moving coil cartridge. When combined with the appropriate amplifier, you'll get results so good you wouldn't have thought it possible.

A record-cleaning machine

Adjustment and Maintenance

It can be stated with confidence that the condition of the average turntable was partly responsible for the success of the CD. Perhaps a plea for the defense is in order.
A good performance from a disk stands or falls by the proper adjustment of the arm/cartridge combination and the suitability of the amplifier. Get advice from an expert if you are in any doubt. Be aware, in any case, that too much stylus pressure is considerably less harmful than too little. Don't skimp on the maintenance of your turntable either. Nowadays, you can buy convenient turntable cleaners that will effectively keep the turntable mat free from dirt, dust, and grease. Clean the turntable and the needle each time you want to play a record. A good carbon fiber turntable brush costs only $7 or $8, while an adequate stylus cleaner costs $5.

Tone arm

Investment

A good new turntable costs at least $250 and a better-quality MC cartridge may cost $120. If you have an older but otherwise still serviceable amplifier, do not connect it to your turntable using the largely outdated PU music input. It is much wiser to buy a modern PU pre-amplifier and then connect that to the line or auxiliary input. Good pre-amplifiers can be bought from around $100.

Tuner

The radio is an underestimated source for music-lovers. Many people identify radio with news reports, the weather, and pop stations. But since the advent of FM, radio has had an outstanding output quality, perfect for listening to serious acoustic music. The public radio stations and commercial stations dedicated to classical music offer a fantastic range. There are often broadcasts of live concerts that give you the feeling of being there in person.
For reception of FM stereo broadcasts you need a piece of equipment called a tuner. This apparatus transforms the incoming signals, from cable or sometimes from an antenna, into (musical) data that can be passed through an amplifier. A tuner

Top-of-the-range turntable.

Tuner.

consists of three parts:

– A reception array, or high frequency amplifier. This is where the antenna signal (frequently a weak one) is amplified and tuned;

– A sort of mid-amplifier, also called the mid-frequency amplifier. This is where further amplification and the "losing" of unwanted by-products of the transmission process occur. At the end of the process the musical signal is said to have been "recovered";

– The stereo decoder. This link takes care of the final transformation. If there's a stereo signal in the transmission, the stereo decoder reconstructs that signal. At the same time, it gets rid of any unwanted parts of

Pickup/preamp

the stereo coding process at the output side.

Sometimes tuner and amplifier are combined in one case (tuner-amp or receiver).

Cable or Antenna

Nowadays, a large number of householders nowadays are connected to cable. This means that all the radio stations that can be accessed by the tuner come, in a certain sense, "pre-packaged." Collaboration between cable providers means that you get a much larger number of stations than you would be able to get through your own antenna. Admittedly you are at the mercy of the cable providers' choice. Because the number of available channels is not infinite, you sometimes have to make difficult choices. Your own antenna will often supply the desired qualities of FM signal but not everyone has their own antenna. If you want to listen to radio using your own antenna on the roof, there are some points to be considered. The number of stations you can receive in FM stereo is restricted to those with transmitters within a radius of about 45 miles from your home. So it makes sense to erect the best possible FM antenna. The sensitivity and selectivity of your tuner components are also quite critical factors. Nowadays, very few tuners are on the market that are best suited to one particular brand of antenna. Also, they're not cheap. One alternative is a satellite dish and tuner. You don't need a huge dish for digital radio reception. A dish of about 20 inches diameter will usually provide excellent results. The location in which you place your dish often benefits from having an open aspect toward the southern sky.

For cable customers, everything is simpler and less expensive. You can sit down and sift through the catalogs of various tuners, confident that your choice is about high-quality music reproduction. Pay a couple of hundred dollars more and the reception from the "classical" stations moves up into a different class. Most tuners nowadays have more than adequate pre-selection options so that you don't have to tune in every time to your favorite station. Facilities like the Radio Data System (RDS) are great if you want to know which station you are listening to.

Digital Equipment

Since the arrival of the CD player in 1982, the market for music media has rapidly switched to digital sources, after an initially hesitant start. The CD seems to have hit the bull's-eye. The convenience, the speedy accessibility of tracks (numbers), the fact that CDs are less easily damaged than phonograph records, and the generally high quality, have all contributed to this success.

To listen to a CD, you need to have the right equipment. This may be a CD drive in a portable stereo radio, a portable CD player, or a CD changer in an automobile. Nowadays, most computers have a CD-ROM device and a sound card. You can listen to your favorite CDs with this set-up, assuming you have loudspeakers connected to your computer.

Tuner-amplifier

Affordable, average quality CD player

CD Player

The self-contained CD player comes in all shapes sizes and prices. You can recognize a good example by the modest equipment and case. Generally speaking, you can take it as a rule in the hi-fi world that a flashy case with lots of bells and whistles is inversely proportional to the quality of the inner workings. A CD player consists of the following components:

– The moving parts. A good CD motor should be able to play CDs without background noise, even if they are smudged or damaged. The slightly better mechanics, mostly found in the more expensive CD players, have the best chance of success. The laser used to read the digital information, now has a three-beam lens fitted as standard, though you can pick up good quality, second-hand CD players at a reasonable price that sometimes have only a single lens. Don't worry about three being better than one. On the contrary, up until now, mechanisms with a single lens were far and away the best as far as scanning quality is concerned. You don't find them in new CD players any more for purely for reasons of economy, because a three-part lens is invariably cheaper.

– The central processing unit (CPU). This takes care of the translation of the CD signal into a fully corrected digital datastream. This is where fault correction takes place. Even if the CD signal is interrupted from the mechanism, the central processor is nearly always able to make a continuous datastream out of the broken signal.

– The converter, the final link. The converter

Top-of-the-range CD player.

A top-of-the-range CD/SACD drive mechanism.

More and Better.....

The CD player has again been overtaken by a couple of new developments that occurred due to the quest for a single storage medium that could handle images, data, and sound. New optical and electronic technologies have made this possible. The problem lies in the fact that these two new developments appeared on the market at the same time but are not mutually compatible.

is designed to ensure that the corrected datastream is reconverted into a music signal. This is also where any unwanted signal elements are filtered out. Finally, this is the stage at which the signal is transmitted to the amplifier. The difference between an inexpensive and a more expensive CD player is all down to the quality of these various links. The result is that you get a more pleasing reproduction of the music.

For a good CD player you should count on paying $250. Paying between $450 and $1,000 gives you the best chance of long-lasting satisfaction.

SACD Logo.

SUPER AUDIO CD

Logo of DVD-Audio.

DVD-Audio player.

DVD Player

The DVD player has been on the market for a few years, primarily to play picture and sound information. The greater storage capacity of the Digital Versatile Disk allows even more and better music information on the disk itself. In 2000, the DVD audio player was introduced, and it is a very high quality product. A DVD player can play back CDs although some types that have difficulty with CD-ROMs and CD–Rs (rewritable CDs). Furthermore, some CDs and DVDs cannot be viewed or played on a personal computer. The industry is presently hard at work trying to think up a solution.

SACD Player

In addition to the DVD player, there is now a Super Audio Compact Disk player. A number of manufacturers have opted for a purely audio solution. But the SACD player goes one step further than the DVD player, as far as musical quality is concerned. The SACD player plays normal CDs, but there are twin-layer SACDs (the so-called hybrid disks) that can be played on your CD player. You don't have to worry about sitting with a music collection on CD that you won't be able to play when the day comes when you can no longer buy a CD player. The prices of present day DVD audio players and SACD players are just about at the same level as top-class CD players.

Satellite Tuner

An alternative source for radio reception is the satellite tuner. Although these were first intended for TV viewers, the TV channels are already transmitting a large number of radio stations, often in outstanding (digital) quality. Some of the broadcasts are coded and you can only receive them if you pay a fixed amount each month to the broadcaster, but there are still many you can listen to for free. For a satellite tuner you need a satellite dish. You can buy a good set from around $550. Watch for the latest developments in the field of satellite technology, as there will soon be options for choosing particular satellites. Some satellite tuners are completely adapted for radio reception. These tuners mostly have a slightly better quality of reproduction than the usual satellite tuner or else they have a digital output that can be connected to a separate Digital-Analog converter. Sometimes

Affordable SACD player

DAB/FM combination tuner

it's possible to use the output side (the DA converter) of a good CD player.

Developments continue apace in the field of digital radio reception. In several countries in Europe, experiments in a Digital Audio Broadcasting (DAB) system are happening which will, in time, replace our current (analog) FM network. The BBC launched its first digital radio station, 6 Music, on 11 March, 2002. The DAB system was originally developed for automobile radio reception, but it will certainly be used in future for domestic purposes.

Recording and Registration Media

The modern household does not give a second thought to the recording of data, pictures, and sound. Originally, recordings were made, both at home and by professionals, on open-reel tape-recorders. These were supplanted by the cassette deck that reached a new and impressive level of quality, thanks to the various extraneous noise suppression systems, such as Dolby. In the late 1970s, the first cautious attempts were made at producing digitized music in a domestic setting, when the combined P(ulse) C(ode) M(odulation) recorder and video-recorder made its appearance. If attached to a pair of high-quality microphones, the recording enthusiast had professional quality recording equipment at home with an acceptably long playing time (up to 180 minutes) that was clearly more manageable than a tape-deck with eight-inch reels.

The D(igital) A(udio) T(ape) recorder appeared on the market in the 1980s. It was a much more compact digital solution with better fault correction capabilities than the PCM system. Although originally intended for purely home use, the DAT recorder never really fulfilled this function, and is mainly used by roving radio reporters and other professionals who need high quality tape that can be edited. The fact that LPs were easily obtained and high-quality was probably responsible for the fact that music-lovers were being significantly more selective with

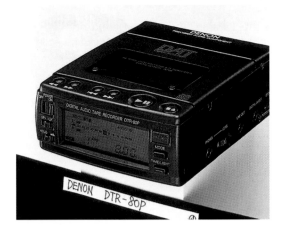

Portable DAT recorder from the early 1990s

their copying. That situation had hardly altered when, 10 years later, the CD made its appearance. In the meantime software copying had really taken off.

Data Compression: Doing the Same with Less...

A remarkable digital development is the use of the data compression systems. On the one hand, the recorded data, picture, and sound information streams take up a huge amount of space (a DVD may contain up to 15 Gb of information!), because optimum quality demands comparably enormous datastreams. On the other hand, there was the development, fueled particularly by communication technology, of a desire for the smallest possible information stream to provide the best possible result. These technologies make use of the fact that our hearing is easily fooled. It is used in the very popular mini-disk recorder and DCC recorder. It is also indispensable for Internet and satellite communications.

The Internet is responsible for the arrival of the MP3 recorder. This music-recording device contains no moving parts at all, the The compressed music datastream being stored in a memory strip. Philips launched the Streamium, a micro music system, in 2003 that claims to be the first capable of playing music direct from the Internet, as well as from radio and CDs. Those who have ADSL or cable broadband, the Streamium can be used to access online music services such as Andante (classical music), Live 365, Musicmatch, MP3.com, and Radio Free Virgin. The Streamium costs around $550.

Cassette Deck

The cassette deck has been the main domestic recording medium for music since the 1990s. The software is inexpensive, so a decent quality of music can be achieved depending on how good the recorder is, and the cassette can be played in any other cassette-player without difficulty.

The role of the cassette deck has certainly drifted into the background with the coming of digital media, but many music lovers still keep their favorite concert recordings, broadcast on public radio, on cassette. New cassette decks have become harder to find in recent years but can still be bought at a number of quality stores. A cassette deck consists of three components:

– The running gear. The quality of the sound reproduction stands or falls by this. A cassette deck with a weak motor will give your piano recordings an unwanted vibrato. Good motors don't come cheap, of course.

– The heads. Ideally, a cassette deck should have three heads, a recording head, a playback head, and an erase head. On many models, the recording and playback heads are combined. This is called a double-head recorder. Although when you're out to buy one you'll be told that three heads are better than two, that's only true to a very limited extent. There are, in fact, very few genuine three-headed recorders on the market. What you'll be offered mostly as a three-

Dolby logo.

headed recorder will in fact be only a two-headed recorder, in which the recording and replay heads are placed closely side-by-side in one box. The weakest spot of this recorder is the pressure pad that holds the tape in the cassette against the head. In the absence of that three-head configuration, the felt pad often doesn't line-up exactly opposite the slots in both heads. This increases the chance of problems such as flutter and high-frequency decay.

– The electronics. A number of amplification circuits ensure the correct tonal balance on recording and replaying.

In every cassette-deck, these circuits should really be customized to suit the make and type of tape you're planning to use. Unfortunately, very few companies can do this for you. For quality music recording we would advise you to use type II (chromium dioxide) tapes. Some of the more expensive recorders can also give good results with the a slightly better grade of type IV (ferric oxide) cassettes. You can buy a good basic cassette deck for occasional recording from around $250. If your musical demands are higher (the reproduction of organ and piano notes needs to be very accurate) or if you want to use the cassette recorder more intensively, then you should count on spending a minimum of $450. A genuine three-head recorder can cost up to $1,000.

DAT Recorder

The DAT recorder was originally intended as domestic recording equipment. It actually had everything going for it, the same high quality as a CD player, the same facilities as a CD player, a playing time of up to three hours at a stretch (double that in long-play mode with an insignificant loss of quality), and ease of use. However, domestic use of the DAT recorder was very marginal. Perhaps it was the high cost of the software that counted against it. Also the acquisition of a CD player and CD collection might already have had too great an impact on the household budget. The DAT recorder is most often found in the professional and semi-professional recording world and is also owned by music and opera lovers who are delighted by its long-playing capabilities. A DAT recorder consists of the following components:

– The motor. In a DAT recorder, the motor looks like a small video motor (the cassettes are slightly smaller than those of an 8-mm camcorder.) They are studies in miniature engineering. The running gear is not as vulnerable as you might think. Proper maintenance is, however, essential.

– The electronic pick-up. This component turns the analog and digital signals being recorded into a digital datastream that can be recorded on tape.

– The electronic replay. These circuits are very similar to those of the CD player.

Just as with the CD player, both processes are controlled by a computer that is permanently connected to all the internal digital processors inside the machine. A DAT recorder will cost at least $800. For a model with higher quality running gear and output circuitry, you could pay up to $1,500.

Minidisk Recorder

A minidisk recorder is a machine you can use for recording digital music information on a disk. This disk is about the same size as a 3½-inch floppy disk and sits inside a similar case. The digital information is, however, burned in optical-magnetically, just like the CD but unlike the floppy disk. A complex internal mechanism is required to burn the musical information onto the digital surface but this mechanism is virtually inaudible. The storage capacity of the minidisk was at first not as large as that of a CD, so data compression was used. The original 650 Mb of a CD can be substantially compressed until it is compact enough to be saved to a minidisk. The minidisk offers outstanding musical performance. Moreover, the music lover has a large number of search and format facilities available. That makes this machine the

equipment of choice for anyone who wants to cut, erase, and paste, in other words, edit the raw input. A minidisk recorder consists of the following components:

– The running gear. The minidisk running gear is a prime example of miniaturized engineering. It is fairly shock-resistant and the access time to any particular track is extremely short.

– The control and encoding circuitry. This is the place for all the digital adaptors and controls including fault correction. A useful facility for music lovers on nearly all minidisk recorders is a second-counter that shows how much of the music being recorded has been stored in memory. The instant you press the "record" button, (and that can sometimes be too late), for that dazzling, unfamiliar aria, you get a few

Minidisk-recorder.

Minidisk with portable recorder.

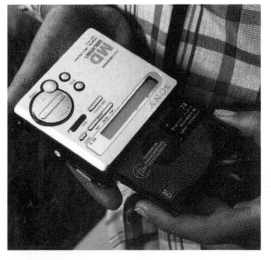

extra seconds in which everything up until then will go on the disk.

– The electronic replay circuits: these electronics are comparable to those of the CD player.

The quality of a minidisk recorder can always be traced back to the running gear but predominantly to the electronic replay circuits and it is here that you can anticipate incisive differences of sound quality. A good minidisk recorder (or CD player) doesn't benefit from internal economies. Good quality consumer electronics need to be carefully engineered in order to ensure that the various links connect up properly with each other, and this is never a cheap option. A minidisk recorder for general use will cost more than $300. For the enthusiast who wants to record live music there are portable minidisk players and recorders. These are compact machines that can give quite excellent results with a good (stereo) microphone. A portable minidisk recorder will cost from around $300 but a quality, stereo microphone will set you back at least $300.

CD Recorder

The CD recorder has become very popular within a short space of time. The first examples came out during the 1990s and were originally intended for professionals. The consumer version came about through very far-reaching integration in the form of multifunction chipsets. The recording process is fairly simple. The digital surface of a CD is simply "cloned." There's nothing more to be done, therefore, than to press the appropriate buttons and start the recorder. Analog sources, such as phonograph records, require a little more effort. The CD recorder has a built-in analog/digital converter (just like the DAT recorder and the minidisk recorder) that transforms the analog signal into a digital datastream. All you have to do is set the recording level correctly. To do this, find the loudest spot on the phonograph record and adjust the recording level so that the meters on the recording instrument don't exceed –3 dB (in the case of very loud music, we would suggest –6 dB). Remember that overloading (going into the red) with digital processing inevitably leads to serious distortion and even signal loss.

Working with CD-Rs in a CD recorder requires some precautionary measures. Always read the instructions for use carefully. When you want to play a recorded CD-R in another CD player then it has to be "burned" or finalized. It makes sense to realize that recording on a CD is irretrievable. There is, of course, an erasable CD-R, the CD-RW, but it does not allow for procedures such as "edit" or "replace." If that's the sort of thing you want to do, you would be better off buying a minidisk recorder. The CD recorder consists of the following components:

– The running gear. This is very similar to mechanisms of the CD player but has an extra heavy-duty laser beam for burning the CDs;

– The recording circuits. These are similar to those of the DAT recorder and the minidisk recorder;

– The control and (de)coding circuits. These are also similar to the DAT recorder and minidisk recorder;

– The replay circuits. Similar to those of the CD player.

There are some useful combination machines on the market, in which a CD recorder is bundled with a CD player in the same box. You can get hold of this sort of equipment for about $400. A high-quality CD recorder designed with high-quality music reproduction in mind will probably cost at least $750.

Just as manufacturers of commercial CDs burn a "tattoo" into their recordings to ensure they can't be copied, now home recording enthusiasts can do the same thing, with the Disk T@2, a disk-labeling system that can be used with the Yamaha CRW-F1 drive. Once the CD has been "burned", it can be labeled with text, images, and logos to be "tatooed" on the underside of the disk.

MP3 player.

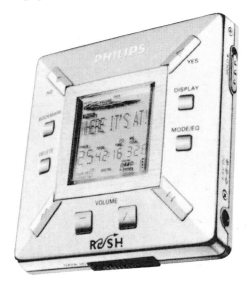

MP3 Recorder/Flashcard Recorder

These recorders are not intended for high quality sound reproduction. The recording medium is a memory card. The MP3 recorder is designed to record music files that can be downloaded from the Internet, as often as not for free. The quality can be reasonable but is nowhere near as good as that of the CD, but it is a simple and inexpensive recording solution.

There is a flashcard recorder, akin to the MP3 recorder, that is now often used by radio journalists. The datastream is also fixed on a memory card and the quality of the spoken word is outstanding, but best of all for the professional, the very fast editing facilities make these recorders very popular in the world of the roving reporter. This medium is not yet suitable for music purposes but that could quickly change.

Amplifier

The central processing and amplification unit in your music system is called the am-

plifier. It has a number of functions. An amplifier consists of two parts, the pre-amplifier and the main amplifier.

In the pre-amplifier, the signal coming from the record player is first strengthened and then corrected. This signal is much weaker than the one that comes from a CD player or tuner. Nowadays, in any case, not every amplifier is fitted with a so-called PU pre-amplifier. If you don't have one in your amplifier, then you can buy a separate PU pre-amplifier (see "Turntable"). This part of the pre-amplifier enables you to select the sound source (CD player, tuner, and so on) and you also get a signal that can be sent out to any recording device that is connected to the amplifier. The "the simpler, the better" rule applies here as well.

The better class of amplifier is remarkable for its smooth sound. Sometimes a simple tone control can be useful, particularly for vinyl disk reproduction, but it doesn't need to be used most of the time. (On some amplifiers, you can bypass the tone control.) This part of the amplifier also ensures that

Preamplifier.

Inside a power amplifier.

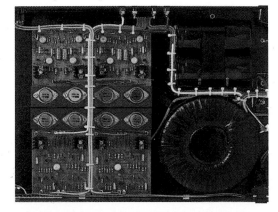

the signal that is exported to the main amplifier is as neutral as possible.

The main amplifier is responsible for maintaining the necessary capacity for your music system. The music information that is output from the pre-amplifier in compressed form is converted into capacity at this stage. This capacity is necessary to energize the loudspeaker. For such an apparently simple task, the amplifier nearly has to perform the impossible in order to retain control over something as complex as a loudspeaker. A good main amplifier therefore requires a robust power supply. Weight is nearly always the guiding factor. In a heavy-duty main amplifier the heat sink is very important. It must ensure that the heat generated by the amplification process can be dissipated, since an amplifier cannot be fitted with a noisy fan, like a computer. The question of necessary capacities will be dealt with under "loudspeaker."

The job of both parts of the amplifier, of course, is to output the musical information stored there as precisely as possible, without adding or losing any detail. This, of course, is true of the whole system.

For a fully functional amplifier, you should pay around $300 but if you're making more serious demands of your amplifier you should expect to pay around $500. Most importantly, if you have to work with lengthy speaker connections (more than 30 feet) it really makes sense to use a separate pre-amplifier–main amplifier setup. The main amplifier should be placed near the loudspeakers and you can work with short

Integrated amplifier.

speaker connection cables. The connection between the pre-amp and main amplifier can be as long as required. This connection produces virtually no signal loss, in contrast to the connection between the main amplifier and the loudspeakers.

Loudspeakers

The loudspeaker is the most complex but often also the most contentious component in your music system. You need two of them for stereo sound production (for a home movie theater setup you need at least five) and these must occupy a visually prominent place in your living-room. Placing the loudspeakers behind a couch or high up on a wall next to the ceiling will have disastrous consequences for your musical enjoyment. A loudspeaker is a converter of electrical information into acoustic information. It usually consists of a minimum of two active elements, each one covering its own particular part of the musical sound spectrum. At all events in this particular case, more definitely not better. To ensure that the loudspeakers don't interfere with each other, there is an electronic filter circuit in each cabinet.

The cabinet has a number of functions, one of which is to ensure that the noise from the front of the loudspeaker is not able to reach the back of the speaker, as this would lead to the sound of being damped down. The cabinet must also provide a form of mounting surface that ensures the loudspeakers are restricted from any movement in relation to each other. Finally, the cabinet must be built in such a way as to avoid unwanted reverberation. A good cabinet is a "dead" cabinet. A good loudspeaker is a neutral and unremarkable loudspeaker that you can listen to for hour after hour without becoming tired of the sound.

The shape has been and remains a matter of debate. If you want to produce a lot of sound, especially with lot of bass, then a large cabinet is indispensable. It is pretty nearly physically impossible to reproduce

The inside of a modern loudspeaker.

Small but high-quality loudspeakers.

power," but it is distortion, rather than capacity, that will knock your speakers out. Handsome, so-called "25-watt" loudspeakers are more likely to run the risk of being destroyed if they are connected up to that neat-looking radio-cassette-recorder just out of the box, even if it clearly states "2 x 20 watt output" on the outside. On the other hand, there's no need to anticipate any

High-end column loudspeaker.

the sub-contra octave of an organ through a 4-inch loudspeaker. That said, you can still experience really musical results from small loudspeakers providing that they are correctly positioned and powered from a good amplifier. A hi-fi specialist store can best help and advise you on the whole process of listening to and trying out equipment (perhaps even in your own home). The expression "loudspeaker wattage" makes no sense. There is a poorly defined and awkward expression "loudspeaker disasters if you wired up your neighbor's 2 x 100-watt amplifier to your own loudspeakers. So long as the output is perfect, there's nothing to worry about.

So, loudspeakers have no wattage, but they certainly have a capacity or output. Most loudspeaker manufacturers indicate the capacity of the loudspeaker in the specifications. You see this translated into a statement of the capacity in dB/watt. If you have chosen loudspeakers with a capacity of 85 dB/watt then it would make sense to choose a robust amplifier (minimum 2 x 50 watt). Certainly if you have a large room or plan to listen to chamber music at a reasonable distance away from the loudspeakers, then these are sensible numbers. Absolute numbers are irrelevant because the audio world does its counting in logarithmic decibel ratios. If you want the music twice as loud (that is 3 dB), then you need 10 times as much amplifier capacity. That's why the capacity of the loudspeakers is so important. Thanks to better quality magnets, compact loudspeakers can produce an output of as much as 91 dB/watt. That makes a difference of four times the volume at best, in relation to a loudspeaker with an output of 85 dB and this can be of overriding importance in a large room.

Take care over positioning, and buy good cables. If you don't have the space to position the loudspeakers correctly, at least buy good headphones. A pair of small, quality loudspeakers will cost around $300. Larger loudspeakers now often come in the shape of elegant columns rather than the dreary teak boxes with black faces with which we were so familiar, will cost at least $600 per pair.

Copying and copyright are a problem area. A CD contains exactly the same information as the original master tape, so the purchaser is actually getting a clone of the master tape. The industry has now introduced copy protection on CD and DAT recorders intended for consumer use. Copy protection allows you to make one copy of each CD for your own use.

THE VOICE AS INSTRUMENT

It might well sound strange but the human voice is not regarded as a musical instrument by musicologists. We would agree with the famous musicologist, Theo Willemze, that the voice is not an instrument in the true sense of the word but we would do the voice an injustice if we ignored it as the oldest, most complete, and natural source of music. It is a musical source directly connected to the human psyche and irretrievably linked with our physical constitution.

There are various theories about how the voice operates, of which the two most important will be summarized. According to the classical theory, the two vocal chords, that lie next to each other when at rest, are caused to vibrate along their length by excess pressure. This happens in the same way as the blowing of the double reed in the oboe. This vibration sets in motion the air that is being breathed out, and the resulting sound is amplified and given a clear tone-color by the mouth, nose, and throat cavities. Sound amplification cavities are called resonators.

Hans Sachs

The most recent theory allocates a much more active role to the vocal chords. They are actively involved in the tone formation process through influencing the speech nerve (the *nervus recurrens*) whose purpose is to stimulate the vocal cords individually in exactly the right way to produce the desired sound. Because of their elasticity, the vocal cords return to their resting position once their work is done.

The human singing voice—leaving the speaking voice out of the reckoning for the moment—according to pitch or height. Accordingly, distinctions are drawn between a number of different registers:

– The chest voice, that uses the chest cavity as resonator. This voice sounds full with plenty of mid-tone volume;

– The head voice, that hardly uses the chest cavity as a resonator at all. This voice sounds bright and gives the vocal sound plenty of articulation.

– The middle register, that lies between chest and head voices;

– The falsetto register, in which the voice is "overblown," as in a flute. What comes out is a harmonically related overtone. This register is most easily detected in yodeling or in the voice of the counter-tenor in medieval and baroque music.

The female voice is categorized as follows:
- The soprano is the highest female voice. Sopranos can further be divided into:

– Dramatic soprano (Maria Callas);
– Lyrical soprano (Elizabeth Schwarzkopf);
– Coloratura soprano (Christina Deutekom);
– Soubrette, with a light sound (Reri Grist);
– Mezzo-soprano, a slightly lower female voice, often with a more mature sound, lively and versatile (Teresa Berganza).
- The contralto is the low female voice. A distinction is often drawn here between two vocal types:
– Dramatic contralto (Marian Anderson);
– Low contralto (Kathleen Ferrier).

The male voice has a somewhat more

Maria Callas.

extended range:

- The boy soprano: until the voice breaks (and boys are always getting a "frog in the throat" during puberty) boy sopranos sing the high parts in mixed choirs. During the baroque period, male voices used to break at around 17 years of age, but nowadays this happens more commonly around 12 years of age. During the baroque period, therefore, there were very elaborate parts for boy sopranos, for example in the many *cantatas* of Johann Sebastian Bach and other church music.
- The tenor, the higher-pitched male voice.

The following are different types of tenor:
- Powerful heroic tenor or dramatic tenor, (opera and oratorios);
- Lyric tenor, often with a wide range and flexibility (Placido Domingo, Luciano Pavarotti);
- Buffo tenor, a light voice often used in comic roles (Jurgen Forster);

The baritone is the mid-range male voice, and is subdivided into:
- Heroic baritone or dramatic baritone (Sigmund Nimsgern);
- Character baritone (Tito Gobbi);
- Lyric baritone (Dietrich Fischer-Dieskau, Gérard Souzay);

The bass is the lowest male voice, recognized as:
- Bass-baritone (Hans Hotter);

- Character bass (Feodor Chaliapin);
- Serious bass (Max van Egmond);
- Buffo bass (Sigmund Nimsgern).

These named singers do not in all cases fall exclusively within the categories indicated, but can also usually take on different characteristics in different roles. Thus, Sigmund Nimsgern is just as much the heroic baritone in Bartok's *Duke Bluebeard's Castle* as the buffo bass in Georg Philipp Telemann's (1681-1767) *Pimpinone* (1725).

The counter-tenor, or alto, is the male voice using the falsetto register. This voice is often used for alto parts that would not, for historical reasons, have been sung by a woman before the end of the eighteenth century. Nowadays these parts (an example is the role of Cherubino in Mozart's *The Marriage*

Feodor Chaliapin (1873-1938). Painting by Korovin.

Carlo Broschi, the *castrato* better known as Farinelli (1705-1782).

FARINELLI.

Capella Pratensis.

of Figaro) are usually sung by men though they may be sung by a female contralto. Alfred Deller, Michael Chance, and Andreas Scholl are all famous counter-tenors.

Castrati were male sopranos who retained their high-pitched boyhood voice as a result of "timely" castration. The larger body of the fully-grown man gave this voice a very particular sound and volume. Castrato voices used to sing in the Vatican Chapel until as late as the early twentieth century. There have been virtually no castrato voices in our times but a few recordings survive from the early twentieth century in which some of the last professional castrati can be heard in the twilight of their careers. The most famous castrato in history was probably Carlo Broschi, better known as Farinelli (1705-1782). In a film about his life, the voice of Farinelli was approximated for the recordings by mixing the voices of a female soprano and a male counter-tenor.

The human voice is heard solo, as often as not in combination with other instruments. When voices sing together we describe it as a choral singing. There are various types of choir formats, each with its own typical sound.

The forerunner of the opera chorus was the Greek chorus, who performed in the ancient tragedies and comedies, the plays plays performed in the open air theaters of Ancient Greece. Later, the choir became an established feature of the church, laying the foundation for a mixed voice choir, as heard in church and for singing oratorios.

The classical standard for the allocation of vocal parts in a choir is: soprano, contralto, tenor and bass, a division according to pitch. Some well-known types of choirs are:

- Male voice choir, tenor and bass voices only;
- Ladies' choir, sopranos and contraltos;
- Opera/oratorio choir, a large mixed choir of all voice types;
- Chamber choir: all voice types, but with fewer singers in each voice;
- Boys' choir: boy sopranos only;
- Children's choir: boy and girl sopranos.

With the arrival of electronics, the voice has gained a quite separate, expressive role in popular music, both on the stage and in the recording studio. Although a certain measure of vocal training is still regarded as desirable for professional popular singers (and it is a must for backing singers who earn their living in the recording studio), the technology has now progressed so far that it can turn a childish squawk into a full-bodied soprano!

Church choir

Internet Sites about Music

General

www.amis.org
American Musical Instrument Society
Has its own journal and news report The site is especially interesting because it contains an international list of museums with musical instrument collections and a list with different categories,

www.cs.Helsinki.fi/u/wikla/music.html
Personal site of Arto Wikla, lecturer at the University of Helsinki (Finland). The site has many links, in particular on the subject of ancient music and music instruments.

www.music.ed.ac.uk/euchmi
Site of the Edinburgh University Collection of Historic Musical Instruments, with many images of historical instruments.

www.si.umich.edu/CHICO/MHN/enclpdia.html
Site of CHICO, the Cultural Heritage Information and Community Outreach project (Michigan, U.S.A.) It contains a beautiful music instruments encyclopedia.

www.classicalmusic.about.com
Lots of information and many links on all sorts of subjects related to classical music, amongst which are musical instruments.

www.siba.fi/Kulttuuripalvelut/instruments.html
Site of the Sibelius Academy, containing many links to specialist musical instrument sites.

www.diabolus.org
Site of the English group Diabolus in Musica with information about medieval and Renaissance music and instruments.

www.musiciansnews.com/encyclopedia
Complete music encyclopedia. There is a keyword search facility, or you can search via the alphabet.

www.orpheon.org
Site of the Orpheon museum in Wenen, Germany with many images of historical stringed instruments.

Brass Instruments

www.hornplanet.com/hornpage
Site dedicated to the horn.

www.petrouska.com
Site dedicated to the trumpet and related instruments.

www.ocr.woodwind.org
The "Online Clarinet Resource," containing many articles about the clarinet.

www.hornplayer.net
Portal for everything there is to know about horns, history, mailing list, purchase, etc.

www.contrabass.com
Site with all sorts of information about the contrabass.

Stringed Instruments

www.jose-sanchez-penzo.net/strad.html
Site about stringed instruments and information about various violins.

www.earlybass.com
A site containing information and links for the double-bass and violin.

www.violadagamba.org
Site about the viola da gamba.

crab.rutgers.edu/~pbutler/rebec.html
Site with information about the rebec.

http://music.tradeworlds.com
Portal about all kinds of instruments.

Keyboard instruments

keyboardtimes.com

Site containing information about all sorts of aspects of keyboard instruments (including teaching and playing techniques), and information about keyboard instruments themseves.

http://orgel.com
Portal about organs: library, MP3..

www.uk-piano.org
English site with information about pianos, including the construction and the history of the instrument.

trfn.clpgh.org/free-reed
The Classical Free-Reed, Inc., an American site containing a lot of informatiom about "free-reed" instruments, such as accordions, harmoniums, and Asian instruments, such as the sheng.

www.bostonclavichord.org
Site of The Boston Clavichord Society containing various articles and information about the clavichord.

www.accordions.com
Site with information and explanation of various kinds accordions.

www.islandnet.com/~arton/barluthp.html
A special site about the lute-harpsichord.

www.ptg.org
Site of the American Piano Technicians Guild containing all sorts of information about pianos.

Glossary

A capella
Literally "in chapel mode". Description of a manner of singing in which the choir comprising soprano, contralto, tenor, and bass sings without instrumental accompaniment and produces its own rhythms.

Acciaccatura
A short grace note. A decoration that is only used by keyboard instruments, in which the note a half-tone above the main note is struck briefly.

Accidental
Sign indicating that a note should be played a half-tone higher or lower than the note itself indicates. An accidental only lasts for the duration of the measure in which it is written.

Adagio
Slow, peaceful. This tempo is somewhere between largo and andante.

Acoustics
Acoustics is the science of sound reproduction, whether it be of a musical instrument, a building, or a space. The term is also used to distinguish between electric and electronic and non-electric or electronic instruments, such as the "acoustic guitar."

Allegro
Indication of a lively playing tempo. Since the eighteenth century, this indication is for a speed that is slower than presto.

Andante
Literally walking. Indicates a measured speed. Andante is a tempo often used where the idea of movement is to be conveyed.

Aria
Solo song with instrumental accompaniment in an opera, oratorio, or cantata. Arias are also performed as self-contained concert pieces.

Arpeggio
Chords (q.v.) played in such a way that the notes sound one after the other rather than simultaneously (as if drawing one's hand across harp strings); an alternative name is "broken chords."

Arrangement
A piece of music for a particular grouping of instruments, often being a re-write of a piece originally written for a different ensemble, different instruments, or in a different mood or tempo.

Articulation
The accurate means of linking and separating notes, e.g. legato,

playing or singing notes connected to each other, and staccato, playing or singing notes separately from each other.

Autophonic   Self-playing; autophonic instruments are those whose shape and/or material is sufficiently flexible that they start vibrating spontaneously by means of rubbing, plucking, striking, or blowing. The aeolian harp (q.v.) is an example of autophony.

Basso Continuo   The bass instrumental voice of the baroque period, whose notes were shown in a sort of code in the score to emphasize the base notes of the chords and the rhythm.

Baton   Stick of wood or ivory, about one foot long, used to emphasize by a conductor to emphasize his gestures as he directs the orchestra.

Bis   Literally "twice." A direction to a musician that the indicated passage should be played one more time.

Bitonality   The simultaneous pressing of two keys. A condition of bitonality is that there should be some tonality present, so that two notes are based on the same tonal center. On the other hand, there is no tonal center in atonality and likewise atonal music is not written in any particular key.

Bocca Chiusa   Literally "closed mouth," the effect in singing of wordless humming with the mouth closed. Used as an accompanying chorus in opera, as in the famous "Humming Chorus" in Puccini's Madam Butterfly.

Bourdon string   A string which may be plucked or strummed on the neck of the instrument, but which is never bowed, during playing. It sounds continuously, freely in sympathy with the plucked string. It is frequently found in ancient music and folk music. Not to be confused with the resonating string, which is never played itself but resonates along with the plucked string.

Breve   The name given to the "full value" note, equivalent to two minims or four crotchets.

Bridge   Piece on a stringed instrument that raises the strings above the sounding-board.

Brush   A metal stick ending in a fan of soft metal threads. The brush is primarily used in jazz on drums or cymbals, making a soft swishing sound.

Calando	A direction to a musician to play less rigidly and that the tempo should become slower.
Cambiare	A direction in a score that a change is required in the orchestra, for example that a different instrument should intervene.
Canzone	A lyrical instrumental composition on a small scale, based on or derived from vocal music.
Capriccio	Literally a caprice or whim. Description of light, lively and—literally—capricious piece of music with many intertwined voices, particularly applicable to seventeenth-century piano pieces. The term has more to do with the mood of a piece than with a clearly defined musical form.
Chamber music	Instrumental music for a small number of set instruments, such as trios and quartets, originally designed to be played in small halls or salons, nowadays used mainly to describe a particular type of music (as opposed to orchestral music).
Chest voice	A register of the voice, usually regarded as the normal singing voice (as opposed to the "head" voice).
Chromatic	Proceeding in half-tones, e.g. c, c#, d, d#, e, f, f# etc; striking all of the keys on a piano in sequence produces a chromatic scale.
Chord	The simultaneous sounding of three or more notes within the same octave (see Arpeggio).
Cluster	Unbroken sequences of notes; a muddle of notes. Easily playable on multi-voiced instruments such as the piano (with the flat of the hand or forearm.) Only playable by wind instruments in ensemble. Also occurs in orchestral and choral music.
Coda	Literally a tail or wisp. The terminal section of a piece of music, which brings the work to a close. It is often short, but sometimes also freely extended and cleverly elaborated.
Collegno	Direction as to the manner of playing a stringed instrument. The strings should not be stroked with the length of the horse-hair of the bow, but hit with the wooden spine of the bow in order, for example, to play a staccato passage.
Compass	The lowest and highest notes an instrument or voice can produce are its compass; this is indicated by the notes at each extreme.

Composition class	Where the principles are taught as to how to write music, in terms of harmony, counterpoint, and rhythm.
Concerto grosso	Instrumental form from the baroque period in which a solo group (the concertino or solo) is set against a larger group (tutti or ripieno).
Conductor	The director of a choir or orchestra. He indicates to the musicians or choristers the beat, rhythm, and tempo, using arm and hand movements, and also conveys his artistic interpretation.
Continuo	Instruments used during the Baroque period for the support of higher voiced instruments; an instrument that plays the bass line or chord progression and so lays down the harmonic foundation of the composition. For example, organ, viola da gamba, and theorbo might accompany two violins in a sonata for two violins and continuo.
Coperto	Literally "covered." A direction for playing percussion instruments, e.g. the timpani, by damping the note with a cloth, a piece of felt, or the fingers.
Crescendo	Literally increasing in size. A direction indicating that the volume of a piece should increase
Crotchet	Note with one-fourth the value of a minim.
Custos	Literally "lookout." A sign at the end of a page, indicating the pitch of the first note on the next page.
Da capo	"From the top", or start over, usually abbreviated to D.C. Instruction that a piece is to be repeated to a particular spot, e.g. "D.C. al fine" (from start to finish) or "D.C. al segno" (from the start to a sign).
Decibel	A measurement of the strength of a sound. The abbreviation is dB.
Descant	Upper voice; the high sounds in any register (descant soprano, descant bass), and passage sung higher than the basic melody, in a choir .
Diatonic	Proceeding in the characteristic variation of whole- or half-tones that forms the basis of the tonic solfa (do, re, mi, fa, so, la ti, do).
Diffusion	The dispersal of a sound through a room. The stronger the dispersal, the greater the diffusion.

Diminuendo	Literally "decreasing." Direction to a player to start playing more softly.
Dissonance	Sounds or intervals that cross over a consonance. There is no single definition of a dissonance, so custom and what people are used to hearing play an important role in the assessment of consonance and dissonance.
Dot	This has various significances in notation. After a note, it indicates that the length of the note is increased by half; above or below a note indicates that it should be played staccato; between a note and a tie indicates the note should be played portato, i.e. between staccato and legato.
Double-stopping	A technique of string playing whereby two or more notes on different strings are fingered at the same time.
Double shake	A particular form of shake in which two shakes are played by one hand at the same time. The notes are usually a third or a sixth apart from each other.
Down-bow	Indication of the direction in which the bow should be moved when playing a stringed instrument.
Dur	Frequently used German term for "major" (French = *majeur*) as opposed to "minor" (French = *mineur*), the two families of keys in tonal music. The "major" scale is made up of steps of half-tones between the 3rd and 4th and 7th and 8th degrees.
Elegy	This term has been used since 1800 for gentle, plaintive music that includes singing as well as for purely instrumental pieces.
Embouchure	Configuration of the lips when playing a wind instrument. Having a good embouchure enables the production of a resounding, clear tone.
Étouffé	A performance instruction for percussionists and harpists. The note should be dampened immediately after it is struck.
Etude	An instrumental piece (French for "study") intended to assist in practicing a particularly difficult technique.
Fantasia	Compositional form which has taken on many different guises , over the centuries. Mostly improvisational and without strong form; contrapuntal from the sixteenth through the eighteenth centuries.

Fifth	1. Interval (q.v.) of five steps.
	2. The fifth note of a scale, counting from the lowest note (root) of the scale.
Fillers	Registers of labial organ pipes with fractured feet; extra registers that can accentuate the most important overtones (q.v.) and thus influence the tone color.
Finale	The ending. The last movement in a multi-movement work such as a sonata or symphony.
Fingering	The position of the fingers when playing an instrument.
Fingering chart	A diagram showing the position of the fingers for playing an instrument, provided in order to help the player.
Flat	Pitch sign, indicating the lowering in pitch of the following note by a half-tone
Forte	Performance direction for louder volume. Abbreviation: f.
Fortissimo	Performance direction: play very loudly. Abbreviation: ff.
Frequency	The number of times a sound vibrates in a specific time, measured in Hertz (Hz).
Fret	Shallow ridges across the neck of some plucked or stringed instruments to assist in the clear production of notes. Frets are placed in exactly the spot at which the string has to be shortened in order to produce a (higher) note that is in tune.
Glissando	Literally "sliding." Sliding the hand up the neck of a stringed or plucked instrument; sliding the hand across the black or white keys on a keyboard instrument. Brass instruments, such as the trombone, can produce a complete glissando, as can the violin, but the horn can only glissando through the harmonic series (q.v.).
Harmonic note	A note with that makes a particular sound on a stringed and plucked instrument, produced by not pressing the string down on the fingerboard but using a light bowing so that the overtones emerge with a flute-like tone quality.
Harmonic series	All the notes on a wind instrument that can be produced merely by different strengths of blowing, without lengthening or shortening the tube.

Harmony	The theoretical basis for the (progression of) chords in the major or minor tonality. Harmony was developed in the eighteenth century from the teaching of counterpoint and was first applied to the music of the eighteenth and nineteenth centuries.
Head voice	The highest register of the singing voice, in which the head becomes the resonating chamber. Also sometimes called "falsetto."
Hemiola	Extremely common since the fifteenth century, a deliberately inserted alteration of the strong beats in a measure as, for example, the insertion of an uneven 3/4 measure in a passage of 6/8 time.
House music	A term that emerged in the seventeenth century as a counterpart to chamber music, which at that time was still the preserve of the aristocracy. House music was played by gatherings of friends or family in an intimate setting.
Idiophonic	See Autophonic.
Improvisation	Music that is made up on the spot and played on stage. It usually begins from a melody or succession of chords, seeking out an appropriate variation. Improvisation is an important component of jazz.
Intermezzo	Music played between during the interval between two acts at the theater or opera. A short nineteenth century piano piece.
Interval	The distance between two notes; the notes of a scale, often called degrees in music teaching. An interval is described numerically. The numbering is counted from one degree to the other of the interval, so that the interval between C and G is a fifth, for example; C D E F G.
Intonation	1. Singing or playing clearly at the right pitch 2. Adjustment made to the sounding apparatus of an instrument so that it produces the desired sounding quality.
Introduction	A normally slow prelude to the first movement of a symphony or chamber music piece.
Largo	A tempo indication; slow, broad, solemn.
Leitmotif	A short, musical motif with a particular musical or dramatic significance in an opera or orchestral work and which recurs throughout the work, a device known since the Classical period.

Manual	Name for organ keyboards played by hand (Latin; manus = hand). The organ usually has between two and four manuals.
March	Name for a piece of music suggesting the impression of a striding movement. According to the circumstances in which a march is played, a distinction is made between the celebratory wedding march, the rousing military march, and the solemn funeral march that is sometimes played on state occasions.
Measure	A means of organizing music in which the duration of the notes is shown. Distinctions are made between common time measures (2/4, 4/4, 2/2 etc.) triple time measures (3/8, 3/4, 3/2 etc.), compound time measures (e.g. 6/8, which can also be viewed as two times 3/8 or common time with triplets) and irregular time measures (e.g. 5/8, 7/4 etc.) that enjoyed a brief popularity in the 1920s.
Melody	A series of notes with a unique character that arises from a logical sequence of notes. Even in instrumental music, a melody can be characterized by its "singing" quality.
Metronome	Mechanical apparatus that indicates the tempo, used primarily in music teaching.
Minim	Name given to a note half the length of a breve.
Mode	In present-day usage, this signifies the major or minor scale covering the twelve semitones of the octave. A more general meaning is that of a scale rising from a particular note of a tonal system (for example, church modes).
Modulation	In tonal music, the name for the change from one key to another within the same piece of music.
Mordant	A sort of decoration in which the main note is embellished by alternating it with the note a second below it.
Motif	The smallest compositional element, making up the themes in a piece.
Mouthpiece	The name applied to the cup-shaped playing end of brass instruments.
Multiphony	A situation in which more than one voice sings or plays a piece of music. This includes homophony as well as polyphony.

Mute	Name of a device by which the volume of a sound can be reduced and the sound color can be altered. On the piano, notes are muted by use of the una-corda pedal that shifts the mechanism, allowing only one string per note, instead of three, to be struck. On stringed instruments, this is accomplished by clamping a mute of wood or rubber to the bridge. Wind instruments are muted by closing them off tightly with the hand or by means of a specially inserted mute. Percussion instruments are muted by placing a cloth over them.
Neck	On instruments in the lute and violin families, the strings pass over a narrow neck, to which a fingerboard is usually fitted. From here, the strings pass across the sounding-board.
Ninth	1. Interval (q.v.) of nine steps. 2. The ninth note in a scale, counting from the lowest note (root) of the scale.
Note	The sign which signifies a sound. In the notation currently in use, the position of the note indicates the pitch. The shape of the note shows its relative length.
Octave	1. Interval (q.v.) of eight steps. 2. The eighth note in a scale, counting from the lowest note (root) of the scale. NB. Notes that lie an octave apart but at different pitches will merge completely with each other if sounded simultaneously.
Offstage	Not on the stage; behind it or in the wings.
Ornamentation	The ornamentation of a melodic line, for example by means of a shake, a turn, or a grace-note, usually indicated in the score by a small note or an extra sign.
Overblowing	Increasing the pressure of air in a wind instrument or organ-pipe so that what emerges is a note higher than normal.
Overtones	When a "note" is produced on a musical instrument, you can also actually hear a whole range of other notes at the same time. The lowest of these notes, the "fundamental," sounds strongest and governs the pitch of the note played. Other, fainter, notes sound above the fundamental; these are called the overtones. Overtones govern the timbre or tonal color of the note played.
Passage-work	The name given to a quick succession of notes, used primarily in virtuoso, solo instrumental, or vocal music.

Passing note	The melodic connection of two notes in one or two chords by intervening notes which do not fit the harmony.
Pedal	A foot-operated lever on various instruments (organ, harpsichord, piano, concert harp, and timpani), used by the player to alter the sound.
Pedal note	A long drawn-out or often repeated note, usually of low pitch, underscoring one or more melodies that continue independently above it. The pedal note serves to increase tension and is therefore mostly used toward the end of a movement.
Piano reduction	A piece of music originally written for an ensemble (e.g. symphony, opera) but arranged in a form playable on the piano.
Pizzicato	Performance instruction for stringed instruments, whereby the strings are plucked instead of bowed. At the end of a pizzicato passage, the term "coll'arco" (with bow) is used to indicate that the bow has to be used again.
Plectrum	A small, flat implement for plucking the strings of a guitar, mandolin, banjo, or similar stringed instrument.
Polyrhythm	Name for the simultaneous appearance of several rhythms in one piece. Polyrhythm has been a very common stylistic device since the Late Romantic period, and particularly in new music. It is also an important feature of jazz and many forms of music outside Europe and North America.
Portamento	Letting the melody slide from one note to the next.
Presto	Indication that the music must be played quickly.
Prima vista	Sight-reading. A piece to be sung or played immediately, without prior practice.
Quadrille	An eighteenth-century French dance in which sets of four couples dance complicated figures.
Quartet	A piece for four (instrumental) voices. The term is also used for a group of four musicians.
Reed	Flexible component part, used mostly on wind instruments, that starts the vibration of the air-stream. Depending on how hard or easy it is to blow, the reed is described as being either hard or soft.

Register	On keyboard instruments (primarily the organ) this is the selectable range of sound colors brought into play by the use of different sounding mechanisms, for example, the strings on the harpsichord or the pipes in an organ.
Reprise	A single repeat of a section within a movement or aria. The reprise is especially elaborately developed as part of a sonata.
Requiem	Roman Catholic mass sung for the dead. The first polyphonic settings were composed in the fifteenth century.
Resonating string	A string on a plucked instrument that is not plucked itself but that vibrates in sympathy with the plucked string.
Retrogression	Name for the repetition of a melody, but back to front, so that all the notes sound in reverse order. The technique is typical of polyphonic music.
Root	In harmony, this is the name of the note on which a chord is built up.
Sautillé	Literally "jumping bow." A manner of bowing in which the bow bounces off the string, so that the string is only bowed very briefly. A very specific, lively sound is produced by this method.
Scale	The arrangement of notes in the tonal system and tonal family, from which a mode is decided. There are other scales besides the major and minor, such as the pentatonic.
Score	The detailed notation of all the voices in a piece of music. The score is set out in such a way that the progress of all the voices can be followed at the same time.
Second	Interval lasting for a semi-tone (minor second) or a full tone (major second). In modern tuning, the former equates precisely to a twelfth of an octave.
Shake	An umbrella term for ornamentation, in which one note is substituted for shorter, rapidly alternating notes above or below it, or both.
Sharp	Sign (#) that makes the pitch of the note following it one semi-tone higher.
Sign	See Accidental. A sharp instructs the pitch of the note to be raised by one semi-tone; a flat means the pitch of the note should be lowered by a semi-tone. A natural cancels out the other signs.

Slur	The curved marking between two notes, indicating that they should be played smoothly and in one continuous run.
Solo	Usually a technically difficult vocal or instrumental piece played by a performer alone and without accompaniment.
Sordino	A mute (q.v.) Score directions are *con sordino* = muted and *senza sordino* = unmuted.
Sound	This expression covers all sorts of audible vibrations that spread out as sound waves. For music, sound waves that spread through the air are most relevant.
Spiritual Music	Collective name for vocals with religious Christian texts. Like church music, it is the antonym of secular music, but has no ties to specific religious institutions.
Speaking	The production of tones on an instrument.
Staccato	A direction that each note should be played spikily and clearly, separately from each other. Staccato is indicated in scores by a dot above or below the note(s).
Staff	The system of horizontal parallel lines on which the notes can be written, to indicate their pitch.
Stop	1. The relationship of notes to each other. 2. "Family" relationships of organ pipes, strings, or wind instruments. 3. The sounding length of a string.
String	A thin, strand of material of natural fiber, metal, nylon, or a combination thereof. The string is the basis for many instruments and twanging a string is one of the oldest known methods of sound production. The sound is produced when the string is set to vibrate and varies depending on the material of which the string is made, as well as its length and thickness.
Strings	The collective name for all stringed instruments played with a bow. "Strings" often signifies this instrumental group in the orchestra, who always sit closest to the conductor.
Stroke	To rub against or along. To stroke a string is to rub against the string in such a way as to make it vibrate.
Swell box	The part of an organ used to mimic an echo of the playing.

Symphony	The best-known and most representative form of orchestral music. The symphony developed during the eighteenth century as a work of three or four movements, of which the first is normally written in sonata form.
Syncopation	Shifting of the rhythm against the proper beat, so that for example in a four beat measure the emphasis falls on the second and fourth beats rather than on the first and third.
Tafelmusik	Literally "table music." Court banquets, held in Europe mostly in the seventeenth and eighteenth centuries, were often accompanied by music composed especially for the occasion.
Tangent	Striking pin or hammer connected to the end of a key that hits or plucks the string when the key is depressed.
Tempo	The speed at which parts of a musical composition are played. The tempo came into being from a subjective assessment of the amount of notes to be played, on the one hand, but became fixed objectively after the arrival of the metronome, that indicates the number of beats per minute. The best-known tempo indications are: largo, adagio, lento (slow), andante, moderato (average speed), allegro, vivace, and presto (quick).
Third	The interval from the root note to the note three diatonic steps above it. A distinction is made between the minor third (C to E–flat) and the major third (C to E) that results in the difference between minor and major tonalities heard in triads.
Timbre	The name given to the definite "color" of the human voice and sometimes also to the "colors" of instrumental sound.
Tonality	The relationship and distribution of notes and chords having a definite basis, by which the harmonic integrity of a work is guaranteed. Hallmarks of tonality are the distinction between major and minor and the functioning of chords as tonic, dominant, and so on. Chords close to the tonal center are consonant, while those further from the tonal center are dissonant.
Transcription	An arrangement of a piece of music for another instrument; arrangement of a song for instrumentals, and vice versa.
Transposition	Transfer of music from one scale to another. Music for so-called "transposing instruments" is written at playing pitch, as opposed to actual sounding pitch.

Tremolo	(Italian = trembling)
	1. Repeated alteration between two notes.
	2. Continuous repetition of one note.
Trill	*See* shake.
Triad	A chord of the tonic, a major or minor third, and a perfect fifth. The simplest form of the chord forms the basis of major/minor tonality.
Tuning fork	A helpful device to assist in establishing intonation (q.v.) The tuning fork is an elongated U-shaped metal fork with a short handle. The note produced by the tuning fork is at a fixed frequency and can be amplified on a sounding-boards.
Twelve-tone technique	A composition technique developed around 1920 by Arnold Schoenberg. It proceeds from a row of the semi-tones within an octave, which, however, may not have a tonal center. The row is elaborated through the piece but still remains in its expositional form. The twelve-tone technique played an important role in new music and in the 1950s it led to serial music.
Unison	The name for the simultaneous singing or playing of the same melody by various voices or instruments.
Valve	By using valves, brass instruments can play all the notes in the chromatic scale through the tuning of the instrument or the alteration of individual notes. In an organ, valves are used to alter the air-flow through the pipes.
Vibrato	A small, fast alteration of the pitch of a note, particularly by string players and singers, resulting in a sort of trembling note; the note is said to "sing". Since the nineteenth century, a regular vibrato has been the norm; prior to that it was an ornamentation applied where it was felt to be appropriate.
Wind cap	A small hood with a blowing aperture, placed over the reed of a crumhorn or bagpipe. When blown, the airflow is directed onto the reed. In labial organ-pipes, the device is known as a "flue."

Index

Acknowledgements

The authors wish to acknowledge the assistance of the following individuals and institutions who contributed to the creation of this book:

J. ten Cate, W. ten Cate van de Kring van Draaiorgelvrienden,
    Haren, Netherlands
Peter Couvée of the Community Museum, The Hague, Netherlands
Marguerite Dütschler-Huber of Claves Records, Thun, Switzerland
De Lachende Fagottist
Tini de Haan van de Stichting Martinikerk, Groningen, Netherlands
Kerstin Hänssler van Hänssler Classic (o.m. Edition Bachakademie),
    Holzgerlingen, Duitsland
Jord Homan, Groningen, Netherlands
Louis Hummel van Hummel Saxofoons, Groningen, Netherlands
Klaas Iwema, Noordwolde, Netherlands
Adam Kania, Groningen, Netherlands
Bram Kijf, Winsum,Netherlands
Dick Kijf, Winsum, Netherlands
Ewald Kooiman
Noord Nederlands Orkest (NNO), Groningen, Netherlands
Rikkers Gitaarbouw, Groningen, Netherlands
Marko Sileon van Sileon's Muziekhuis, Ter Borg, Netherlands
Stichting Jazz in Nederland
Jaap Stiggelbout van Stiggelbout Slagwerk, Groningen, Netherlands
The Dutch Tuba Site
Dick Verel, Onnen, Netherlands
Woldrings Strijkershuis, Groningen, Netherlands
Willem Wolthuis, Glimmen, Netherlands
Yamaha Musical Instruments
Peter Roovers
Lambert Smit
Yke Toepod
Gesina Liedmeyer
Vincent van Ballegooyen
Edwin Beunk

Photo Credits

The authors availed themselves of photographs from the following collections in order to illustrate the book:
- The Hague Community Museum Collection
- Verel Collection (photographed by E.B. Oling)
- Stiggelbout Collection
- Hummel Collection
- Woldring Strijkershuis Collection
- Rikkers Guitar-making Collection
- Willem Wolthuis Collection
- Blauwe Schuyt Collection
- Adriana Brenkink Collection
- Edwin Beunk Collection
- Liedmeyer Collection (photographed by O.A.J. Achterberg, S. Doering, and F. Dries)
- Studio Imago, Heros Awanis

In addition, thanks are due to the Music School in Amersfoort for giving permission to photograph some unusual instruments.

The editors have also tried to trace all possible copyright holders of the photographs used. Any copyright holders who have not (yet) been approached for permission to use their photographs are invited to contact the editors.

Bibliography

1.   Arnold, Bruce, *Keynote Recognition*, Muse Eek Publishing Company, New York, NY., September, 1999.

2.   Bond, Anne, *A Guide to the Harpsichord*, Amadeus Press, an imprint of Timber Press, Inc., Portland Oregon, November, 1997.

3.   Deutsch, Diana, *The Psychology of Music*, second edition, Academic Press, a division of Elsevier, New York, N.Y., September, 1998.

4.   Dickreiter, Michael, *Score Reading: A Key to the Music Experience*, Amadeus Press, an imprint of Timber Press, Inc. Portland, Oregon, September, 2000.

5.   Godwin, Andrew, *Dancing in the Distraction Factory: Music and Popular Culture*. Published by University of Minnesota, Minneapolis, 1992.

6.   Green, Barry, Galway, W. Timothy, *The Inner Game of Music*, Doubleday, New York, NY, March, 1986.

7.   Gurney, Edmund, *The Power of Sound*. First published in 1880. Reprint by Basic Books, New York–London, 1966.

8.   Little, Karen R. *Notes*, Scarecrow Press; (January 1995)

9.   Miller, T. and Miller, Fred, *Music in Advertising*, Music Sales Corp, New York, NY, December, 1987.

10.   MacDonald, Raymond A. R., Hargreaves, David J, Miell, Dorothy, *Musical Identities*, O.U.P., July, 2002.

11.   Mark, Michael L., *Source Readings in Music Education*, second edition, Routledge, New York and London, January, 2002.

12.   Parncutt, Richard (Ed.), McPherson, Gary (Ed.), *The Science and Psychology of Music Performance*, O.U.P., Oxford, UK. (March 2002)

13.   Sloboda, John (ed.), *Generative Processes in Music - The Psychology of Performance, Improvisation, and Composition*, Oxford University Press, Oxford, UK. January, 2001.

14.   Ord-Hume, W.J.G. *Barrel Organ: The Story Of The Mechanical Organ And Its Repairs*, A. S. Barnes and Co, New York, N.Y., 1978.

15.   Sadie Stanley, (Ed.), *New Grove Dictionary of Musical Instruments*, Macmillan Press Limited, London and Grove's Dictionaries of Music, New York,1984.

16.   Tame, David, *The Secret Power of Music*, Destiny Books, Rochester, Vermont, March, 1984.